PC LEARNING LABS TEACHES MICROSOFT ACCESS FOR WINDOWS 95

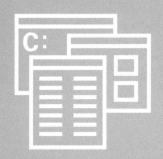

PC LEARNING LABS TEACHES MICROSOFT ACCESS FOR WINDOWS 95

By Julie Nichols Kulik for

Ziff-Davis Press
Emeryville, California

Writer	Julie Nichols Kulik
Curriculum Development	Logical Operations
Copy Editor	Heidi Steele
Technical Reviewer	Heidi Steele
Project Coordinators	Ami Knox and Madhu Prasher
Proofreader	Jeff Barrash
Cover Illustration and Design	Regan Honda
Book Design	Laura Lamar/MAX, San Francisco
Technical Illustration	Steph Bradshaw, Cherie Plumlee
Word Processing	Howard Blechman
Page Layout	Janet Piercy
Indexer	Anne Leach

Ziff-Davis Press, ZD Press, PC Learning Labs, and PC Learning Labs Teaches are licensed to Macmillan Computer Publishing USA by Ziff-Davis Publishing Company, New York, New York.

Ziff-Davis Press imprint books are produced on a Macintosh computer system with the following applications: FrameMaker®, Microsoft® Word, QuarkXPress®, Adobe Illustrator®, Adobe Photoshop®, Adobe Streamline™, MacLink®*Plus*, Aldus® FreeHand™, Collage Plus™.

If you have comments or questions or would like to receive a free catalog, call or write:
Macmillan Computer Publishing USA
Ziff-Davis Press Line of Books
5903 Christie Avenue
Emeryville, CA 94608
1-800-688-0448

ISBN 1-56276-330-X

Manufactured in the United States of America
10 9 8 7 6 5 4 3 2 1

CONTENTS AT A GLANCE

TABLE OF CONTENTS

Chapter 11: Using Macros with Forms 272

Chapter 12: Enhanced Report Design 294

INTRODUCTION

Welcome to *PC Learning Labs Teaches Microsoft Access for Windows 95*, a hands-on instruction book that will help you attain a high level of Access fluency in the shortest time possible. And congratulations on choosing Access for Windows 95, an easy-to-use, feature-packed database program that will help you store, retrieve, and report data in many useful ways.

We at PC Learning Labs believe this book to be a unique and welcome addition to the ranks of "how to" computer publications. Our instructional approach stems directly from over a decade of successful teaching in a hands-on classroom environment. Throughout the book, we mix theory with practice by presenting new techniques and then applying them in hands-on activities. These activities use specially prepared sample Access files, which are stored on the enclosed Data Disk.

Unlike a class, this book allows you to proceed at your own pace. And we'll be right there to guide you along every step of the way, providing landmarks to help you chart your progress and hold to a steady course.

When you're done working your way through this book, you'll have a solid foundation of skills in

- Creating tables to store data

- Finding and editing table records

- Using queries to manipulate the data in your tables

- Creating and using forms to see data the way you want

- Creating and printing reports based on Access data

- Creating macros to automate Access tasks

WHO THIS BOOK IS FOR

This book was written with the beginner in mind. Although experience with databases and personal computers is certainly helpful, little or none is required. You should know how to turn on your computer and use your keyboard. We explain everything beyond that.

HOW TO USE THIS BOOK

You can use this book as a learning guide, a review tool, and a quick reference.

 ### AS A LEARNING GUIDE

Each chapter covers one broad topic or set of related topics. Chapters are arranged in order of increasing proficiency; skills you acquire in one chapter are used and elaborated on in later chapters. For this reason, you should work through the chapters in sequence.

Each chapter is organized into explanatory topics and step-by-step activities. Topics provide the theory you need to master Access; activities allow you to apply this theory to practical, hands-on examples.

You get to try out each new skill on a specially prepared sample Access file stored on the enclosed Data Disk. This saves you typing time and allows you to concentrate on the technique at hand. Through the use of sample files, hands-on activities, illustrations that give you feedback at crucial steps, and supporting background information, this book provides you with the foundation and structure to learn Access quickly and easily.

 ### AS A REVIEW TOOL

Any method of instruction is only as effective as the time and effort you are willing to invest in it. For this reason, we strongly encourage you to spend some time reviewing the book's more challenging topics and activities.

AS A QUICK REFERENCE

General procedures such as opening a worksheet or changing the number format of a cell are presented as a series of bulleted steps; you can find these bullets (•) easily by skimming through the book. These procedures can serve as a handy reference.

At the end of every chapter, you'll find a quick reference that lists the mouse/keyboard actions needed to perform the techniques introduced in that chapter.

 SPECIAL LEARNING FEATURES

The following features of this book will facilitate your learning:

- Carefully sequenced topics that build on the knowledge you've acquired from previous topics

- Frequent hands-on activities that sharpen your Access skills

- Numerous illustrations that show how your screen should look at key points during these activities

- The Data Disk, which contains all the files you will need to complete the activities (as explained in the next section)

- Easy-to-spot, bulleted procedures that provide the general, step-by-step instructions you'll need to perform Access tasks

- A quick reference at the end of each chapter, listing the mouse/keyboard actions needed to perform the techniques introduced in the chapter

THE DATA DISK

One of the most important learning features of this book is the *Data Disk*, the 3½-inch floppy disk that accompanies the book. This disk contains the sample Access files you'll retrieve and work on throughout the book.

To perform the activities in this book, you will first need to create a work folder on your hard disk (see Chapter 1). You'll then copy the sample files from the Data Disk to your work folder. This folder will also hold all the Access files that you will be creating, editing, and saving during the course of this book.

WHAT YOU NEED TO USE THIS BOOK

To run Access 7.0 for Windows 95 and complete this book, you need a computer with a hard disk and at least one floppy-disk drive, a monitor, a keyboard, and a mouse (or compatible tracking device). Although you don't absolutely need a printer, we strongly recommend that you have one. Windows 95 must be installed on your computer; if it is not, see your Windows 95 reference manual for instructions. Access for Windows 95 must also be installed; for help, see Appendix A.

 COMPUTER AND MONITOR

You need an IBM or IBM-compatible personal computer and monitor that are capable of running Microsoft Windows (version 95 or higher). We recommend that you use a 3860DX or higher (486, and so on) computer.

You need a hard disk with at least 42 megabytes (42 million bytes) of free storage space (if Access for Windows 95 is not yet installed), or 1 megabyte of free space (if Access for Windows 95 is installed).

Finally, you need an EGA or higher (VGA, SVGA, and so on) graphics card and monitor to display Windows 95 and Access 7.0 for Windows 95 at their intended screen resolution. (**Note:** The Access 7.0 for Windows

95 screens shown in this book are taken from a VGA monitor. Depending upon your monitor type, your screens may look slightly different.)

 KEYBOARD

IBM-compatible computers come with various styles of keyboards; these keyboards function identically but have different layouts. Figures I.1, I.2, and I.3 show the three main keyboard styles and their key arrangements.

Figure I.1   **IBM PC–style keyboard**

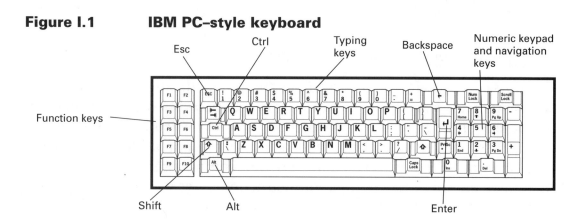

Figure I.2   **XT/AT–style keyboard**

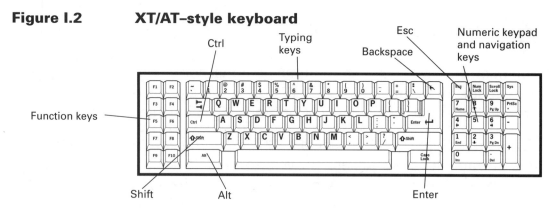

Figure I.3 **The 101-key Enhanced Keyboard**

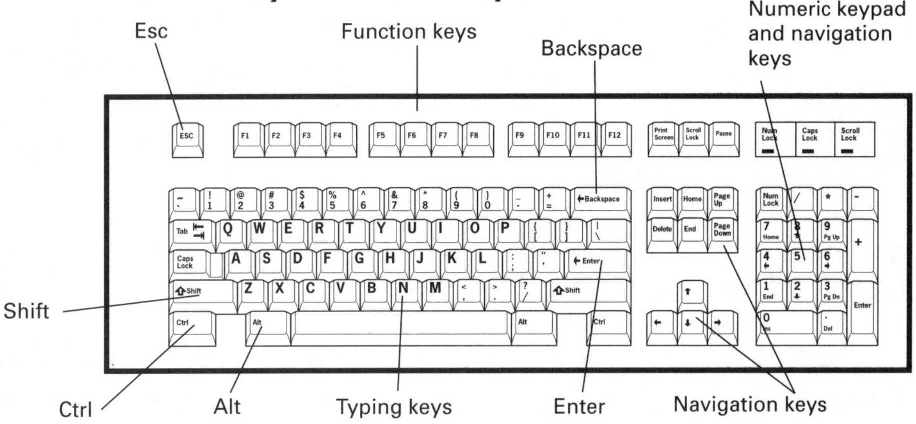

Access uses all main areas of the keyboard:

- The *function keys*, which you can use to issue some Access commands. On the PC-, XT-, and AT-style keyboards, there are 10 function keys at the left end of the keyboard; on the 101-key Enhanced Keyboard there are 12 at the top of the keyboard.

- The *typing keys*, which you use to enter letters, numbers, and punctuation marks. These keys include the Shift, Ctrl, and Alt keys, which you need to use several of Access's special features. The typing keys are located in the main body of all the keyboards.

- The *numeric keypad*, which you use either to enter numeric data or to navigate through a document. When *Num Lock* is turned on, you use the numeric keypad to enter numeric data, just as you would on a standard calculator keypad. When Num Lock is turned off, you use the numeric keypad to navigate through a worksheet by using the cursor-movement keys: Up, Down, Left, and Right Arrows; Home, End, PgUp (Page Up), and PgDn (Page Down). To turn Num Lock on or off, simply press the Num Lock key. To enter numeric data when Num Lock is off, use the number keys in the top row of the typing area.

- The *cursor-movement keypad*, which is available only on the Enhanced Keyboard, lets you navigate through a document by using the Home, End, Page Up, and Page Down keys. The cursor-movement keypad works the same when Num Lock is turned on or off. This makes it possible for you to keep Num Lock on and still be able to use the cursor-movement keys.

 MOUSE OR OTHER TYPE OF TRACKING DEVICE

You need a mouse or other type of tracking device to work through the activities in this book. Any standard PC mouse or tracking device (a track-ball, for example) will do.

Note: Throughout this book, we direct you to use a mouse. If you have a different tracking device, simply use your device to perform all the mousing tasks: pointing, clicking, dragging, and so on.

 PRINTER

Although you don't absolutely need a printer to work through the activities in this book, we strongly recommend that you have one. A laser printer is ideal, but an ink-jet or dot-matrix will do just fine. Your printer must be selected for use with Access for Windows 95.

CONVENTIONS USED IN THIS BOOK

The following conventions used in this book will help you learn Access for Windows 95 easily and efficiently.

- Each chapter begins with a short introduction and ends with a summary that includes a quick-reference guide to the techniques introduced in the chapter.

- Main chapter topics (large, capitalized headings) and subtopics (headings preceded by a cube) explain Access features. Hands-on activities allow you to practice using these features.

  In these activities, keystrokes, menu choices, and anything you are asked to type are printed in boldface. Here's an example from Chapter 3:

  > Click on the **New** button to open a new table window in Design view.

- Activities adhere to a cause-and-effect approach. Each step tells you what to do (cause) and then what will happen (effect). From the example above,

  > Cause: Click on the **New** button.
  >
  > Effect: A new table window opens in Design view.

- A plus sign (+) is used with the Shift, Ctrl, and Alt keys to indicate a multikey keystroke. For example, press Ctrl+F10 means "Press and hold down the Ctrl key, then press the F10 key, and then release them both."

- To help you distinguish between steps presented for reference purposes (general procedures) and steps you should carry out at your computer as you read (specific procedures), we use the following system:

  - A bulleted step, like this, is provided for your information and reference only.

  1. A numbered step, like this, indicates one in a series of steps that you should carry out in sequence at your computer.

BEFORE YOU START

Each chapter's activities proceed sequentially. In many cases, you cannot perform an activity until you have performed one or more of the activities preceding it. For this reason, we recommend that you allot enough time to work through an entire chapter in one continuous session.

Feel free to take as many breaks as you need. Stand up, stretch, take a walk, drink some decaf. Don't try to absorb too much information at one time. Studies show that people assimilate and retain information most effectively when it is presented in digestible chunks and followed by a liberal amount of hands-on practice.

You are now ready to begin. Good learning and...*bon voyage!*

CHAPTER 1: GETTING STARTED

A Quick Review of
Mouse Skills

Creating Your
Work Folder

Introduction to
Database
Concepts

Starting Access

Please Read
This—It's
Important!

Exiting Access

Welcome to Access and the world of electronic databases. Access provides you with a set of powerful tools for collecting, retrieving, and presenting data. In this first chapter, we'll get you up and running in Access and introduce you to the Access working environment. Then you'll learn how to exit the program.

When you're done working through this chapter, you will know

- How to use the mouse
- How to start Access
- How to exit Access

A QUICK REVIEW OF MOUSE SKILLS

The *mouse* is a hand-operated device that enables you to communicate with Access by manipulating (selecting, deselecting, moving, deleting, and so on) graphical and text objects that are displayed on your computer screen. When you move the mouse across the surface of your mouse pad (or roll a trackball in its base), a symbol called the *mouse pointer* moves across the screen. You use this mouse pointer to point to the on-screen object that you want to manipulate. The mouse has two or more buttons. You use these buttons to communicate with Access in various ways, as detailed in Table 1.1.

Note: Read through the following table to familiarize yourself with standard Access mousing techniques. Do not, however, try to memorize these techniques. Instead, use this table as a quick reference, referring to it whenever you need to refresh your memory.

Table 1.1   **Mousing Techniques**

Technique	How to Do It
Point	Move the mouse until the tip of the mouse pointer is over the desired object. "Point to the word *File*" means "move the mouse until the tip of the mouse pointer is over the word *File*."
Click	Press and release the left or right mouse button. When we want you to click the left mouse button, we'll simply say "click." For example, "click on the word *File*" means "point to the word *File* and then press and release the left mouse button." When we want you to click the right mouse button, we'll say so. For example, "point to the Standard toolbar and click the right mouse button."

Table 1.1 **Mousing Techniques (Continued)**

Double-click	Press and release the left mouse button twice in rapid succession. "Double-click on the Preview 1 file" means "point to the file name *Preview 1* and then press and release the left mouse button twice in rapid succession."
Choose	Click on a menu command or a dialog-box button. "Choose File, Open" means "click on the word *File* (in the menu bar), and then click on the word *Open* (in the File menu)."
Drag	Press and hold the left mouse button while moving the mouse. "Drag the scroll box upward" means "point to the scroll box, press and hold the left mouse button, move the mouse upward, and then release the mouse button."
Scroll	Click on a scroll arrow or within a scroll bar, or drag a scroll box.
Select	Click on an object (to select the entire object), or drag over part of a text object (to select part of the text). "Select the Chapter 2 file" means "click on the file name *Chapter 2.*" "Select the first three letters of the label "*Last Name*" means "drag over the letters *Las.*"
Check	Click on a check box to check (turn on) that option. "Check the Match Case option" means "click on the Match Case check box to check it."
Uncheck	Click on a check box to uncheck (turn off) that option. "Uncheck the Match Case option" means "click on the Match Case check box to uncheck it."

CREATING YOUR WORK FOLDER

Throughout this book, you'll be creating, editing, and saving a number of files. To keep these files in one place, you'll need to create a work folder for them on your hard disk. Your work folder will also hold the sample files contained on the enclosed Data Disk.

Let's create our work folder.

1. Turn on your computer. After a brief internal self-check, Windows 95 will load and prompt you for a password.

2. Type your password, if prompted, and press **Enter**. Momentarily, the Windows 95 desktop will be displayed (see Figure 1.1).

Figure 1.1 **The Windows 95 desktop**

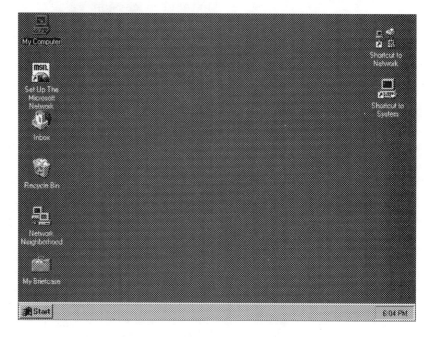

3. From the Windows 95 desktop, click on the **Start** button to open the Start menu. Point to Programs to open the Programs menu, and select **Windows Explorer**. The Windows Explorer can be used to manage the folders and files on your computer.

4. In the Tree pane, click on the plus sign (+) to the left of the My Computer branch to expand it so that you can view both the floppy-disk drive and the hard drive. (The branch might already be expanded.) This branch may also contain folders, such as the Control Panel and Printers folders.

5. Click on the hard-disk icon **(C:)**. From the menu bar, choose **File, New, Folder** to create a new folder. You will copy the contents of the Data Disk into this folder. The new folder is

displayed in the Contents pane and is highlighted so that you can rename it now.

6. Type **Access Work** and press **Enter** to assign the name to the new folder.

7. Select (click on) the hard-disk icon **(C:)** and choose **File, Properties** to view the amount of available hard-disk space. On the General tab, the amount of free space is displayed. If you have fewer than 1,000,000 free bytes (1MB), you will not be able to store the practice files in your work folder and perform the hands-on activities in this book (while still maintaining an adequate amount of free hard-disk space for your other computer activities). In this case, you will have to delete enough files from your hard disk to increase the free space total to at least 1,000,000. To do this, refer to your Windows 95 reference manual, or better yet, enlist the aid of an experienced Windows 95 user. (**Note:** Make sure you back up all your important files before deleting them!)

8. Click on **Cancel** to close the Properties dialog box. (Do *not* proceed to step 9 until you have made room for the Data Disk files on your hard disk.)

9. Remove the Data Disk from its envelope at the back of this book. Insert the Data Disk (label up) into the 3 1/2-inch floppy-disk drive. Determine whether this is drive A or drive B. (On a single floppy-disk system, the drive is generally designated as A. On a double floppy-disk system, the upper or left drive is generally designated as A and the lower or right as B.)

10. The easiest way to copy the files from the floppy disk to your Access Work folder is by dragging them. Display the contents of the **3 1/2 Floppy (A:)** branch. (Use the same technique that you used in step 4.) Then, choose **Edit, Select All** from the menu to select all the files in the Contents pane.

11. Drag the selected files to the Access Work folder in the Tree pane. (The folder name should be highlighted before you release the mouse button.) As the files are copied, a message box graphically displays the files flying from one folder to another.

All the files that you need for this book are now stored in your Access Work folder. As a final step, you can create a shortcut to this folder and display it on your desktop. A shortcut will give you quick access to the files in the folder. This procedure is strictly optional; you don't need the shortcut to access the files as you work through the chapters in the book. However, if you would like to create such a shortcut, you can use the following drag-and-drop technique.

- If the Windows Explorer window is maximized, click on the *Restore* button (to the left of the Close button in the upper-right corner of the window) so that you can see part of the desktop.

- Select the *Access Work* folder icon. Press and hold the right mouse button and drag the icon to the desktop. Release the mouse button and choose *Create Shortcut(s) Here* from the shortcut's object menu.

Important Note: The hands-on activities in this book assume that your work folder is on the hard drive and is named Access Work. If you specified a different location or name for this folder, remember to substitute this location and/or name whenever we mention the Access Work folder.

INTRODUCTION TO DATABASE CONCEPTS

A *database* is a collection of related information, or data. It may sound like a complicated word, but in fact you work with many databases every day. A telephone book, a calendar, and a card catalog all are examples of common databases.

Access is an electronic database-management system; its purpose is to help you collect, retrieve, and present data. For example, you might want to keep an Access database of personnel information. You could then retrieve data about new employees (name, address, telephone number, and so on), retrieve a list of employees according to their hire dates, or print a list of employee telephone numbers.

The main advantages of electronic database-management systems over their paper-based counterparts are that they can store very large amounts of data, and make it much easier—and quicker—to extract and rearrange that data.

Before we start Access, let's take a minute to examine the database in Figure 1.2. We'll need to be sure we understand a few terms before we plunge into the software. The database in the figure is in the form of a table that includes names, addresses, and telephone extensions. In Access, your databases will be made up of one or more tables like this one.

Figure 1.2   **A sample paper database**

```
Last        First       Adr                   City          St  Zip    Ext
----------  ----------  --------------------  ------------  --  -----  ---
Abel        Marie       127 Ford Avenue       Shackelford   TX  76430  339
Abot        Robert      99 Stonecreek Rd.     Trenton       NJ  08618  350
Beaton      Robert      391 State Street      West Seneca   NY  14224  323
Bell        William     66 Big Hill Rd.       Troy          NY  12182  340
Binder      Julia       10 Cory Drive         Trenton       NJ  08753  324
Binga       Sam         50 Dallas Street      Pasadena      CA  91106  348
Carter      Andrea      718 Prole Road        Rockville     SC  29204  360
Chase       Wilma       52 Pempleton Dr.      Albany        NY  12205  309
Conner      Bill        32 Ash Lane           Allentown     NJ  08501  328
DeMarco     Alice       34 Sable Ave.         Bentwood      IL  61820  332
Desoto      Frank       P.O. Box 7234         Trenton       NJ  07092  356
Easter      Ester       21 Stonecreek Rd.     Trenton       NJ  08620  390
Harper      Harry       82 East Avenue        Long Beach    CA  90745  395
Haslam      David       453 Lakeshore Dr.     Evans Mills   ND  58352  338
Henley      Albert      12 Divine Drive       San Pueblo    CO  80403  318
James       Ted         34 Fields Street      Fort Worth    TX  76116  300
Jones       Homer       466 Fairhaven St.     Los Alamos    MI  48104  337
Kyler       Dennis      273 Fireside Dr.      Great Neck    NY  11023  362
Martin      Jane        50 Smart Drive        Oceanside     CA  91762  349
McDonald    Ronald      8165 Main Street      Trenton       NJ  08690  303
Naylor      Ruth        532 Union Street      Nashville     TN  38109  334
Osowski     Dominick    23 Lakeside Ave.      S Granbury    TX  76048  368
Packer      Penny       9929 Clearview        Vienna        VA  22181  346
Sanders     Maria       12 East Avenue        Denton        TX  76201  310
Stira       Joe         200 Nester Street     Bath          NY  76708  315
Ward        Junior      7 Chamberlin St.      Massena       NC  28210  317
Zambito     Joseph      81 Pleasing Lane      Alhambra      CA  91801  311
```

Notice that:

- Each column contains a single kind of data (last names, first names, addresses, and so on). In a table, each column of data is called a *field*.

- Each row contains one piece of data from each field relating to a single person. In a table, each row of data is called a *record*.

It's very important that we understand the difference between fields and records. In a phone book, for example, each line would be a record; last names, first names, and phone numbers would be fields. Got it?

A paper table (or database) presents many problems when you actually want to use it. What if you wanted to arrange the records in Figure 1.2 by city? You'd have to get out a new sheet of paper, figure out the order, and then copy all the records to the new sheet. Many common database tasks would present this sort of problem. What if you wanted to list only three of the fields (columns)? Or perhaps only those people who live in California? Even something as simple as finding a specific person in the table could lead to some nasty eye strain. Not only would such tasks be drudgery, but also your work would be prone to errors—you might, for example, mistype a name or miss a record.

Let's take a look at the sample database in Figure 1.3. This database contains some of the same data we saw in Figure 1.2, but in a different arrangement. Here, each record is on a separate card, making the information easier to read and understand. Access lets you create *forms* so that you can see database information in whatever layout you choose.

Figure 1.4 shows another sample database. There are three tables that contain different types of data (one for employees, another for customers, and a third for suppliers). In Access, as in this example, a database can comprise many related tables. The sample database in Figure 1.4 also includes tools for viewing and working with the data in the table, namely forms, reports, and queries. Access provides all these tools, each of which we'll see in action later in this chapter.

To summarize, a database is a collection of related information. In Access, the data are stored in tables. Tables contain columns of information called fields, and rows of related field information called records. Forms, queries, and reports are tools for viewing and manipulating the data in the tables. This will all become clearer when we see some examples.

STARTING ACCESS

Before you start Access, both Microsoft Windows 95 and Access 7.0 must be installed on your hard disk. If either of these programs

Figure 1.3   A sample paper database with forms

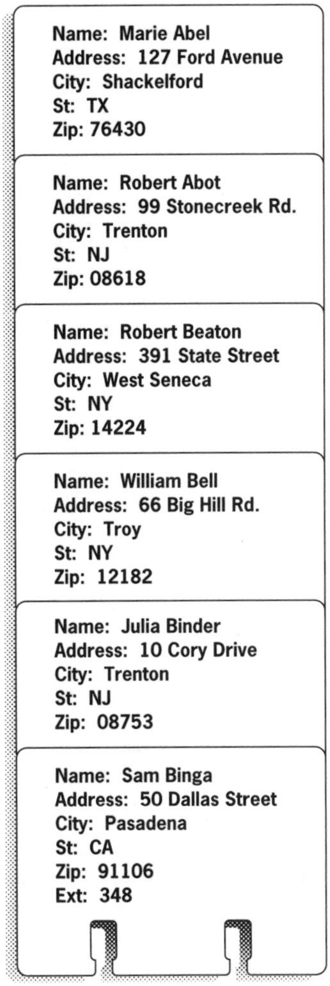

Name: Marie Abel
Address: 127 Ford Avenue
City: Shackelford
St: TX
Zip: 76430

Name: Robert Abot
Address: 99 Stonecreek Rd.
City: Trenton
St: NJ
Zip: 08618

Name: Robert Beaton
Address: 391 State Street
City: West Seneca
St: NY
Zip: 14224

Name: William Bell
Address: 66 Big Hill Rd.
City: Troy
St: NY
Zip: 12182

Name: Julia Binder
Address: 10 Cory Drive
City: Trenton
St: NJ
Zip: 08753

Name: Sam Binga
Address: 50 Dallas Street
City: Pasadena
St: CA
Zip: 91106
Ext: 348

is not installed, please install it now. For help installing Windows 95, see your Windows documentation. For help installing Access 7.0, see Appendix A of this book.

You also need to have created a work folder on your hard disk and copied the files from the enclosed Data Disk to this folder. If you have not done this, please do so now; for instructions, see "Creating Your Work Folder" earlier in this chapter.

Figure 1.4   **A sample database with three tables and other tools**

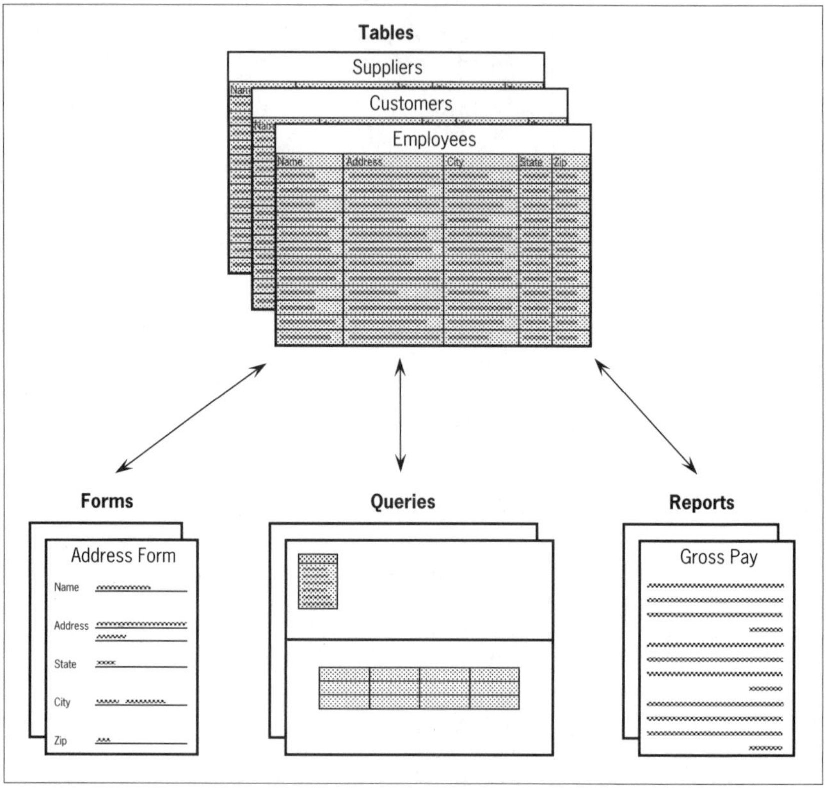

Note: In this book, we present two types of procedures: bulleted and numbered. A *bulleted* procedure—one whose steps are preceded by bullets (•)—serves as a general reference; you should read its steps without actually performing them. A *numbered* procedure—one whose steps are preceded by numbers (1., 2., and so on)—is a specific hands-on activity; you should perform its steps as instructed.

To start Access:

• Turn on your computer.

• Enter your Windows 95 password if prompted.

• From the Start menu, open the Programs menu, and select *Microsoft Access*.

Note: To start Access, we must first locate the program in the Start menu. Because Windows 95 is a customizable program, we cannot know the details of your Windows 95 setup. So please bear with us as we search for your Microsoft Access program.

With Windows 95 already running, let's start Access:

1. Click on the **Start** button in the taskbar.

2. Highlight (point to) **Programs** to display the available programs (see Figure 1.2; your menu choices will vary). Depending on your Windows 95 setup, you might need to search through a few layers of menus to find Microsoft Access (or you might have created a shortcut to it on your desktop).

3. Click on the **Microsoft Access** choice to start the program. Your screen should match—or closely resemble—Figure 1.5.

Figure 1.5   **Access 7.0, after startup**

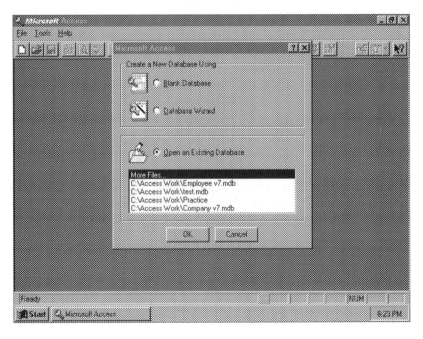

4. Click on the **Cancel** button to close the Startup dialog box. We will be opening existing databases and creating new databases by clicking on buttons on the toolbar.

5. If your Access window does not fill the entire screen, click on the **Maximize** button, in the upper-right corner of the screen (to the left of the Close button).

PLEASE READ THIS—IT'S IMPORTANT!

Like Windows 95, Access can be customized. Depending on how you (or perhaps a colleague) have set up your Access program, it may look very different from another user's Access setup, or from the Access setup used in this book.

To write this book for an "invisible" audience—with hundreds, if not thousands, of different Access setups—we had to assume that you are running Access with the same *default* (standard) settings that were automatically chosen when you first installed the application. Of course, this assumption may be false. You or a colleague may have customized your Access program to show additional toolbars, run in full-screen view, display on-screen text in a 20-point Gargantuan Urdu font, hide the status bar, and so on.

Here's our recommendation: First of all, relax. Chances are your program settings are fine. But if you should run into a snag while working through this book—for example, if your screen displays differ markedly from ours, or if tools we ask you to use are missing from your screen—simply use your ever-increasing Access expertise to make the changes necessary to match your Access setup as closely as possible to ours.

EXITING ACCESS

Your final step of every Access session is to exit Access. Never just turn off your computer while Access, Windows 95, or any other program is open and running, as this could result in the loss of data.

There are multiple ways to issue many of the commands available in Access. Exiting Access is no exception; for example, you could exit the program by using any one of the following techniques.

- Choose *File, Exit* from the menu bar.

- Click on the application-window *Control menu* icon (it looks like a gold key in the top-left corner of the window), and choose *Close*.

- Double-click on the application-window *Control menu* icon.

- Click on the application-window *Close* button.

The method that you choose to issue any command is to some extent a matter of preference. For example, if you like to compute by mouse alone, you might not want to learn any keyboard shortcuts; if, on the other hand, you're a dyed-in-the-wool keywhacker, you might be violently allergic to mouse pointers.

For the remainder of this book, rather than confuse you with a plethora of techniques to accomplish the same thing, we will, in each case, try to provide you with what we believe is the simplest method of accomplishing a task. For the long haul, it's up to you to determine which techniques will be the most comfortable for you.

Let's exit Access:

1. Observe the button to the right of the application-window Maximize/Restore button: This is the Close button.

2. Click on the application-window **Close** button to exit Access.

SUMMARY

In this chapter, you learned how to start and exit Access, and you've been introduced to database concepts.

Here's a quick reference guide to the Access features introduced in this chapter:

Desired Result	How to Do It
Start Access	Start Windows; choose **Start, Programs**; locate and click on **Microsoft Access** choice
Exit Access	Click on application-window **Close** button

In the next chapter, we'll show you the basics of using Access: how to open a database, how to explore some objects contained in that database (including tables, forms, queries, and reports), and how to close the database. You'll also learn how to obtain online help.

A NOTE ON HOW TO PROCEED

If you wish to stop here, please feel free to do so now. If you feel energetic and wish to press onward, please proceed directly to the next chapter. Remember to allot enough time to work through an entire chapter in one sitting.

CHAPTER 2: TOURING ACCESS

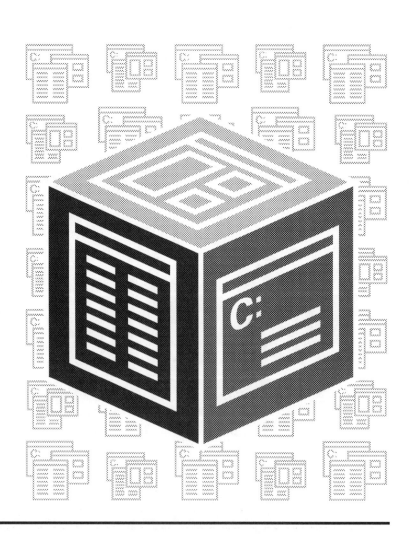

In Chapter 1, we were introduced to the Access environment. In this chapter we will take a brief tour of the elements of an Access database.

When you're done working through this chapter, you will know

- How to open, navigate in, and close a table

- How to open, navigate in, and close a form

- How to sort records and run queries

- How to preview a report

- How to close a database

As you work through this chapter, remember this is just a tour. In later chapters, we'll explore many of Access's features in greater detail.

THE ACCESS APPLICATION WINDOW

Because Access is a Windows application, its environment contains some items that are common to all programs that run under Windows 95. Table 2.1 lists some parts of the Access application window and their uses. You can refer to Figure 2.1 to see where each of these elements is located.

Table 2.1   **Access Application Window Elements**

Element	Description/Use
Application window	The window that contains the entire program.
Title bar	The bar at the top of the window; it contains the Control menu icon, the application title, the Minimize button, the Maximize button or Restore button, and the Close button.
Control menu icon	The icon shaped like a key in the upper-left corner of the window; clicking on it provides a list of commands for controlling the window.
Minimize button	The button with a horizontal bar on the right of the title bar; clicking on it minimizes the Application window to show only the task button for the application in the taskbar at the bottom of the screen.

Table 2.1   **Access Application Window Elements (Continued)**

Element	Description/Use
Maximize button	The button with a rectangle on the right side of the title bar; clicking on it enlarges the Application window to fill the entire screen. (This button does not appear in Figure 2.1 because the window is already maximized.)
Restore button	The button with two overlapping rectangles in the upper-right corner of the screen; clicking on it returns the window to the size and place it was before being maximized.
Close button	The button with an X in the upper-right corner of the screen; clicking on it closes Access, removing the program from your computer's memory.
Menu bar	The area below the title bar that contains the names of the various menus; clicking on a menu name displays a drop-down menu from which you can choose commands. (In Figure 2.1, Access displays only the File and Help menu options. Access will display more menu options, however, as they become relevant to the task at hand.) You can open an Access menu by clicking on the menu name.
Toolbar	The bar just below the menu bar; its buttons give you access to some of the most frequently used commands without going through the menu. The buttons available on the toolbar will change depending upon what you are doing. In Figure 2.1, many of the tools are dimmed because they cannot be used at the moment.
Status bar	The bar at the bottom of the application window; it displays information relevant to the task at hand.

If you are not currently running Access, please follow the steps outlined in Chapter 1 "Starting Access" to start the program, and close the Startup dialog box.

Let's take a closer look at some of these screen elements.

1. Click on the application **Control menu icon** to open the application Control menu (see Figure 2.2). Make sure you don't double-click, as this would exit Access. You can use the commands in the Control menu to control the application window.

Figure 2.1   Access application window

Application Control
menu icon

Menu bar

Toolbar

Title bar

Application
Minimize button

Application Maximize/
Restore button

Application
Close button

Application
window

Status bar

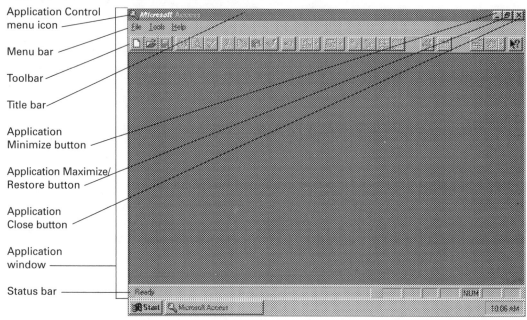

Figure 2.2   The Control menu

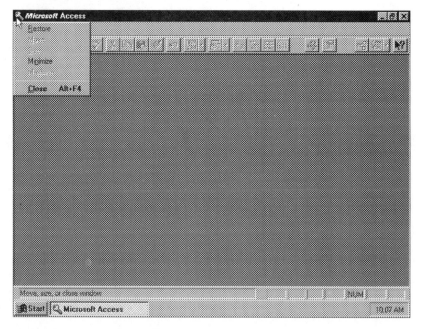

2. Click on the application **Control menu icon** again to close the Control menu, and then click on the **Maximize/Restore** button to change the application window to a smaller size. Notice that the Restore button has changed into a Maximize button (it contains only a single rectangle).

3. Click on the **Maximize** button to enlarge the window so that it once again fills the entire screen, and then click on **File** in the menu bar to open the File menu. Some of the menu items, or commands, are dimmed because they are not currently available. Move the mouse pointer over the menu choice New Database. Notice that the status bar displays a short description of the highlighted command, New Database.

4. Click on **File** again to close the File menu, and then double-click on the **Help** button in the toolbar (don't click on the Help *menu*). This opens the Help Topics window.

5. Click on the **Close button** to close the Help Topics window.

USING MENUS

Many tasks in Access require you to use the menu system to issue commands. To issue a command through the menu system,

- Click on the desired menu name in the menu bar. When you click on a menu name, a *drop-down menu* appears containing the names of several commands (as we saw with the Control and File menus).

- Click on the desired command name to issue the command or to display further options. Sometimes information to the right of a command name gives you a clue as to what will happen when you choose that command:

  - An ellipsis (...) after a command name tells you that choosing the command will display a dialog box from which you can choose further options.

  - A triangle pointing to the right after a command name means that choosing the command will display a sub-menu from which you can choose another command.

- A key combination (such as Ctrl+S) to the right of the command means you can issue the command without going through the menu by pressing those keys in combination.

A nice feature of the menu system is that when you highlight a menu or command name, Access displays a descriptive message in the status bar (at the bottom of the application window). These messages can help you understand the menu system.

OPENING A DATABASE

When you first start Access, no databases are open. To open a database, you follow these steps:

- Click on the Open Database button in the toolbar to display the Open dialog box.

- Select the desired drive and folder, if necessary.

- In the list of files, double-click on the desired file (or click on the file, and then click on Open).

Let's open a database now:

1. Click on the **Open Database** button in the toolbar. The Open dialog box appears.

2. Click on the **Up One Level** button to display the contents of the folder up one level.

Repeat the procedure as necessary, until drive C (or whatever drive your hard disk is) is displayed. The drive's contents are displayed in the large box below the Look in box.

3. If necessary, use the horizontal scroll bar to display the Access Work folder. This is the work folder we created in Chapter 1; you'll use this folder to store all of the documents you work with in this book.

4. Double-click on the Access Work folder to display its contents (see Figure 2.3).

5. In the list of files, double-click on the **Employee** file to open the Employee database file. After a moment, a window with

Figure 2.3   **Opening a database from the Access Work folder**

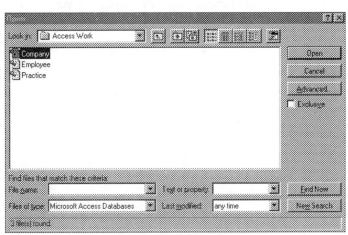

the title *Employee:Database* will appear. This window is
called the *Database window*.

6. Click on the Database window's Maximize button to enlarge
the window so that it uses all the available space in the application window. You'll notice that there are two Control menu
icons in the upper-left corner of the screen. The upper Control
menu icon is for the Access window, and the lower one is for
the Database window.

ORIENTATION TO THE DATABASE WINDOW

The Database window appears within the Access application window when you open a database. You can have only one database
and Database window open at a time.

The Database window serves as a command center for the database, providing you with access to all the objects within the database. (In Access, major items within a database—such as tables
and forms—are called *objects*.)

Let's take a closer look at the Database window:

1. Examine the Database window (see Figure 2.4); like the
Access application window, the Database window has a
Control menu icon, a title bar, a Minimize button, and a
Maximize/Restore button. The window also has Open,

Design, and New command buttons on the right side. Notice also the series of *object tabs* along the top of the window. Objects that can comprise an Access database include tables, queries, forms, reports, macros, and modules. Because the Tables tab is selected, a list of table object names appears in the main area of the Database window.

Figure 2.4   **The Employee: Database window**

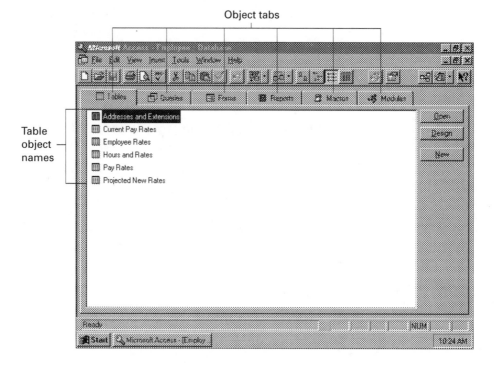

2. Click on the **Forms** tab to display a list of form object names. Note that the icon next to each form object name matches the icon on the Forms tab.

3. Click on the **Tables** tab to return to the list of table object names.

4. Examine the menu bar. Because a Database window is open, the number of menu options has increased. The menu options are now File, Edit, View, Insert, Tools, Window, and Help. (Note also that some additional buttons are available on the toolbar.)

5. Click on **File** to open the File menu. Because the Database window is open, some different menu items are available.

6. Move the mouse pointer over the Edit Menu choice to open the Edit menu. Note that the File menu closes automatically when you open another menu.

7. Click on **Edit** to close the Edit menu.

INTRODUCTION TO HELP

Access Help is an extensive online help system that provides you with "how-to" information on every aspect of the Access program. One way to access the help system is through the Help menu.

THE HELP TOPICS WINDOW

The Access Help Topics window provides an overview of the topics for which help information is available. To use the Help Topics window:

- Press F1 (or double-click on the Help button in the toolbar) to open the Help Topics window, which contains the following tabs designed to give you access to information in different ways:

  - *Contents*—displays a list of common procedures, which contain further subtopics that expand in outline style.

  - *Index*—contains a comprehensive list of terms and procedures.

  - *Find*—allows you to search for specific information. (The first time you use this feature, Access guides you through the creation of a database of information that is customized to your particular setup.)

  - *Answer Wizard*—gives you step-by-step guidance on topics you request.

- To exit the Access Help Topics window, click on its Close button.

Note: All the tabs available in the Help Topics window contain built-in instructions for their use.

Let's briefly use the Help Topics window to search for help on toolbars.

1. Press **F1** to open the Help Topics window, and select (click on) the Index tab (see Figure 2.5).

Figure 2.5 **The Index tab in the Help Topics window**

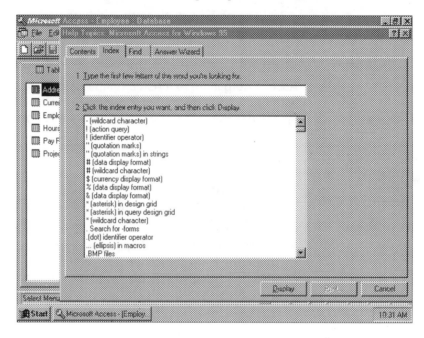

2. Type **t**. Notice how the list of topics now shows subjects that begin with *t*.

3. Type **o**. The list of subjects now shows subjects that begin with *to*.

4. Type the second **o**. The selected subject is now *toolbar buttons*.

5. Select the Index entry **built-in** under the toolbars category. Click on the **Display** button to open the Help window *About built-in and custom toolbars*.

6. Point to the green text **built-in toolbars** toward the top of the window (the pointer will take the shape of a pointing hand), and then click to display the definition window about built-in toolbars.

7. Click on the definition window to close it, and then click on the **Close button** to close the Help window. The Help Topics window is automatically closed.

ORIENTATION TO TABLES

Tables are the only type of Access object that actually stores data. The other objects—including forms and reports—serve as tools to manipulate that data.

Tables store data in a grid of rows and columns. Like the sample paper table in Chapter 1, each column of a table stores a certain category of data (or field), and each row stores one unit of data (or record) that span those categories.

Because Access lets you have multiple tables within a database, you can store different types of data in separate tables. For example, you might have one table that stores data about your customers, and a second that stores information about your purchase orders. The advantage of using two tables in this manner is that you wouldn't have to repeat *all* the customer information in every record of the purchase order table. Instead, you could have a common customer ID in both tables. That way, if you needed more detail about a customer, you could look it up in your customer information table.

OPENING AND EXAMINING A TABLE

To view or edit information contained within a table, you must first open the table. Let's open a table in our database:

1. Observe the Database window. Table object names are listed alphabetically. The first table object name, Addresses and Extensions, is selected.

2. Click on the **Open** button to open the Addresses and Extensions table in its own window (you also can open a table by double-clicking on its object name in the Database window). Your screen should now look like Figure 2.6.

3. Examine the Table window. The status bar indicates that this is the *Datasheet view*; that means we're viewing the data contained in the table. Because a table is open, buttons relevant to working with tables appear on the toolbar.

Figure 2.6 The Addresses and Extensions table

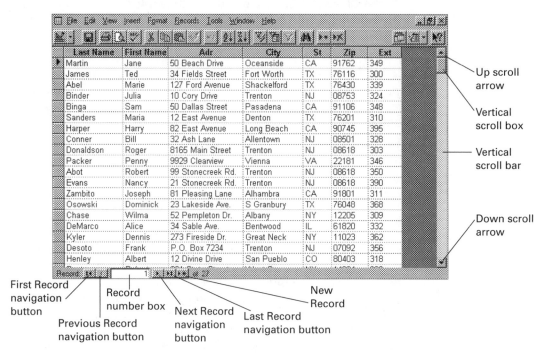

Last Name	First Name	Adr	City	St	Zip	Ext
Martin	Jane	50 Beach Drive	Oceanside	CA	91762	349
James	Ted	34 Fields Street	Fort Worth	TX	76116	300
Abel	Marie	127 Ford Avenue	Shackelford	TX	76430	339
Binder	Julia	10 Cory Drive	Trenton	NJ	08753	324
Binga	Sam	50 Dallas Street	Pasadena	CA	91106	348
Sanders	Maria	12 East Avenue	Denton	TX	76201	310
Harper	Harry	82 East Avenue	Long Beach	CA	90745	395
Conner	Bill	32 Ash Lane	Allentown	NJ	08501	328
Donaldson	Roger	8165 Main Street	Trenton	NJ	08618	303
Packer	Penny	9929 Clearview	Vienna	VA	22181	346
Abot	Robert	99 Stonecreek Rd.	Trenton	NJ	08618	350
Evans	Nancy	21 Stonecreek Rd.	Trenton	NJ	08618	390
Zambito	Joseph	81 Pleasing Lane	Alhambra	CA	91801	311
Osowski	Dominick	23 Lakeside Ave.	S Granbury	TX	76048	368
Chase	Wilma	52 Pempleton Dr.	Albany	NY	12205	309
DeMarco	Alice	34 Sable Ave.	Bentwood	IL	61820	332
Kyler	Dennis	273 Fireside Dr.	Great Neck	NY	11023	362
Desoto	Frank	P.O. Box 7234	Trenton	NJ	07092	356
Henley	Albert	12 Divine Drive	San Pueblo	CO	80403	318

Up scroll arrow

Vertical scroll box

Vertical scroll bar

Down scroll arrow

First Record navigation button

Record number box

Previous Record navigation button

Next Record navigation button

Last Record navigation button

New Record

4. Examine the table itself. Each column is a field and the field names appear at the tops of the columns. Each row is a record.

USING THE MOUSE TO MOVE IN A TABLE

Access provides many ways to move through a table. Let's take a look at some ways to navigate by using the mouse:

1. Point to the contents of the City field for the third record (Marie Abel's record; the field contains the text *Shackelford*). The pointer now appears as an I-beam, which means it is over an area where you can type text. Click once to place an insertion point in the City field. (The *insertion point* is the flashing vertical line Access uses to determine where text you type will appear.)

2. Click once on the **down scroll arrow** to scroll down one record (it is the downward-pointing arrow in the bottom-right corner of the window; refer to Figure 2.6, if necessary).

3. Point to the **vertical scroll box** (again, use Figure 2.6 if you need help finding it), press and hold the mouse button, drag the box to the bottom of the scroll bar, and then release the mouse button. Now you can see the bottom of the table, which contains a blank record. Dragging a scroll box is a quick way to move through a table.

4. Click on the **up scroll arrow** (refer to Figure 2.6) to scroll up one record per click.

5. Drag the **vertical scroll box** to the top of the scroll bar to move back to the top of the table.

6. Examine the Table window's navigation buttons, which are located in the lower-left corner of the Table window, directly above the status bar (as shown in Figure 2.6). These buttons allow you to either move through the table one record at a time, or to move quickly to the top or the bottom of a table. The box between the navigation buttons indicates the current record number. The total number of records in the table is indicated to the right of the navigation buttons.

7. Click on the **Next Record** navigation button to move to the next record, and then click on the **Previous Record** navigation button to move back to the previous record.

8. Click on the **Last Record** navigation button to move to the last record in the table, and then click on the **First Record** navigation button to move to the first record in the table.

9. Double-click on the number **1** in the Record Number box to select it, type **9**, and then press **Enter** to move to the ninth record (Roger Donaldson).

 ## Navigating in a Table with the Keyboard

You also can use the keyboard to move within a table. Let's try it:

1. First, use the mouse to place the insertion point in the City field for the first record in the table (Jane Martin's record; the field contains the text *Oceanside*).

2. Press the **Tab** key to move to the next field to the right, *St.*

3. While holding down the **Shift** key, press **Tab** to move back to the field to the left, City, and then release the Shift key. (In the future, when we want you to combine two keys in this manner, we'll say simply, "Press Shift+Tab.")

4. Press the **End** key to move to the final field in the current record (Ext), and then press the **Home** key to move to the first field in the current record (Last Name).

5. Press the **Down Arrow** key to move to the same field in the next record, and then press the **Up Arrow** key to move to the same field in the previous record.

6. Press **Ctrl+End** to move to the last field in the last record in the table (remember, that means hold down the **Ctrl** key, press **End**, and then release **Ctrl**); then press **Ctrl+Home** to move to the first field in the first record in the table.

FINDING A RECORD IN A TABLE

As tables get very large, it can become quite difficult to find a specific record. In the table we have open now, it wouldn't be too hard to locate Julia Binder's record because there are so few records in the table. However, imagine if you had to find her record in a table of *1,000* records.

Fortunately, Access provides a *Find* command you can use to locate records in tables of any size. To find a specific record, you would follow these steps:

• Place an insertion point within the field in which you want to search. For example, if you want to search for the record of someone whose last name is Smith, move to the Last Name field.

• Choose *Edit, Find* to open the Find dialog box for that field.

• In the Find What text box, type the text for which you want to search (for example, *Smith*).

• Click on *Find First* to find the first record that contains the text you typed in the current field. If you haven't found the correct record, click on *Find Next* to find the next occurrence of the text. You can repeat this process until you find the correct record.

• Click on *Close* to close the Find dialog box.

Let's find Andrea Carter's record in our table:

1. If necessary, move to the Last Name field (click within the Last Name column).

2. Choose **Edit, Find** to display the Find In Field: 'Last Name' dialog box. Notice that the title of the dialog box reflects our current field.

3. In the Find What box, type **Carter** (see Figure 2.7). You will search for a record that contains this text in the Last Name field.

Figure 2.7   **Finding a record**

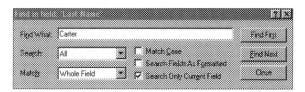

4. Click on the **Find First** button and then examine the table. Access selected the last name *Carter* in Record 25 (Andrea Carter's record), but the Find dialog box remains open.

5. Click on **Close** to close the dialog box.

USING THE TOOLBAR

You can perform many actions without going through the menu by clicking on a button in the toolbar. We saw an example of this the first time we opened a Help window. When you point to any button, Access will display the name of the tool, which can help you determine which tool you wish to use. Let's experiment briefly with the toolbar:

1. In the toolbar, point to the button with a picture of a pair of binoculars on it. If you keep pointing to it, Access displays a small box that tells you the name of the button, in this case, *Find*.

2. Click on the **Find** button in the toolbar to display the Find In Field: 'Last Name' dialog box. This is an alternative to choosing the Edit, Find command. The buttons that are available will change depending upon what you are doing, but you always can display the name of a button simply by pointing to it.

3. Click on **Close** to close the dialog box.

CLOSING A TABLE

When you finish viewing or editing a table, you may want to close it to clear it from the screen and from your computer's memory. (When you clear the table from memory, it will still remain in storage on your hard disk.) You close a table by clicking on the Table window's Close button, or by choosing File, Close.

Let's close the table:

1. Locate the Table window's Close button. It's in the upper-right corner of the screen, directly below the Application window's Close button.

2. Click on the **Close** button. (Don't click on the Application Close button, as this will close Access itself.) The Table window closes, revealing the Database window, which actually has been open all along.

PRACTICE YOUR SKILLS

You've already learned a great deal about getting around in Access. The following activity will give you a chance to apply some of this knowledge. Please don't think of this activity as a test, but rather as an opportunity to hone your Access skills. After all, it's only through practice that you'll really get good at the techniques you've learned.

In this activity, you'll open a table, navigate through the table, find a record, and close the table.

1. Open the Addresses and Extensions table.

2. Move to the last field in the last record in the table (Record 27).

3. Move to the first field in the last record.

4. Move to record number 4 (Julia Binder's record).

5. Find David Haslam's record.

6. Move to the first field in the first record.

7. Close the Table window (but leave the Database window open).

ORIENTATION TO FORMS

You use forms to view and edit data that is stored in a table. Like the sample paper form we saw in Chapter 1, Access forms allow you to create a custom layout for your data.

Access lets you create forms that show your data in almost any layout you can imagine. For simplicity's sake, however, we'll start by looking at a fairly simple form that is based on the Addresses and Extensions table. You open a form the same way that you open a table: display the form object names in the Database window, select the one you want, and click on the Open button (you also can double-click on the object name).

Let's open and examine a form:

1. In the Database window, click on the **Forms** tab to display the list of form object names. There are three form objects in this database.

2. Double-click on **Address Data Entry** to open the Address Data Entry form (see Figure 2.8). Only one record from the Addresses and Extensions table appears in the form window. The field names (Last Name, First Name, Adr, and so on) appear to the left of each field. There also are some different buttons available on the toolbar.

3. At the bottom of the Form window, click on the **Next Record** navigation button to view the next record. This works just as it does in the Datasheet view of a table.

4. Click on the **Last Record** navigation button to move to the last record in the table, and then click on the **First Record** navigation button to move to Record 1.

You also can find records from a Form window just as you would from a Table window. Let's try it:

1. Click on the **First Name** label to select the text *Jane* and to make First Name the current field. Notice that the Record Number box says the current record is Record 1.

2. In the toolbar, click on the **Find button** (the pair of binoculars) to open the Find In Field: 'First Name' dialog box. Notice that the last search value you used still appears in the Find What text box.

Figure 2.8　　　**The Address Data Entry form**

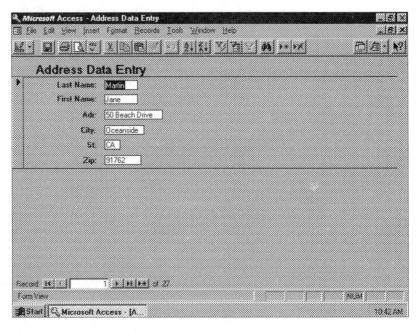

3. Type **Roger,** and then click on **Find First** to find the first record that contains the text *Roger* in the First Name field. Access has found the record. If you look at the Record Number box, you'll notice that the current record is now 9; you'll also notice that the status bar displays the message *Search succeeded*.

4. Click on **Close** to close the dialog box. The text *Roger* is selected in the record for Roger Donaldson.

5. Click on the Form window's **Close** button to close the Form window and return to the Database window.

ORIENTATION TO SORTING AND QUERYING

As your database tables grow larger, you will need to control the order and amount of data that you see on the screen. Two ways that you can accomplish this are through sorting and querying.

SORTING RECORDS

By default, records appear in tables in the order in which you enter them. However, when you are working with large tables, you might prefer to sort the records in some other order. For example, you might want to sort a table of invoices by invoice number, or a table of employees by department.

When working in a form, you can sort records by any single field, or by a combination of fields. For example, in a telephone book, entries are sorted by last name and then by first name, so that Mary Smith appears after John Smith.

To sort records by a single field, from a form:

• Place the insertion point in the field you want to sort on.

• Click on the Sort Ascending or Sort Descending button in the toolbar.

Let's sort some records by last name:

1. In the Database window, double-click on **Internal Phone List** to open the Internal Phone List form shown in Figure 2.9. This form is based on the Addresses and Extensions table. However, instead of a single-column layout, this form is in a tabular layout that lets you see more than one record at a time. Notice that the records are in no apparent order.

2. To sort the data in this form alphabetically by last name, make sure that the insertion point is in the Last Name field, then click on the **Sort Ascending** button.

3. Close the Form window.

RUNNING A QUERY

A *query*, as its name suggests, lets you ask questions about data. Keep in mind that a query is the actual question you ask, and not the data that answers that question. Because of this, you get up-to-date information every time you run a query.

Figure 2.9　　　**The Internal Phone List form**

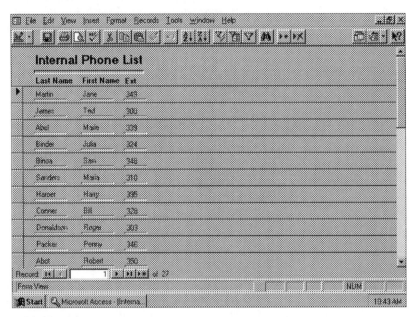

For example, you might run a query to see a list of the people in your company who make more than $10 per hour. A month later, you could run the same query (ask the same question) but get a new list of employees because some salaries have increased (or decreased, for that matter!).

Let's run a query that asks for a list of the people who live in California from the Addresses and Extensions table:

1. In the Database window, click on the **Tables** tab to display the list of table object names, and then double-click on **Addresses and Extensions** to open the table. The records are in no apparent order and list all employees, regardless of their state.

2. Close the Table window (click on the Table window's Close button or choose **File, Close**).

3. In the Database window, click on the **Queries** tab to view the list of query object names.

4. Double-click on **CA Addresses** to run the CA Addresses query (see Figure 2.10). The employees appear in alphabetical order by last name, and only employees who live in California

are listed. Although the result of a query looks like a table, the data you see is not stored as a table. The query object stored with the database is simply the request, *Show me California employees*.

Figure 2.10   **The result of the CA Addresses query**

Last Name	First Name	Adr	City	St	Zip
Binga	Sam	50 Dallas Street	Pasadena	CA	91106
Harper	Harry	82 East Avenue	Long Beach	CA	90745
Martin	Jane	50 Beach Drive	Oceanside	CA	91762
Zambito	Joseph	81 Pleasing Lane	Alhambra	CA	91801

5. Close the Query window (click on the Query window's Close button or choose **File, Close**).

ORIENTATION TO REPORTS

Reports are the last database object we'll explore in this chapter. Although you can print from tables, forms, and queries, reports provide the best way to present your data as a printed document.

You might think of telephone lists, mailing labels, invoices, and sales summaries as examples of reports. You can base reports on tables or queries, and you can include summary information. On an invoice, for example, you may want to include summary information such as the number of items purchased and the total cost of those items.

PREVIEWING A BASIC REPORT

When you *preview* a report you can see how it will look when printed. Previewing reports, especially when you are working with and creating new reports, can save you both time and paper.

Let's preview a basic report that is based on the Pay Rates table:

1. Open the Pay Rates table. (Display the list of table object names, and then double-click on **Pay Rates**.) It includes data on employees' hours and pay rates.

2. Close the Table window.

3. In the Database window, click on the **Reports** tab to display the list of report object names.

4. Select **Employee Hours and Rates**, and then click on the **Preview** button to preview the report. (The mouse pointer may change to an hourglass while Access generates the report.) Except for the report's date, which will vary, your report should look like the one in Figure 2.11. The toolbar displays several buttons you can use to control the preview.

Figure 2.11   **Previewing the Employee Hours and Rates report**

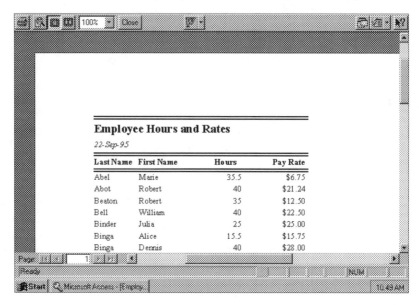

5. Click on the **Zoom** button to view the full page (it looks like a magnifying glass over a document).

6. Click on the **Zoom** button again to return to a close-up view.

7. Use the vertical and horizontal scroll bars to scroll through the report. The report has a title, displays the current date, and lists employees alphabetically with their hours and pay rates.

8. Scroll to the bottom of the report to view the summary information: grand totals for hours and pay rates.

9. On the Preview toolbar, click on the **Close** button to close the Report window.

PREVIEWING A REPORT WITH GROUPS AND TOTALS

Reports also let you arrange your data in groups, and total each group of data separately. For example, if you are creating a gross-pay report, you may want to group employees by department and then calculate each department's total gross pay.

Let's preview a report that does just that:

1. In the Database window, double-click on **Dept Gross Pay** to preview the report. (Double-clicking on a report object name is an alternative to selecting the name and then clicking on the Preview button.) Your screen should resemble Figure 2.12.

Figure 2.12   **Previewing the Dept Gross Pay report**

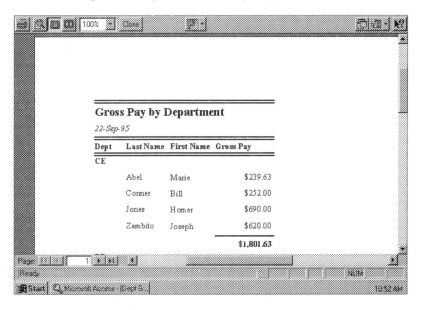

2. Use the vertical scroll bar to scroll down through the first page of the report. The records appear in groups by department. Within each department, the records are in alphabetical order, and the total gross pay for the department appears at the bottom of each group.

3. Click on the **Last Page** navigation button and then scroll up or down, as necessary, to view the grand total at the end of the report. (When you preview a report, Access displays page navigation buttons rather than record navigation buttons.)

4. Close the Report window.

SUMMARY

In this chapter, you learned how to start and exit Access, how to open a database, and how to use some key database objects: tables, forms, queries, and reports. Congratulations! You're well on your way to mastering Access.

Here's a quick reference guide to some of the techniques introduced in this chapter:

Desired Result	How to Do It
Maximize (restore) window	Click on window's **Maximize** or **Restore** button
Choose command	Click on menu name and then click on command name
Open Help Topics window	Press **F1**
Close window	Double-click on window's **Control menu icon**, or click on **Close** button
Open database	Click on **Open Database** button; select drive and directory; select database file name; click on **Open**
View database object names	In Database window, click on appropriate object tabs

Desired Result	How to Do It
Open table	Click on **Tables** tab in Database window, select **table object name**, and click on **Open** (or double-click on **table object name**)
Place insertion point in field	Click on field
Scroll down (up) one record in table	Click on **down scroll arrow** (**up scroll arrow**)
Scroll to the bottom (top) of table	Drag **vertical scroll box** to bottom (top) of vertical scroll bar
Move to next (previous) record in table	Click on **Next Record** (**Previous Record**) navigation button (or press appropriate **Arrow key**)
Move to first (last) record in table	Click on **First Record** (**Last Record**) navigation button
Move to specific record in table	Double-click in **Record Number** box, type desired record number, and press **Enter**
Move to next (previous) field in record	Press **Tab** (**Shift+Tab**)
Move to the first (last) field in record	Press **Home** (**End**)
Move to first field in first record in table	Press **Ctrl+Home**
Move to last field in last record in table	Press **Ctrl+End**
Find record	Move to field in which you want to search, choose **Edit, Find** (or click on Find button in toolbar), type text you want to find, click on **Find First** (or **Find Next**), and then click on **Close**

Desired Result	How to Do It
Open form	Click on **Forms** tab, select **form object name**, and click on **Open** (or double-click on **form object name**)
Sort records in form	Select field you wish to sort by, click on the **Sort Ascending** or **Sort Descending** buttons
Run a query	Click on **Queries** tab, select **query object name**, and click on **Open** (or double-click on **query object name**)
Preview a report	Click on **Reports** tab, select the **report object name**, and click on **Preview** (or double-click on the **report object name**)
Zoom in and out on previewed report	Click on **Zoom** button
Close previewed report	Click on **Close** button in the middle of the Preview toolbar

A NOTE ON HOW TO PROCEED

If you wish to stop here, please feel free to do so. If you want to press onward, please proceed directly to the next chapter. If you are going on, you should try to allow enough time to work through the entire chapter in one sitting.

CHAPTER 3: TABLE BASICS

Examining a Table
and Its Design

Designing and
Creating a Table

Adding Records
to a Table

Modifying a Table
Design

Using the Table
Wizard to Create a
Table

In Chapter 2, we took a passing glance at some of the major elements of an Access database: objects (including tables, forms, queries, and reports). In this chapter, we'll take a closer look at Access's cornerstone objects: tables.

When you're done working through this chapter, you will know

- About the design of a table
- How to create, save, and modify a table design
- How to create and modify fields
- How to set a primary key
- How to add and save records
- How to modify the Datasheet-view layout
- How to preview and print a table

EXAMINING A TABLE AND ITS DESIGN

You learned in Chapter 2 that tables are the only type of database objects that actually store data. There is more to a table, however, than its contents; there is also its design.

A table design is like the foundation of a house: While you don't see it most of the time, it determines how the table will look and function. Without a good foundation, a house will fall apart; without a good design, a table won't work properly.

The design of a table includes

- The assignment of field names
- The order in which fields will appear in the table
- The type of data each field will contain
- Field properties (which can determine, among other things, a field's size, appearance, and behavior)
- Field descriptions

An Access table can contain up to 255 fields.

You can observe and modify the design of a table through the table's *Design view*. To switch to the Design view of an open table, choose View, Table Design (or click on the Design View button on the far left side of the toolbar).

If you are not currently running Access with the Employee Database window open, please follow the steps outlined in Chapters 1 and 2 under "Starting Access" and "Opening a Database" to start the program and open the Employee database.

To become more familiar with table design before you create your own table, let's first take a look at an existing table and its design:

1. If they aren't already maximized, maximize the application window and the Database window. (Click on each window's **Maximize** button until the windows completely fill the screen.)

2. Open the Hours and Rates table. (In the Database window, display the list of table object names, and then double-click on **Hours and Rates**.) The table's fields include ID, Last Name, First Name, Hired, Dept, Hours, Pay Rate, and Health. Values in the ID field begin with zeros. Values in the Hired field appear in the *mm/dd/yy* format. Values in the Hours field display decimals only when necessary. Values in the Pay Rate field display dollar signs and two decimal places. Values in the Health field are either Yes or No. Notice also that the status bar indicates that this is the Datasheet view of the table.

3. Choose **View, Table Design** to switch to the table's Design view, and then compare your screen to Figure 3.1. The window is split into two panes: The upper pane contains a *design grid*, and the lower pane displays field properties. Each row in the design grid defines one of the table's fields. The columns in the grid define different aspects of each field, specifically field name, data type, and field description. (We'll discuss each of these in greater detail shortly.) Notice that the data type for the ID field is *Text*.

4. Click on the **field selector** to the left of the text *ID* to select that row, and then examine the Field Properties pane of the window (refer to Figure 3.1). It displays properties for the ID field: The Field Size property is set to 4, and the Indexed property is set to Yes (No Duplicates). You will learn more about the elements of a Table window's Design view later in this chapter when you create your own table.

5. Close the Table window. (Click on its **Close button**.)

DESIGNING AND CREATING A TABLE

The keys to a well-designed database are well-designed tables. Before you create a table, carefully consider the type of information you will need to store and retrieve. Then, plan your table design around those needs.

Figure 3.1   The Hours and Rates table in Design view

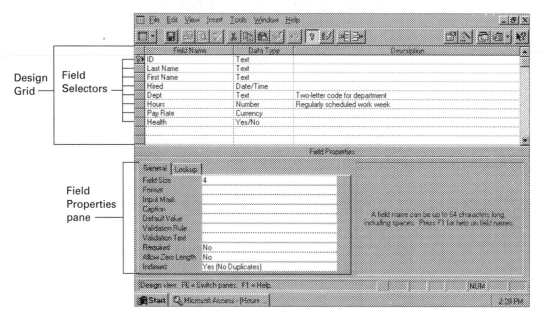

When you're planning a table, follow these steps:

- Determine the fields (categories) of data you need and what data types they should be. (Table 3.1 describes the data types available in Access.) If you use paper forms to collect data, they are excellent tools for determining fields and data types. Proper data types are important; for example, you wouldn't want to use text as the data type for a field if you intended to perform calculations on that field's data.

- Decide if the data are closely related and should be in one table or if they can be split into multiple tables. For example, you might divide your data into one table for employee information and a second table for supplier information. Or, as we discussed earlier, you might have one table for customers and another for invoices. When possible, using more than one *related* table will make your databases more efficient.

- Try to anticipate what questions you will need to ask about the data; for example, "How will I want to sort the data?" or "In what groups will I want to see the data?"

Table 3.1   **Data Types**

Data Type	Use for
Text	Text, numbers on which you will not do calculations, and numbers that will display leading zeros. Examples include names, telephone numbers, zip codes, and product-identification codes. You can define text fields to contain up to 255 characters; the default field size is 50 characters.
Yes/No	Values that are restricted to one of two logical values (such as Yes or No, True or False, and On or Off).
Date/Time	Dates and times that you can use for date arithmetic.
Number	Numerical data on which you will perform calculations (except for money). Number fields can store numbers with up to 15 digits of precision.
Currency	Values representing money. Currency fields can store numbers with up to 15 digits to the left of the decimal point and up to 4 digits to the right. By default, currency-field values display dollar signs ($) and thousands separators (commas).
Memo	Lengthy text and numbers, such as comments or explanations. Memo fields can store up to 32,000 characters per record.
OLE Object	Object Linking and Embedding (OLE) objects created in another application and linked to Access using Windows's OLE protocol. (Refer to Access's online Help for an overview of OLE.)
Auto-Number	Numbers that are automatically inserted when a record is added.
Lookup Wizard	Creates a field that allows you to choose (through a series of Wizard dialog boxes) values from another table.

- Identify the types of reports you will need to produce from your data. There may well be existing reports you can use as models.

For each field in a table, you will need to specify a unique field name. In Microsoft Access, field names can be up to 64 characters long and can include any combination of letters (upper- and lowercase), numbers, spaces, and special characters with the following exceptions:

- Leading spaces

- Periods (.)

- Exclamation points (!)

- Square brackets ([])

- Control characters (ASCII values 0 through 31)

DESIGNING THE TABLE

Let's plan the design of your first table, an employee-information table. First, examine Figure 3.2, which shows a paper data-collection form upon which we will base our table. Table 3.2 poses some questions about how we should design our table, and suggests some answers. Bear in mind that there are not necessarily "right" or "wrong" answers to these questions.

Figure 3.2   **A sample paper data-collection form**

Employee Information Form

Employee ID: _____   Date Hired: _____

Name (Last, First): _____

Hours/Week: _____   Rate/Hour:_____

Gross Pay: _____

Health Insurance: ___ Yes   ___ No

Table 3.2   **Planning Our Design**

Question	Answer
Should an employee's name be one field, as it is on the form, or two fields (one for first name and one for last name)?	We will make it two fields so that we can sort employee records by last name, first name, or both.
Should the ID field be a text field or a number field?	Because we want our ID numbers to include leading zeros—and we'll never need to use them in calculations—we'll make ID a text field.
What data type should we use for the hire-date field?	Date/Time is the obvious choice, but one reason why isn't so obvious. The Date/Time data type will allow us to use these dates in date arithmetic—for example, to find all employees hired before a certain date.
What data type should we use for the hours field?	Because we'll use this field in calculations, we'll use the Number data type.
Should we also use Number as the data type for the hourly rate field?	Because the hourly rate is a currency value, we'll do best by using the Currency data type.
Should we include a field for gross pay?	It's not necessary to include this field because we can always calculate gross pay by multiplying hours worked by hourly rate. To increase accuracy and efficiency in your tables, never include a field that you can calculate from other fields. We can create reports and queries that will show us any calculation we can imagine.
Should the health-insurance field be two fields (as on the form) or one?	If we use the Yes/No data type, we can use just one field.

Now examine Figure 3.3. This is a report that displays selected information on members of the Marketing department. When looking at such a report, the question you should ask yourself is, "What additional information do I need in my table to be able to create this report?" The answer in this case is that we need a field to identify each employee's department.

Figure 3.3   **A sample report**

Marketing Department - Wages

Dept	Last	First	Gross Pay
MK			
	Abot	Robert	$849.60
	Bell	William	$900.00
	Binder	Julia	$625.00
	Binga	Dennis	$1,120.00
	James	Ted	$898.70
	Naylor	Ruth	$1,080.00
	Osowski	Dominick	$880.00
	Packer	Penny	$840.00
	Stira	Barbara	$1,040.00
			$8,233.30

CREATING THE TABLE AND A TEXT FIELD

Once you determine your needs for a table, you can create a new table by following these steps:

- Display the table object names in the Database window and click on *New,* select *Design View,* and click on *OK* to display an empty Table window in Design view.

- Use the design grid to enter a field name and data type for each field you need in your table. If you wish, you also can specify a description and field properties for each field.

- Decide whether you want to set a primary key and, if so, on what field or fields. (We'll discuss primary keys later in this chapter.)

- Choose *File, Save As* to display the Save As dialog box.
- Type a name for the new table and then click on *OK*.

Let's begin to create our employee table:

1. Be sure that the list of table objects appears in the Database window, and then click on the **New** button to display the New Table dialog box. Access gives you the choice of creating a new table, or using the Table Wizard to help you create the table. *Wizards* are features that lead you through the process of creating various objects.

2. Click on **Design View** to open a new Table window in Design view (see Figure 3.4). Because this is a new table, the design grid is empty. Because there are no fields, Access does not display any field properties in the lower pane. The insertion point is in the Field Name cell of the first row, ready for you to add the table's first field name.

Figure 3.4   **The Design view of the new table**

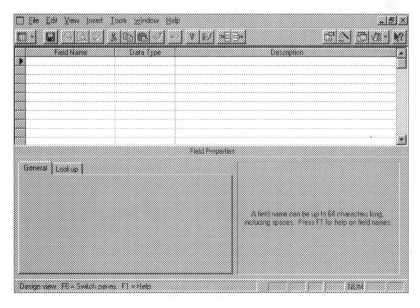

Now let's create your first field, ID, as a text field:

1. In the Field Name cell of the first row of the design grid, type **ID**; then press **Tab** to move to the Data Type column. Access selects the default data type, Text. Note that Access now displays field properties applicable to text fields at the bottom of the Table window, and has filled in default values for Field Size and several other properties. (You will learn more about the Indexed property later in this chapter under "Setting a Primary Key.") The status bar indicates that you can use the F6 function key to switch to the Field Properties pane.

2. Press **F6** to move to the Field Properties pane and if neccessary, select the default value of 50 in the Field Size box. (You also can double-click in the Field Size box to achieve the same result.)

3. Because the ID numbers will be only four digits long, type **4** to replace the default value. Your screen should now look like Figure 3.5.

Figure 3.5   **Defining the ID field**

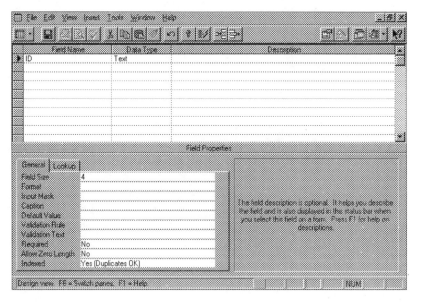

USING ONLINE HELP TO LEARN ABOUT DATA TYPES

Access provides an extensive help system which, among other things, can help you figure out which data type would be appropriate for your fields.

Let's create your last-name field (which we'll call LN), and try out this online help in the process:

1. Place the insertion point in the Field Name cell of the second row. (Use the mouse to point to the cell, and then click.)

2. Type **LN** and then press **Tab** to move to the Data Type column. (Later, you'll change this field name so that it's more descriptive.)

3. Click on the **drop-down arrow** on the right of the current Data Type cell to display a list of data types. There are nine types from which to choose.

4. Click on the **drop-down arrow** once more to close the list, and then choose **Help, Microsoft Access Help Topics** to open the Help Topics window. Select the **Index** tab.

5. Type *data type* to list the topics having to do with data types. Under the data types category, select **described**, and click on the **Display** button.

6. Scroll down the Help window until the information about the *text* data type is displayed, and click on the **More Information** button. (When you point at the button, the mouse pointer becomes a pointing hand.) Scroll through and read about the Text data type.

7. Click off of the Help window and onto the lower pane of the Table window. Notice that the Help window is still displayed.

8. Select the number in the Field Size box and type **15** to allow up to 15 characters for data in the LN field.

9. Close the Help window by clicking on its Close button.

PRACTICE YOUR SKILLS

1. Add a third field, called **Dept**, to the table.

2. Define Dept as a text field.

3. Change the field size to **2**. (Your screen should resemble Figure 3.6.)

Figure 3.6   **The table design after adding the Dept field**

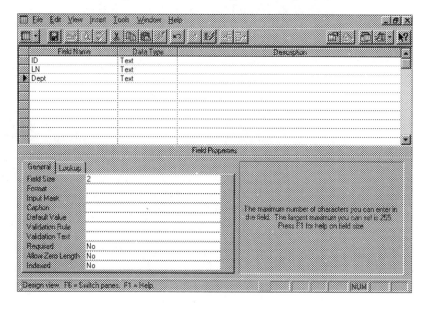

 CREATING A YES/NO FIELD

As we discussed earlier, a single field with the Yes/No data type would be ideal for the health-insurance field. Let's create a yes/no field for health insurance:

1. Place the insertion point in the Field Name cell of the next row in the design grid.

2. Type **Health**, and then press **Tab** to move to the Data Type column.

3. In the Data Type column, select **Yes/No** from the drop-down list. (Click on the drop-down arrow and then click on

Yes/No.) Your screen should now match the one shown in Figure 3.7. Notice that fewer field properties are applicable to yes/no fields than to text fields. The Format box displays *Yes/No* by default, but a yes/no field also can be formatted to display *True/False* or *On/Off*.

Figure 3.7   **The design of the Health field**

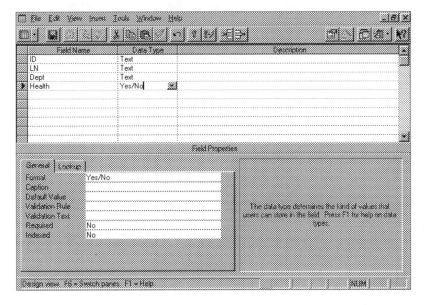

 CREATING A DATE FIELD

The Date/Time data type is the clear choice for our hire-date field; it is ideal not only because it can store dates and times, but also because you can use values in date/time fields to perform date arithmetic. Among other things, you can use date arithmetic to sort records by date, or to calculate the average number of days it takes between accepting and shipping an order.

By using a hired-date field in your employee table, you'll be able to generate a seniority list or schedule annual performance appraisals and raises. Let's create that field now:

1. Place the insertion point in the Field Name cell of the next blank row in the design grid.

2. Type **HD** (for *hired date*), and then press **Tab** to move to the Data Type column.

3. Select **Date/Time** from the Data Type drop-down list (see Figure 3.8).

Figure 3.8   **The design of the HD field**

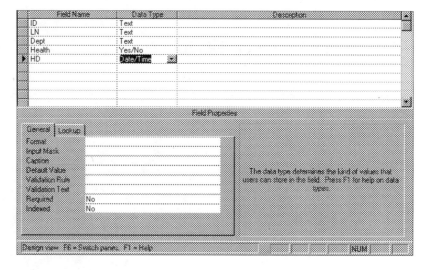

CREATING A NUMBER FIELD

Next we'll create the hours-worked field. Because you'll want to be able to use this field in calculations, its data type should be Number. Another twist we'll add with this field is a description that will appear in the status bar when the insertion point is in the field. Not surprisingly, you add a description to a field by using the Description column in the design grid.

Let's create the hours-worked field:

1. Place the insertion point in the Field Name cell of the next blank row in the design grid, type **Hours**, and then press **Tab**.

2. Select **Number** from the Data Type drop-down list, and then press **Tab** to move to the Description column.

3. In the Description column, type **Normal weekly hours**. This description will appear in the status bar whenever a user selects a value in this field.

4. Observe the default values Access has set for the Hours field. The Field Size is set to Long Integer by default. Press **F6** to move to the Field Properties pane. From the Field Size drop-down list select **Double** (see Figure 3.9). Double is a flexible and accurate number-field size. Decimal Places is set to *Auto*, so decimal places will be displayed only when necessary. The Default Value is set to *0*, meaning that the value will appear in the field if you do not enter any other value. Required is set to *No*, meaning that it is not necessary to enter a value in this field for every record.

Figure 3.9 **The design of the Hours field**

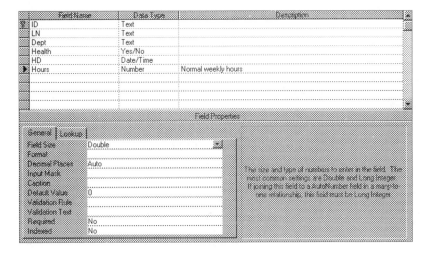

CREATING A CURRENCY FIELD

You'll be using your hourly-rate field for calculations, but because it will store currency values, you'll assign it the Currency data type.

Let's create a currency field named *Pay Rate:*

1. Place the insertion point in the Field Name cell of the next blank row in the design grid, type **Pay Rate**, and then press **Tab**.

2. Select **Currency** from the Data Type drop-down list. Notice the default field property values for currency fields: *Auto* for Decimal Places, *0* for Default Value, *No* for Indexed (see Figure 3.10).

Figure 3.10   **The design of the Pay Rate field**

Field Name	Data Type	Description
ID	Text	
LN	Text	
Dept	Text	
Health	Yes/No	
HD	Date/Time	
Hours	Number	Normal weekly hours
Pay Rate	Currency	

Field Properties

General	Lookup	
Format	Currency
Decimal Places	Auto
Input Mask	
Caption	
Default Value	0
Validation Rule	
Validation Text	
Required	No
Indexed	No

The data type determines the kind of values that users can store in the field. Press F1 for help on data types.

SETTING A PRIMARY KEY

A primary key is any field or combination of fields in a table that uniquely identifies each table record. In an inventory table, for example, you might use a product part number as a primary-key field. When you set a primary key, Access will

- Not permit you to enter records that contain duplicate values in the primary key. For example, no two employees can have the same ID number if the ID field is set as the primary key.

- Use the primary key as a main index to speed data retrieval from large tables. Access uses a primary key as you would use the index in the back of this book to locate data quickly.

Primary keys also help define relationships between tables so that you can use them in concert. You will learn more about table relationships in Chapter 10.

Although Access does not require you to set a primary key for a table, it strongly encourages you to do so. In fact, if you try to save the design of a new or modified table and have not set a primary key, Access offers to create a primary-key field for you. You will learn how to instruct Access to create a primary-key field for you in Chapter 10.

To set a primary key in the Design view of a table, select the appropriate field or fields, and then choose Edit, Set Primary Key (or click on the Primary Key button in the toolbar; it looks like a key).

Because our ID numbers always will be unique, let's set the ID field as the primary key for our table:

1. Click on the **field selector** for the ID row to select it (the field selector is the button just to the left of the row).

2. Click on the **Primary Key** button in the toolbar to set the ID field as the primary key for the table (see Figure 3.11). Notice that a key indicator now appears on the ID row's field selector. This indicates that you have successfully set ID as the primary key.

Figure 3.11   **Setting a primary key**

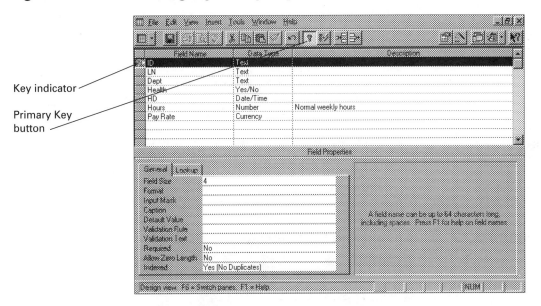

3. Observe the Indexed property box. When you set ID as the primary key, Access automatically changed the property from *No* to *Yes (No Duplicates)*. This property prevents anyone entering data into this table from duplicating an ID number. This precaution ensures that Access can identify records uniquely.

SAVING THE TABLE DESIGN

After you have created your fields and set a primary key, you are ready to save your table design. *Saving* is the process of taking information stored in computer memory (a temporary storage area) and copying it to a more permanent storage area, such as your hard disk. If you don't save your work, you could lose it in the event of a power failure, or if you accidentally turn your computer off. If you've saved it, however, your table design will still be available from your hard disk the next time you load Access.

To save a table design, you would follow these steps:

• From the table's Design view, choose *File, Save As/Export* to open the Save As dialog box.

• Type a name for the table. Table names can be up to 64 characters long and must follow the same naming conventions as field names (see "Designing and Creating a Table" earlier in this chapter).

• Click on *OK*.

Let's save the design of our new table:

1. Choose **File, Save As/Export** to display the Save As dialog box. By default, Access suggests that you use the name *Table1*. Unfortunately, this is not a particularly descriptive name.

2. Type **My Rates and Hours** to give the table a more descriptive name, as shown in Figure 3.12. (In this book, anytime you create a new object you'll begin its name with the text *My* so that you can distinguish it from other objects.)

Figure 3.12   **Saving the table design**

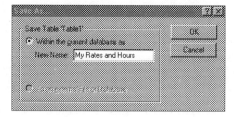

3. Click on **OK** to name the table and close the dialog box. The title bar now displays your new table name.

ADDING RECORDS TO A TABLE

After you design your table, you can begin adding records to it. To add records to a table, you must be in the Datasheet view (or a Form view, which we'll discuss further in Chapter 6). You can switch to the Datasheet view either by choosing View, Datasheet or by clicking on the Datasheet View button in the toolbar.

The Datasheet view for a new table will show only the table's field names across the top of the table and a blank record underneath. If any fields have default values (such as the Hours and Pay Rate fields in our new table), Access will show those default values in the otherwise blank record. No matter how many records are in a table, it always will contain one blank record at the bottom. This allows you to add more records.

To add records in the Datasheet view of a table, simply begin typing in the blank record. As you begin to enter data in the first record, Access will automatically add a new blank record below the first. To move to the next field in a record, you can press either Tab or Enter. You can move to the previous field in a record by pressing Shift+Tab.

To save a record, simply move to a different one. You can do this by using the mouse, or by pressing Tab or Enter when the last field in a record is active. (This moves you to the first field of the next record.) You also can save data in a record without leaving the record by choosing Records, Save Record.

As you enter data in the Datasheet view, you can get information about a record by observing its record selector. (Like the field selector in the Design view, this is the button to the left of the record's row.) The indicators that appear on the record selectors have different meanings:

- A triangle pointing to the right indicates the current record (that is, the record that contains the insertion point).

- A pencil means the current record has been edited but not yet saved.

- An asterisk indicates the last row in the table (which is blank).

- A circle with a slash through it means the record is locked. (See your Access documentation for more information on locked records.)

ADDING AND SAVING RECORDS

Let's switch to the Datasheet view of our table and add some records to it:

1. Choose **View, Datasheet** to switch to the Datasheet view of the table (see Figure 3.13). The names of the fields you created in the Design view appear at the top; other than that, the table contains only a single blank record. Notice also that all the columns, or fields, do not fit within the width of the screen. A triangle pointing to the right appears on the record selector for the blank record, meaning that it is the current record.

Figure 3.13   **The empty Datasheet view of the My Rates and Hours table**

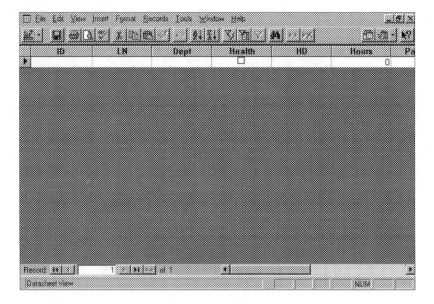

2. Click once on the **right scroll arrow** so that you can see the right edge of the table. Both the Hours and Pay Rate fields show default values in the blank record.

3. Click on the **left scroll arrow** to return to the left side of the table, and then verify that the insertion point is in the ID field. (If it is not, point to the ID field in the blank record and click once.)

4. Type **0020** to enter a value in the ID field. As you begin typing in this record, Access automatically adds a new, blank record beneath it. The record selector for the current field now displays a pencil, which means you've made changes to the record that have not yet been saved. The second record selector displays an asterisk to indicate that it is the last record in the table.

5. Press **Tab** to move to the next field in the record (LN), type **Hanover**, and then press **Tab** again to move to the Dept field.

6. Type **MS** (the two-letter code for the Marketing Support Department), and then press **Tab** to move to the Health field. This field shows a blank check box, which means No.

7. Click in the check box in the Health field to indicate that the employee is covered by health insurance; then press **Tab** to move to the HD field.

8. Type **2–20–90** to enter the date of hire, and then press **Tab** to move to the Hours field. Access automatically adjusts the date in the HD field to *2/20/90*. Also notice that with the Hours field active, the status bar displays the field description you entered in Design view: *Normal weekly hours*.

9. Type **32.5** to enter the normal weekly hours, and then press **Tab**. Access automatically scrolls to the right as you move to the Pay Rate field.

10. Type **15** to enter the hourly pay rate. Because this is a currency field, you do not need to type a dollar sign before the value. Access will take care of that for you.

11. Press **Tab** once more to move to the first field of the next record (see Figure 3.14). Access automatically scrolls back to the left side of the table and saves the last record. The record selector for the first record is now blank, meaning that the record is no longer current and has been saved. The second selector displays a triangle pointing to the right because it is now the current record.

Figure 3.14   **The table after entering the first record**

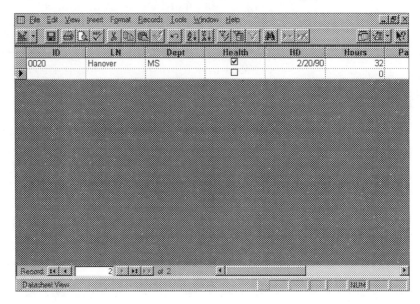

PRACTICE YOUR SKILLS

1. Enter the following records into the table:

ID:	LN:	Dept	Health:	HD:	Hours:	Pay Rate:
0021	Jaen	MK	Yes	6/15/86	40	12
0022	Monder	EE	No	1/6/90	40	20.75
0023	Tallon	MK	Yes	11/17/91	32.5	21.5

2. Move the insertion point to the blank record to save the last record. Your screen should resemble Figure 3.15.

MODIFYING A TABLE DESIGN

Even with the best planning, you may find that you need to modify your table design. Through a table's Design view, you can add, rename, delete, move, or change the data type or properties of any field. After you make modifications to a table design, you should choose File, Save to save those changes.

Figure 3.15   **The table after adding three more records**

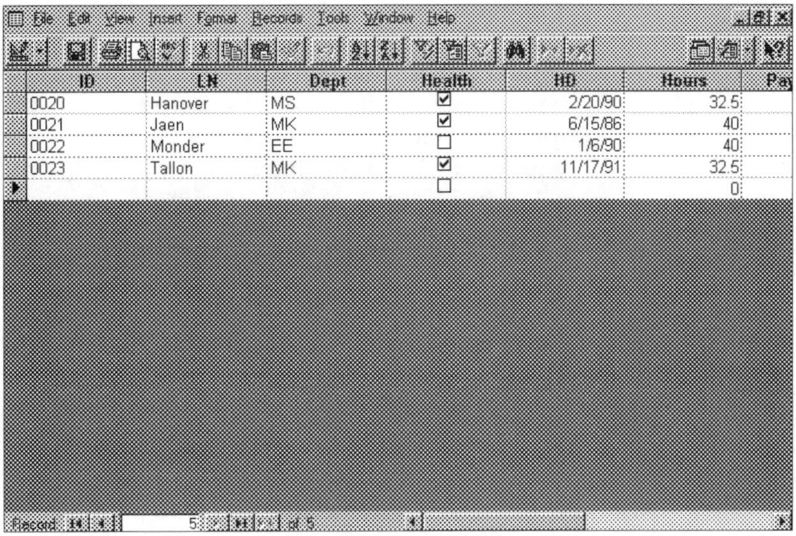

ID	LN	Dept	Health	HD	Hours	Pa
0020	Hanover	MS	☑	2/20/90	32.5	
0021	Jaen	MK	☑	6/15/86	40	
0022	Monder	EE	☐	1/6/90	40	
0023	Tallon	MK	☑	11/17/91	32.5	
			☐		0	

Modifying the design of a table can have far-reaching effects on your database. For this reason, you should consider the following things before you make such changes:

- It is a good idea to make a backup copy of a table (or of the entire database) before modifying a table design.

- If you delete a field, Access also will delete any data it contains.

- When you delete or rename a field in the table design, you also must delete it from or rename it in related objects. Until you do, any queries, forms, or reports in which the field appears may not work properly.

- If you reduce a field to a smaller size, Access may *truncate,* or cut off, data that will not fit in the smaller field.

- If you change a field's data type, Access will attempt to convert your existing data, which may create unexpected results. (Refer to Access's online Help for information on the possibilities and pitfalls of data conversion.)

IDENTIFYING THE NEED FOR IMPROVEMENTS TO A TABLE

You will save considerable time and effort in the long run by thinking carefully about your table designs before entering data and creating other objects. However, some design problems will not be apparent until you have entered at least some data, or have tried to create other objects based on your table. And, of course, your needs from the database may change over time.

Table 3.3 poses some questions about the design of our new table, and suggests some ways in which we might improve that design.

Table 3.3

Considering the Design of the My Rates and Hours Table

Question	Answer
Are the field names useful?	You could change the name of the LN field to Last Name to make it more descriptive. You might wish to do the same with the HD field.
What if there are two employees with the same last name?	Right now, we wouldn't be able to tell two such employees apart. We should add a first-name field to the table so we can distinguish employees with the same last name.
What if a new company policy stated that all employees would receive health insurance?	Such a policy would make the Health field irrelevant.

CHANGING FIELD NAMES

In a table's Design view, you can edit a field name by selecting it and then typing. Let's change the names of a couple of our fields:

1. Click on the **Design View** button on the toolbar to switch to the Design view of the My Rates and Hours table.

2. In the Field Name column, double-click on **LN** to select the field name.

3. Type **Last Name** to create a more descriptive name for the field.

4. In the Field Name column, double-click on **HD** to select the field name.

5. Type **Hired** to create a new name for this field, and then compare your screen to Figure 3.16.

Figure 3.16   **Changing field names**

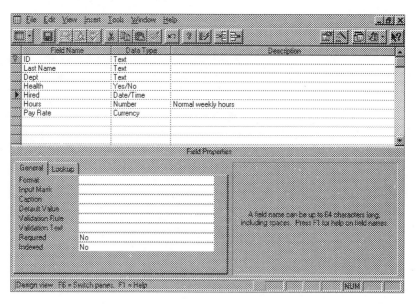

 ## USING SHORTCUT MENUS

There are often many ways to issue commands in Access. We've already seen that the toolbar, in many cases, offers buttons that act as shortcuts for menu commands. Another useful feature for issuing commands is the *shortcut menu*. When you point to many parts of the Access screen and click the right mouse button, Access displays a menu containing commands that are appropriate to the part of the screen on which you click. You then choose the commands as you would in any menu.

INSERTING AND DELETING FIELDS

You can add a field to the end of a table simply by adding a new row to the design grid. To add a field between two other fields in the table, however, you need to create a new field row to make room. To insert a new row between existing field rows:

- Click on the field selector for the field above which you would like the new row to appear.

- Choose *Insert, Field* to insert a blank row and move the remaining fields down one row (or press the *Insert* key). You then can create a new field in the blank row.

To delete a field:

- Select the field you wish to delete (click on its field selector).

- Choose *Edit, Delete Row* to delete the selected field and its row from the design grid (or press the *Delete* key). Access will display a dialog box reminding you that by deleting a field, you also delete any data contained within that field.

- Click on **Yes** to confirm the deletion, or click on **No** if you decide not to delete the field after all.

Note: Both the Insert Row and Delete Row commands are available in the shortcut menu for any part of the design grid.

Let's add a first-name field and delete the Health field:

1. Click on the **field selector** for the Dept row in the design grid. We will insert a new row for the first-name field above this field.

2. Point to any part of the selected row, and then click the *right* mouse button to display a shortcut menu. Your screen should resemble Figure 3.17. Notice that Insert Field and Delete Field are two of the choices in this menu.

Figure 3.17   **Displaying a shortcut menu**

Shortcut menu —

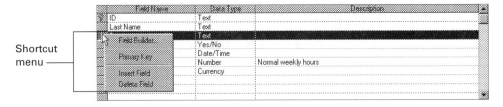

3. Choose **Insert Field** from the shortcut menu to insert a new, blank row above the selected row.

4. Place the insertion point in the Field Name column of the new row (if necessary), type **First Name** to name the field, and then press **Tab** to move to the Data Type column. We will use the default data type *Text*.

5. Change the field size from the default of *50* to **15**. (You can press **F6** to switch to the Field Properties pane, or simply double-click on **50** and then type **15**.)

6. Click the **right mouse button** on the **field selector** to display the Health row's shortcut menu, and then choose **Delete Row** to attempt to delete the Health field. Access asks you to confirm the deletion of the Health field.

7. Click on **Yes** to delete the Health field and the data that it contains, and then compare your screen to Figure 3.18.

Figure 3.18   **The table with the new field and the Health field**

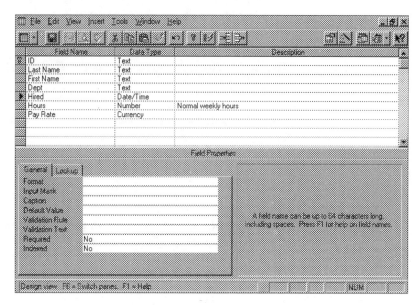

MOVING A FIELD

In the Datasheet view of a table, fields appear from left to right in the order in which they appear from top to bottom in the Design view. To change the order of a field, you can select and then drag it to a new location. As you drag, Access displays a dark line to indicate where it will place the field when you release the mouse button.

Because it might be easier to enter employee names if the First Name field precedes the Last Name field, let's move the First Name field:

1. Click on the **field selector** for the First Name row to select the field.

2. Point to the field selector for the selected field until the pointer changes to the standard mouse-pointer arrow.

3. While still pointing to the field selector, press and hold down the mouse button and drag upward. As you do so, a dark line appears showing where the field will be when you release the mouse button (see Figure 3.19). When this line is between the ID and Last Name rows, release the mouse button. The First Name row now appears before the Last Name row.

Figure 3.19   **Moving a field by dragging its field selector deleted**

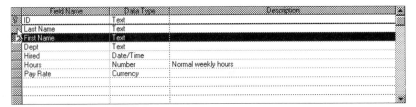

4. Choose **File, Save** to save all the changes you've made to the table design. (**Note:** Because the table is already named, you can update it by using the Save command. If you wanted to give the table a new name, you would use the Save As/Export command.)

ADDING VALUES TO THE MODIFIED TABLE

Now that you've finished modifying the table design, let's take a look at its Datasheet view:

1. Click on the **Datasheet View** button on the toolbar to change to Datasheet view.

2. Examine the modified table (refer to Figure 3.20). You will need to use the horizontal scroll bar to view the entire table. The First Name field is now part of the table. The LN field is now named Last Name and the HD field is now named Hired. There is no longer a Health field.

Figure 3.20   **The Datasheet view of the modified table**

ID	First Name	Last Name	Dept	Hired	Hours	Pay
0020		Hanover	MS	2/20/90	32.5	
0021		Jaen	MK	6/15/86	40	
0022		Monder	EE	1/6/90	40	
0023		Tallon	MK	11/17/91	32.5	
*					0	

PRACTICE YOUR SKILLS

1. Add the following names to the First Name field. (Remember, you can move to the same field in the next record by pressing the Down Arrow key).

ID:	First Name:
0020	James
0021	Enrique
0022	Marsha
0023	Norma

2. Place the insertion point in the blank record to save the changes to the last record (see Figure 3.21).

Figure 3.21 **The modified table with first names added**

ID	First Name	Last Name	Dept	Hired	Hours	Pa
0020	James	Hanover	MS	2/20/90	32.5	
0021	Enrique	Jaen	MK	6/15/86	40	
0022	Marsha	Monder	EE	1/6/90	40	
0023	Norma	Tallon	MK	11/17/91	32.5	
					0	

CHANGING COLUMN WIDTHS IN THE DATASHEET VIEW

In the Datasheet view, the default width of field columns is 15.6 characters. If this isn't convenient—for example, if you can't see the entire width of a field or a table—you can change each column's width to suit your needs.

The easiest way to change column widths is by using the mouse. To do so:

● Point to the right edge of the column's *field selector* until the pointer takes the shape of a two-headed arrow. (In the Datasheet view, field selectors run across the top of the table and bear field names.)

● Drag the column boundary to the left to make the column narrower, or to the right to widen the column.

After you make changes to the layout of a table's Datasheet view, you should choose File, Save Layout to save them. Such changes affect only the appearance of the table in the Datasheet view; they have no effect on a table's design or any of its field's properties.

Let's reduce the width of some columns in your table so that you can view the entire table without scrolling:

1. Place the mouse pointer on the right edge of the ID **field selector** (at the top of the column). When you are pointing to the right spot, the mouse pointer will turn into a two-headed arrow.

2. Drag the edge of the field selector to the left until it touches the *D* in *ID*, and then release the mouse button. The ID field column should now be about half of its original width.

3. Narrow the Dept field to about half of its original width (see Figure 3.22). Now that you've reduced the width of two columns, you can see the entire table without scrolling. (You may have noticed that Access no longer displays a horizontal scroll bar.)

Figure 3.22   **The table after narrowing two columns**

ID	First Name	Last Name	Dept	Hired	Hours	Pay Rate
0020	James	Hanover	MS	2/20/90	32.5	$15.00
0021	Enrique	Jaen	MK	6/15/86	40	$12.00
0022	Marsha	Monder	EE	1/6/90	40	$20.75
0023	Norma	Tallon	MK	11/17/91	32.5	$21.50
					0	$0.00

4. Choose **File, Save Layout** to save the new layout of the Datasheet view of the table.

5. Close the table, and then open it once again. Your layout changes remain in effect.

PREVIEWING THE TABLE

In Chapter 2 we said that reports are the best way to present your data in print. However, if you just want a quick printout of a table, Access can accommodate you. As with reports, you can—and should—preview tables before you print them in order to make sure you're going to get what you want.

Let's preview a printout of our table:

1. Click on the **Print Preview** button in the toolbar to preview the printed table. Access shows you a full-page view of the table as it would print.

2. Point to the table until the mouse pointer changes to a magnifying glass, and then click the left mouse button to view the page close up. (This technique is an alternative to clicking on the Zoom button.)

3. Use the scroll bars as necessary to view the table as it will print (see Figure 3.23). Notice that the printed table will include field names and grid lines, and will use the custom column widths you set in the Datasheet view.

Figure 3.23   **Previewing the table**

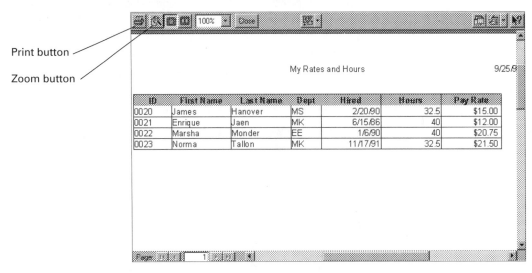

Print button

Zoom button

4. Click on the **Close** button in the toolbar to close the preview screen without printing. (**Note:** If you want to print and your printer is on and properly connected, choose the **File Print** command to open the Print dialog box, and then click on **OK** to print the table.)

5. Close the table.

USING THE TABLE WIZARD TO CREATE A TABLE

The Table Wizard leads you through a series of dialog boxes to help you create a table. There are many sample tables, and there are many sample fields for each table from which to choose. You will lose some control over details when you use the Table Wizard (names of fields, for example), but it can be a great way to produce many tables. Let's use the Table Wizard to create a simple employee table:

1. Be sure the table objects are displayed in the Database window, and then click on the **New** button to display the New Table dialog box.

2. Select **Table Wizard** and click on **OK** to indicate that you wish to use the Table Wizard to create a table. When you use any

Wizard feature, Access will present you with a series of steps containing direct, easy-to-follow instructions. The first Table Wizard pane asks you to choose a sample table, and then to choose fields.

3. In the Sample Tables box, select **Employees**. When you select a different sample table, different sample fields appear in the Sample Fields box.

4. In the Sample Fields box, double-click on **Employee ID** to move the field into the Fields In My New Table box. Access will set the data type and the field properties for you. If you want to change any of this later, you can do so by using the Design view of the table.

5. In the Sample Fields box, double-click on **First Name** and **Last Name** to add those fields to the Fields In My New Table box (see Figure 3.24). These are all the fields we'll be putting in this table, so you're now ready to move to the next Table Wizard step.

Figure 3.24   **Picking a sample table and fields**

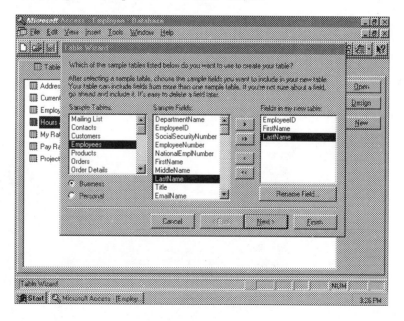

6. Click on **Next** to display the next Table Wizard pane, which lets you name your table. This pane also gives you the option of setting a primary key.

7. Type **My Employees** to give the table a name, and then click on **Next** to move to the next step. (We'll let Access create a primary key in this table for us.) The next pane deals with setting up relationships for the table. We won't relate this table to any of the others. (Chapter 10 discusses relating tables in more detail.)

8. Click on **Next** to display the final Table Wizard pane, and then click on **Finish** to create the table and display its Datasheet view.

9. Click on the **Design View** button (the leftmost button on the toolbar) to see the Design view of the table (see Figure 3.25). Access has done all the design-grid work for you! If you were not happy with the default field properties (or field names, or data types, and so on) that Access used, you could change them here in the Design view.

Figure 3.25   **The Design view of the new table**

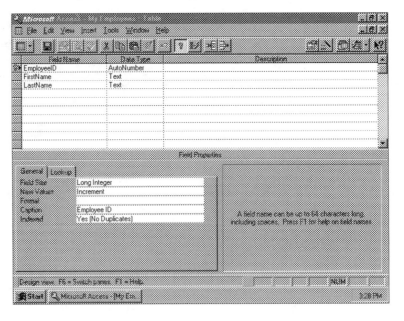

10. Close the table.

SUMMARY

In this chapter, you developed a firm foundation for creating and working with tables. You now know how to design and create a table, create and modify fields, set a primary key, save a table design, add and save records, change column widths, and preview and print a table.

Here's a quick reference guide to the Access features introduced in this chapter:

Desired Result	How to Do It
Switch to Design view of table	Choose **View, Table Design** or click on **Design View** button
Select field	Click on **field selector**
Create table	Display table object names in Database window, click on **New**, click on one of the New Table selections, and click on **OK**
Create field	In table's design grid, type field name in Field Name column and select data type in Data Type column. (You also may type description or set field properties.)
Set field properties	In design grid, press **F6** (or use mouse) to move to Field Properties pane; type or select desired properties
Set a primary key	Select row or rows to include in primary key; choose **Edit, Set Primary Key** or click on **Primary Key** button
Save new table design	From Design view, choose **File, Save As/Export**; type table name; click on **OK**
Save modified table design	From Design view, choose **File, Save**
Switch to table's Datasheet view	Choose **View, Datasheet** or click on **Datasheet View** button
Add record to table	Place insertion point in last blank record, then enter data in each field

Desired Result	How to Do It
Save edited record	Move insertion point to different record
Change field name	In Design view, edit or replace the field name
Insert field	In Design view, select row above which you want to insert field; choose **Insert, Field** (or press **Insert** key); use new blank field row to define field
Delete a field	In Design view, select field row; then choose **Edit, Delete Row** (or press **Delete** key)
Move field	In Design view, drag **field selector** for field up or down to desired position
Change column width in Datasheet view	Point to right edge of column's field selector, then drag to left (to narrow column) or to right (to widen column)
Save changes to Datasheet-view layout	Choose **File, Save Layout**
Preview table	From Datasheet view, choose **File, Print Preview** (or click on **Print Preview** button)
Print table	Preview table, and click on **Print** button

In the next chapter, you'll learn how to find and edit records in a table, and how to undo mistakes you might make while editing. With these skills, you'll be able to work quickly, efficiently, and confidently in tables of any size.

CHAPTER 4: FINDING AND EDITING RECORDS

Finding Records

Editing Records

In Chapter 3, you learned how to design, create, add records to, preview, and print tables. In this chapter, you'll learn how to work efficiently with tables once they contain many records. First, you'll learn more about finding records. Then you'll learn a number of techniques for editing records once you've found them, including how to undo mistakes you may make.

When you're done working through this chapter, you will know

- How to find records by searching through a specific field
- How to find records by searching through all fields in a table
- How to select and delete records
- How to use Undo commands
- How to copy values and records

FINDING RECORDS

Data management frequently involves finding and then editing specific records. As you learned in Chapter 2, you can use the Find command to search for a record that contains a specific value in a particular field. We'll learn more about this technique in this chapter, as well as some other ways you can search for a record.

FINDING RECORDS WITH EDIT, FIND

We'll start by finding a record in the same way we did in Chapter 2. This time, however, we'll examine what we're doing a bit more closely. The Find dialog box offers options that make it possible to search for values in many ways.

If you do not have both the Access application and Employee Database windows opened and maximized, please open and maximize them now. (Refer to Chapters 1 and 2 if you don't remember how to do this.)

Let's find a record based on a particular last name:

1. Open and examine the Projected New Rates table. It's similar to the table you created in Chapter 3.

2. Press **Tab** twice to select the contents of the Last Name field in the first record.

3. Click on the **Find** button to open the Find In Field: 'Last Name' dialog box. Because Last Name is the current field, Access assumes you want to search only through that field.

4. In the Find What box, type **evans**, and then click on the **Find First** button to find the first occurrence of the text *evans* in the Last Name field. (Access will always start searching from the first record in a table when you click on Find First.) Notice that the status bar says *Search succeeded*. Access has found and selected a record.

5. If the dialog box is blocking your view of the found record, point to the title bar of the dialog box, and then drag it down so that you can see the selected record (see Figure 4.1). You can use this technique to move almost any window that has a title bar. You now can see that Access has selected the text *Evans* in Nancy Evans's record. Notice that although you entered the text *evans*, Access found the text *Evans*. If you want Access to search for the exact combination of upper- and lowercase letters that you type, you can check the *Match Case* option in the Find dialog box.

Figure 4.1   **The found record after moving the dialog box**

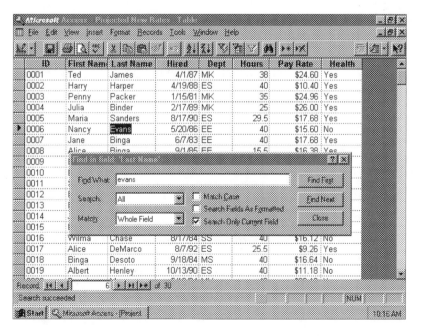

6. Click on **Close** to close the dialog box.

7. Verify that the insertion point is still in the Last Name field and then click on the **Find** button to open the Find In Field: 'Last Name' dialog box again. The last value you used, *evans*, is still in the Find What box.

8. Type **carter** to replace *evans*, and then click on **Find First**.

9. Click on **Close** to close the dialog box, and then observe the table. Access has selected the text *Carter* in Andrea Carter's record.

USING FIND TO SEARCH ALL FIELDS

So far, you've searched for values only in the current field. However, if you do not know what field holds the value for which you are searching, or if you know that the value is not in the current field, you can uncheck the Search Only Current Field option. Access then will search every field in the table for the value you specify. The chief disadvantage of unchecking this option is that it can take Access significantly longer to perform searches. This is particularly true in large tables.

Let's try searching through all the fields in the table:

1. Press **Ctrl+Home** to move to the first field in the first record.

2. Click on the **Find** button to open the Find in field: 'ID' dialog box.

3. Type **binga** to replace *carter*, and then click on **Find First** to find the first occurrence of the text *binga*. Access opens a dialog box telling you that it has finished searching the records, and the search item was not found.

4. Click on **OK** to close the dialog box. The search was not successful because Access searched through only the ID field in the table.

5. In the Find In Field: 'ID' dialog box, uncheck the **Search Only Current Field** option. Notice that the title of the dialog box has changed from *Find in field: 'ID'* to simply *Find* (see Figure 4.2).

6. Click on **Find First**, and then observe the table. Access has found Jane Binga's record.

7. Click on **Find First** again. Because Jane Binga's record is the first in the table containing the text *binga*, her record remains active.

Figure 4.2   **Searching through all fields**

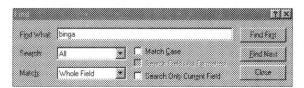

8. Click on **Find Next** and then observe the table. Access has found the next record containing the text *binga:* Alice Binga's record.

9. Click on **Find Next** three more times. Access finds Sam Binga's record, then Binga Desoto's (in this case, the text *binga* occurs in the First Name field), and then displays a dialog box indicating that the search is complete.

10. Click on **OK** to close the dialog box.

11. Close the Find dialog box.

PRACTICE YOUR SKILLS

1. Find Barbara Stira's record (Record 25).

2. Close the Find dialog box.

EDITING RECORDS

In Chapter 3, you learned how to add new records to a table. You will also need to know how to alter records after you enter them. Access provides many techniques for editing records. We'll introduce you to several of these techniques, and you can choose the ones that are most appropriate for your situation.

SELECTING VALUES AND RECORDS

In Chapter 3, you learned that you can select a single word by double-clicking on it. You've also seen that you can replace selected text simply by typing. Now, you're going to learn a wider variety of ways to select and delete information in Access, from fields to entire tables. The following is a list of ways in which you can select the contents of a field:

- Drag over the field's contents.

- Point to the left edge of the field (the pointer will take the shape of a white cross), and then click once.

- Press *Tab* to select the contents of the field to the right, or press *Shift+Tab* to select the contents of the field to the left.

You also might find it useful to be able to select entire records. There also are several ways to do this:

- Click on the *record selector* (to the left of the record).

- Place the insertion point anywhere in the record, and then choose *Edit, Select Record.*

- Drag over several adjacent record selectors to select several adjacent records.

- Choose *Edit, Select All Records* or click on the selector in the upper-left corner of the table to select all the records in the table.

Don't let this long list of options intimidate you. We'll use a sampling of techniques as we go through this chapter. You can use whichever methods you find the easiest.

DELETING A RECORD

After you select a field or record, you can delete it either by choosing Edit, Delete or by pressing the Delete key. Let's find Bill Conner's record, select it, and then delete it:

1. Open and observe the Find dialog box (click on the **Find** button). The Search Only Current Field option is still unchecked.

2. In the Find What box, type **conner**, and then click on **Find First** to find the first occurrence of the text *conner* in the table (regardless of field).

3. Close the dialog box, and then observe the table. Access has found Bill Conner's record (Record 9).

4. Click on the **record selector** for Bill Conner's record to select it.

5. Press the **Delete** key to delete the selected record. For safety's sake, Access displays a dialog box asking you to

confirm the deletion (see Figure 4.3). After you delete a record, it cannot be retrieved, so you should think carefully before you delete a record.

Figure 4.3   **Deleting a record**

6. Click on **Yes** to delete the record. Bill Conner's record no longer appears in the table.

USING UNDO COMMANDS

As you edit records, there may be times when you want to reverse, or undo, a change that you've just made. Often, the Edit menu will contain an Undo command you can use to reverse the action you've just taken. The command name will vary, depending upon what you've been doing. For example, if you've just edited a field, but have not left it, the command will be *Undo Typing,* or perhaps *Undo Current Field/Record* (you also can undo any editing in the current field by pressing Esc). Clicking on the Undo button is a shortcut for choosing an Undo command.

Note: All forms of the Undo commands are available only until you perform another action that can be undone. For example, once you begin editing another record, you no longer will be able to undo changes to the previous record. For safety's sake, use Undo commands only when you need them, and use them right away. If you start depending upon the commands, you are likely to find yourself in trouble.

Let's undo some edits:

1. Find Maria Sanders's record (click on the **Find** button, type **sanders**, click on **Find First**, and then close the Find dialog box).

2. Be sure the text **Sanders** is selected, and then type **Kossowski** to change the Last Name for this record. What if you typed the wrong name? Access has a nice way to handle such a mistake.

3. Choose **Edit** to display the Edit menu.

4. Choose **Undo Typing** and then observe the field. (Use the **Undo Current Field/Record** command if Undo Typing is not available.) Access has changed *Kossowski* back to the original value, *Sanders* (see Figure 4.4).

Figure 4.4   **Undoing an edit**

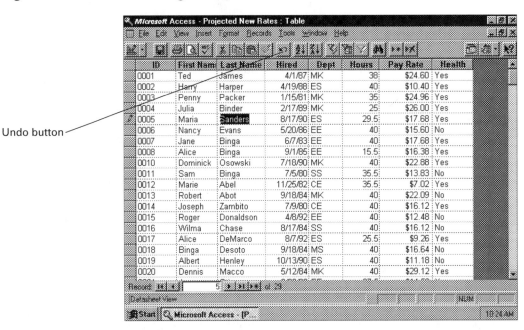

5. Be sure the text Sanders is selected, then once again type **Kossowski**.

6. Click on the **Undo** button to change the name to *Sanders* again (refer to Figure 4.4). The Undo button is a shortcut for choosing an Undo command.

7. Change the name back to *Kossowski*.

8. Press **Shift+Tab** to select the text *Maria* in the First Name field.

9. Click on **Edit** to display the Edit menu. Because you moved from the field you just changed, the Undo Typing option is no longer available.

10. Click on **Edit** again to close the menu, and then click at the end of the text *Maria* to place an insertion point there. We will change this name to Marianne.

11. Type **nne** to change Maria to Marianne, and then press the **Down Arrow key** to move to the next record and save Marianne's.

12. Choose **Edit, Undo Saved Record** and then observe Record 5. Access has restored both the first and last names.

PRACTICE YOUR SKILLS

1. Change Maria's last name back to Kossowski.

2. Save the record. Your screen should resemble Figure 4.5.

Figure 4.5　　**The table after changing the last name and saving the record**

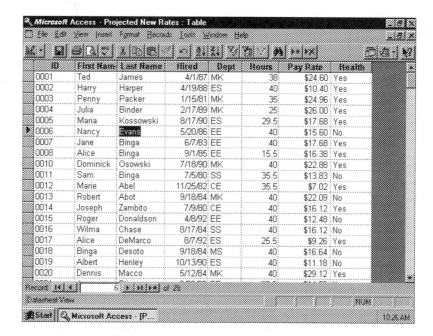

COPYING VALUES

As you add records to a table, you may find that you often repeat values from record to record. For example, in an employee information table, several employees may have been hired on the same date, may work in the same department, or may work the same number of hours.

When this happens, you can save yourself some typing—and perhaps some time—by copying values from other records. If the same field in the previous record contains the value you need, you can copy that value to the next record by placing the insertion point in the field of the lower record, and then pressing Ctrl+' (the single quotation mark key).

To copy a value from a record that is not directly above the record you are adding, you would follow these steps:

- Select the value you wish to copy.

- Choose *Edit, Copy* to place a copy of the selected data in a temporary storage place called *the Clipboard*. (You also can click on the *Copy* button.)

- Move to the field where you want to paste the value.

- Choose *Edit, Paste* to place a copy of the value on the Clipboard at the insertion point (or click on the *Paste* button).

Let's add a record, filling in some fields by copying values from other records:

1. Click on the **New Record** navigation button to move to the blank record at the end of the table.

2. Press **Home** to move to the ID field (if necessary), type **0031**, and then press **Tab** to move to the First Name field.

3. Type your first name and press **Tab** to move to the Last Name field; then type your last name and press **Tab** to move to the Hired field.

4. Type today's date (use the *mm/dd/yy* format) and press **Tab** to move to the Dept field. You will be in the same department as Robert Beaton, whose record is directly above yours. It certainly wouldn't be difficult to type the department code, but we're going to copy it from the record above instead.

5. Press **Ctrl+'** and then observe your record. Access has copied the value from the field above into the current record (*SS*).

Not a big deal with a field containing two letters, but if you have a large text field and are entering many records, this technique can be very useful.

6. Press **Tab** to move to the Hours field, and then press **Ctrl+'** to copy *35* from Robert Beaton's record into your record. This is nice, but what if we want to copy a value from a record that is not directly above the current one?

7. Press **Tab** to move to the Pay Rate field, and then observe Robert Beaton's pay rate. Robert Beaton makes $13.00 per hour. However, your pay rate will match that of William Bell (Record 28).

8. Select the value in William Bell's Pay Rate field, **$23.40** (drag over the value). When you copy something, the first step is to select what you wish to copy.

9. Click on the **Copy** button to place a copy of the selected value in the Clipboard, a temporary storage space you cannot see.

10. Now place the insertion point back in the Pay Rate field for your record. Before you paste the value from the Clipboard, you must specify where you want the value to go.

11. Click on the **Paste** button to paste the value from the Clipboard into your field, and then press **Tab** to move to the Health field. The Pay Rate field for your record now displays *$23.40*.

12. Press **Ctrl+'** to copy the value *Yes* from the previous record to your Health field. Your screen should resemble Figure 4.6, except that you'll see your own name instead of the author's and a different hire date.

Figure 4.6   **Your completed record**

ID	First Name	Last Name	Hired	Dept	Hours	Pay Rate	Health
0014	Joseph	Zambito	7/9/80	CE	40	$16.12	Yes
0015	Roger	Donaldson	4/8/92	EE	40	$12.48	No
0016	Wilma	Chase	8/17/84	SS	40	$16.12	No
0017	Alice	DeMarco	8/7/92	ES	25.5	$9.26	Yes
0018	Binga	Desoto	9/18/84	MS	40	$16.64	No
0019	Albert	Henley	10/13/90	ES	40	$11.18	No
0020	Dennis	Macco	5/12/84	MK	40	$29.12	Yes
0021	Joe	Stira	2/22/89	EE	37.5	$14.56	Yes
0022	Homer	Jones	4/13/90	CE	40	$17.94	Yes
0023	Opal	Packer	3/31/85	SS	25	$14.56	No
0024	David	Haslam	5/13/87	SS	40	$14.04	Yes
0025	Barbara	Stira	11/1/86	MK	40	$27.04	Yes
0026	Ruth	Naylor	9/1/83	MK	40	$28.08	Yes
0027	John	Ward	4/24/92	ES	25	$8.84	No
0028	William	Bell	4/24/84	MK	40	$23.40	Yes
0029	Andrea	Carter	8/23/84	EE	40	$16.64	Yes
0030	Robert	Beaton	11/23/83	SS	35	$13.00	Yes
0031	Julie	Kulik	9/28/95	SS	35	$23.40	Yes

COPYING RECORDS

If most of the values you want in a new record match those of an existing record, it might be easier to modify a copy of the entire existing record than it would be to enter the new record from scratch. For example, if two employees were hired on the same day for the same job, it's possible that the only differences in their records would be their names and IDs.

To copy an entire record to the blank record at the end of the table, you would follow these steps:

• Select the record you wish to copy (use the record selector).

• Choose *Edit, Copy* (or click on the *Copy* button).

• Choose *Edit, Paste Append* to paste a copy of the record in the blank record at the end of the table.

You also can replace one existing record with a copy of another. To do this, you would follow these steps:

• Copy the record (select it and click on the *Copy* button).

• Select the record to which you wish to copy.

• Choose *Edit, Paste* (or click on the *Paste* button).

Let's try each of these methods for copying a record:

1. Select Opal Packer's record. This is the record you will copy.

2. Click on the **Copy** button to place a copy of the selected record on the Clipboard. If you don't remember where a button is, keep in mind that you can see the names of the buttons simply by pointing to them.

3. Select William Bell's record and then click on the **Paste** button. The values from Opal Packer's record have replaced the original values in the record (see Figure 4.7).

Figure 4.7   **Pasting a copy of a record over another record**

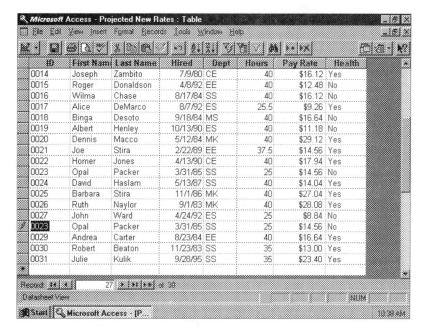

ID	First Name	Last Name	Hired	Dept	Hours	Pay Rate	Health
0014	Joseph	Zambito	7/9/80	CE	40	$16.12	Yes
0015	Roger	Donaldson	4/8/92	EE	40	$12.48	No
0016	Wilma	Chase	8/17/84	SS	40	$16.12	No
0017	Alice	DeMarco	8/7/92	ES	25.5	$9.26	Yes
0018	Binga	Desoto	9/18/84	MS	40	$16.64	No
0019	Albert	Henley	10/13/90	ES	40	$11.18	No
0020	Dennis	Macco	5/12/84	MK	40	$29.12	Yes
0021	Joe	Stira	2/22/89	EE	37.5	$14.56	Yes
0022	Homer	Jones	4/13/90	CE	40	$17.94	Yes
0023	Opal	Packer	3/31/85	SS	25	$14.56	No
0024	David	Haslam	5/13/87	SS	40	$14.04	Yes
0025	Barbara	Stira	11/1/86	MK	40	$27.04	Yes
0026	Ruth	Naylor	9/1/83	MK	40	$28.08	Yes
0027	John	Ward	4/24/92	ES	25	$8.84	No
0028	Opal	Packer	3/31/85	SS	25	$14.56	No
0029	Andrea	Carter	8/23/84	EE	40	$16.64	Yes
0030	Robert	Beaton	11/23/83	SS	35	$13.00	Yes
0031	Julie	Kulik	9/28/95	SS	35	$23.40	Yes

Record: 27 of 30

4. Click on the **Undo** button to restore the original values to William Bell's record.

5. Now choose **Edit, Paste Append** to place a copy of Opal Packer's record at the *end* of the table. This probably is a more useful technique than replacing an existing record. We now can modify the new record to suit our needs.

PRACTICE YOUR SKILLS

1. In the new record, change the following values. (The other fields can remain as they are.)

Field:	New value:
ID	0042
First Name	Robert
Hired	today's date
Pay Rate	$11.00

2. Save the record. Your record should resemble the one at the bottom of Figure 4.8, although the value in the Hired field will be different.

Figure 4.8   **The table after editing and saving the pasted record**

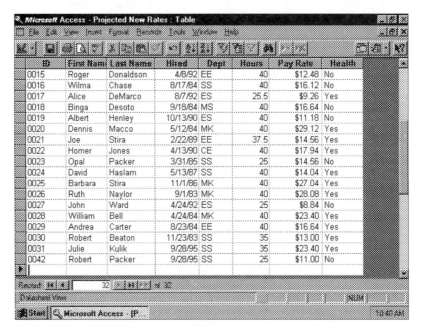

3. Close the Table window.

4. Close the Database window.

PRACTICE YOUR SKILLS

In Chapters 1 through 4, you have learned how to open and create tables, and how to add, find, and edit records. The following two activities will give you an opportunity to practice these techniques.

We've provided a chapter reference after each step in case you need to refer back to the chapter in which we introduced the technique relevant to that step.

Follow the steps below to produce the table shown in Figure 4.9.

Figure 4.9   **Previewing the completed My Inventory table**

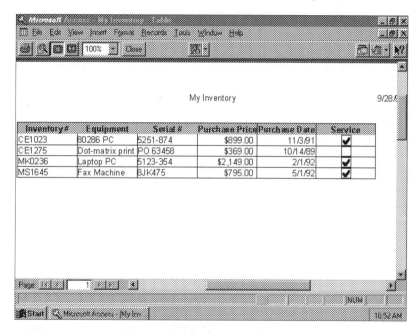

1. Open the **Practice** database file and then maximize the Database window (Chapter 2).

2. Create a new table with the following fields (Chapter 3):

Field Name:	Data Type:	Field Size:
ID #	Text	6

Field Name:	Data Type:	Field Size:
Equipment	Text	25
Serial #	Text	15
Purchase Date	Date/Time	
Service	Yes/No	
Purchase Price	Currency	

3. Set the ID # field as the primary key; then save the table as **My Inventory** (Chapter 3).

4. Switch to Datasheet view, and then enter and save the following records (Chapter 3):

ID #:	Equipment:	Serial #:	Purchase Date:	Service:	Purchase Price:
CE1023	80286 PC	5251-874	11/3/91	Yes	$899.00
CE1275	Dot-matrix printer	PO 63458	10/14/89	No	$369.00
MK0236	Laptop PC	5123-354	2/1/92	No	$2,149.00
MS1645	Fax machine	TO/444	5/1/92	Yes	$795.00

5. Return to Design view and change the name of the ID # field to **Inventory #** (Chapter 3).

6. Move the Purchase Price field between the Serial # and Purchase Date fields (Chapter 3).

7. Save the modified table design (Chapter 3).

8. Switch to the Datasheet view and change the contents of the Laptop PC record's Service field to **Yes** (check the check box).

9. In the record for the fax machine, change the contents of the Serial # field to **8JK475**.

10. Preview the table, zoom in, and compare your screen to Figure 4.9 (Chapter 3).

11. Close the preview screen, and then close the Table window (Chapter 2).

Follow the steps below to produce the table shown in Figure 4.10.

Figure 4.10   **Previewing the completed Parking table**

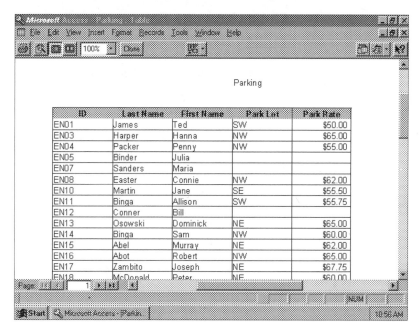

1. Open the Parking table (Chapter 2).

2. Add a new record with the following data (Chapter 3):

ID:	Last Name:	First Name:	Park Lot:	Park Rate:
EN90	(*your last name*)	(*your first name*)	NE	$65.50

3. Find Eugene Davis's record and then copy it to the end of the table.

4. In the new record, change the contents of the ID field to **EN91**, and the contents of the First Name field to **Peter**.

5. Find the record in which the value in the ID field is EN39; then change the contents of that employee's Last Name field to **Cook**.

6. Save the record; then undo the change you just made.

7. Change the contents of the Last Name field to **Ellis-Cook**, and then save the record.

8. Find Luke Nelson's record; then copy the values **SE** and **$57.50** from the previous record into the Park Lot and Park Rate fields.

9. Find and then delete David Stevens's record.

10. Preview the table, zoom in, and then compare your screen to Figure 4.10 (Chapter 3).

11. Close the preview window, and then close the Table and Database windows (Chapter 2).

SUMMARY

In this chapter, you learned how to search for, select, and delete records. You also learned how to undo edits, copy values, and copy records.

Here's a quick reference guide to the Access features introduced in this chapter:

Desired Result	How to Do It
Search for value in specific field	Move to field in which you want to search; choose **Edit, Find** (or click on **Find** button); type search value in Find What box; uncheck **Search Only Current Field** (if necessary); click on **Find First** or **Find Next**
Search for value in all fields	Choose **Edit, Find** (or click on **Find** button); type search value in Find What box; uncheck **Search Only Current Field**; click on **Find First** or **Find Next**
Select field	Drag over field; or, point to left edge and click once; or, place insertion point in adjacent field and press **Tab** to select field to right (or press **Shift+Tab** to select field to left)

Select record	Click on **record selector** (or place insertion point within record, and then choose **Edit, Select Record**)
Select multiple records	Drag over **record selectors** (when records are next to each other)
Select all records	Click on **selector** in upper-left corner of table (or choose **Edit, Select All Records**)
Undo last action	Choose appropriate **Undo** command from Edit menu (or click on **Undo** button)
Copy value down from same field in previous record	Place insertion point in appropriate field in second record and press **Ctrl+'**
Copy value from nonadjacent record	Select value to be copied; choose **Edit, Copy** (or click on **Copy** button); place insertion point in field to which to copy; choose **Edit, Paste** (or click on **Paste** button)
Copy record	Select record to be copied; choose **Edit, Copy** (or click on **Copy** button); select record to which to copy; choose **Edit, Paste** (or click on **Paste** button)
Copy record to end of table	Copy record and then choose **Edit, Paste Append**

In the next chapter, you'll learn how to create, save, and run queries. You'll also learn how to sort records, set criteria, and perform calculations in queries.

CHAPTER 5: QUERY BASICS

Choosing Fields
and Sort Order
for a Query

Setting Criteria in
a Query

Performing
Calculations in
Queries

In Chapters 3 and 4, you learned how to create tables, add data to tables, and find and edit that data. In this chapter, we'll take a look at using queries to control and ask questions about that data. Queries let you use the same data in many ways to suit many tasks. For example, from the same employee information table, you could use one query to review employee pay rates, a second query to update home addresses, and a third query to calculate each department's weekly salary expenses.

When you're done working through this chapter, you will know

- How to run a select query

- How to view a query's design

- How to create, design, and save queries

- How to control the number of visible fields

- How to control the order of records in a query

- How to control which records appear in a query

- How to edit values in a datasheet resulting from a query

- How to perform calculations in a query

CHOOSING FIELDS AND SORT ORDER FOR A QUERY

Because the amount of data in tables is often very large, the two primary uses of queries are to limit the number of visible fields and to sort records in the most useful order. (In Chapter 2, you learned how to sort records by using a form's Filter window. We'll soon see that queries provide a more powerful and convenient way to sort records.)

For example, if you need to review data about employee work hours, you might want to

- View only employee names and work hours, rather than wading through all the data in the table

- Sort the data in a useful order, such as alphabetically by employee last name, or numerically by number of hours worked

Access calls this type of query—a query in which you select and view records—a *select query*. Unlike *action queries*, which can change data, select queries never change data; they only rearrange your view of it. Throughout this chapter, we'll be working solely with select queries. You'll learn more about other types of queries in Chapter 8.

 ### RUNNING A SELECT QUERY

As a review of Chapter 2, we'll begin by examining an employee information table. Then we'll run a select query that is based on that table.

Access displays the result of running a query in a datasheet. These resulting datasheets are considered to be dynamic (changeable), because they can change as the data in your tables changes. As you may recall from Chapter 2, a query is a stored question, not the answer to that question. Because of this, the datasheet that answers that question can change as data in an underlying table change.

If you do not have both the Access application and Employee Database windows open and maximized, please open and maximize them now.

Let's run a select query:

1. Open and examine the Hours and Rates table. The table contains information about employees, including ID, Last Name, First Name, Hired, Dept, Hours, Pay Rate, and Health fields.

2. Close the Table window.

3. In the Database window, click on the **Queries** tab to display the list of query object names.

4. Double-click on **MK Staff and Rates** to run the query (see Figure 5.1). The Query window contains a datasheet that displays department codes, last names, first names, and pay rates for *only* MK department employees. Unlike the Hours and Rates table from which it takes its data, this datasheet displays only some of the fields and records from this table. In all superficial ways, a datasheet displayed after running a query looks just like a table.

EXAMINING THE QUERY DESIGN

Like Table windows, Query windows have two views: Design view and Datasheet view. The Datasheet view (the only view of the Query window you've seen so far) displays a query's data; the Design view displays the query's design.

To switch a Query window from Datasheet view to Design view, choose View, Query Design or click on the Design View button. You also can open a Query window in Design view from the Database window by selecting the query object name and then clicking on the Design button.

Figure 5.1   **The result of running the MK Staff and Rates query**

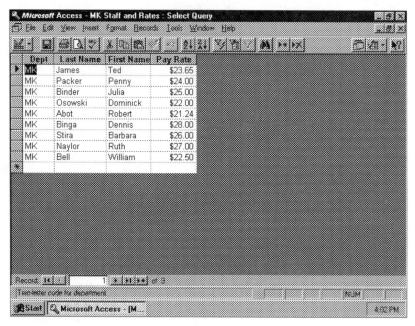

In the Design view, Access divides the Query window into two panes. The upper pane contains the field list or lists for the tables or queries upon which the query is based. (We'll look at queries based upon multiple tables in Chapter 8.) The lower pane contains a design grid that you use to define the query. Each column specifies a field or expression in the query. Within each column, you use the different rows to specify

- The order in which the query should sort records

- Whether the query should show fields in its resulting datasheet

- Criteria to determine which records the query should include in its resulting datasheet

Let's look at the design of the MK Staff and Rates query:

1. Click on the **Design View** button to switch to the Design view for this query (see Figure 5.2). The upper pane of the window contains a list of fields for the table upon which this query is based, Hours and Rates. The lower pane contains a design grid that defines the query.

Figure 5.2   **The Design view of the MK Staff and Rates query**

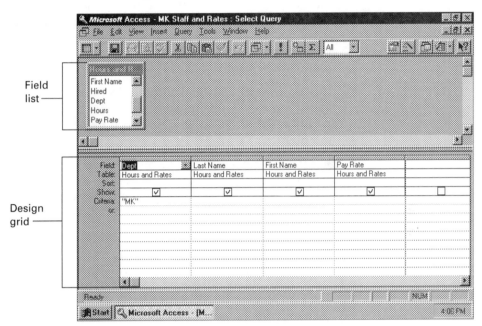

Field list

Design grid

2. Examine the Dept column in the design grid. The Criteria cell is set to "MK." This means the query will show records only if they contain the text *MK* in the Dept field.

3. Compare the design grid to Figure 5.1. For each column in the grid, there is a corresponding column in the resulting datasheet. The order of columns in the design grid determines the order of columns in the resulting datasheet.

4. Close the Query window.

CREATING A QUERY AND SELECTING A TABLE

You can create your own query by opening a new, blank Query window, or by modifying an existing query and saving it with a new name. We'll begin by creating a new query from scratch. By default, Access sets all new queries as select queries. (You'll learn how to modify the query type in Chapter 8.)

To create a new query you

- Display the list of query object names in the Database window, and then click on the *New* button to display the New Query dialog box. You have the choice of creating a new query on your own or using Query Wizards. Query Wizards are helpful in creating more complex types of queries, such as crosstab queries (which we'll discuss in Chapter 8).

- Click on *Design View* and click on *OK* to display a new, blank Query window in Design view. Access will present you with the Show Table dialog box, which contains a list of tables and queries.

- Select each table or query upon which to base your query and click on *Add*. In this chapter, you'll create queries based upon single tables. In Chapter 8, you'll learn how to create queries based upon other queries, or upon multiple tables.

- Click on *Close*.

Let's create a new query now:

1. With query object names displayed in the Database window, click on **New** to display the New Query dialog box. You can either create a new query from scratch, or use Query Wizards to help you.

2. Click on **Design View** and click on **OK** to open a blank Query window in Design view, and to display the Show Table dialog box. This is where you choose the tables and/or queries upon which to base your new query.

3. Select **Hours and Rates**, and then click on **Add** to base your query upon the Hours and Rates table.

4. Click on **Close** to close the Show Table dialog box (see Figure 5.3). The upper pane of the Query window contains a list of fields in the Hours and Rates table; the design grid in the lower pane is empty, because we're creating the query from scratch.

5. Click on **Query** to display the Query menu. There is a dot next to the Select command; by default, Access will make a new query a select query.

6. Click on **Query** again to close the Query menu.

Figure 5.3   **The new Query window**

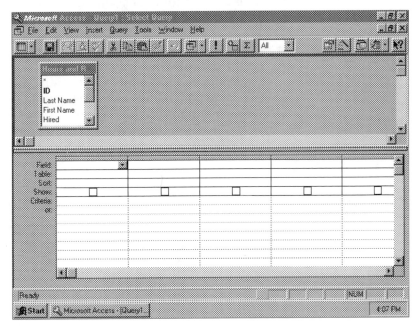

 ## ADDING FIELDS TO THE DESIGN GRID

You use each column in the design grid to specify one field or expression that you wish to see in the query's resulting datasheet. To add a field to the design grid, you would enter the name of the field in the Field row. You can do this in several ways:

- Place the insertion point in a Field cell and type the name of the field.

- Place the insertion point in a Field cell, click on the drop-down arrow that appears in the cell, and then select the desired field name from the list that opens.

- Drag the field name from the table's field list in the upper pane to the desired Field cell.

- Double-click on a field name in the field list to place that name in the Field cell of the first blank column in the grid.

When you place a field name in a Field cell, Access automatically checks the Show option for the field to indicate that it should appear in the resulting datasheet. If you do not wish to have a field displayed in the datasheet, you can uncheck the Show box. (You'll see some reasons for unchecking the Show box in Chapter 8.)

Let's build a query now by specifying some fields:

1. In the Field cell for the first column in the design grid, click on the **drop-down arrow** to display a list of field names from the Hours and Rates table (see Figure 5.4). This list contains the same field names as the field list in the upper pane. As we've mentioned before, many features in Access work this way: When you place the insertion point in a cell, a drop-down arrow appears.

Figure 5.4   **Selecting a field name in the design grid**

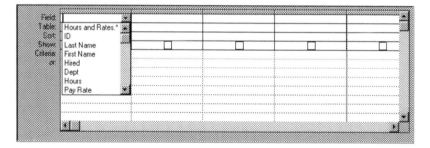

2. In the list of fields, select **Dept** to place the field name in the cell. Notice also that Access has checked the box in the Show row for the column. This means that when the query is run, it will display the Dept field in its resulting datasheet.

3. In the Hours and Rates field list (in the upper pane), double-click on **Last Name**. The field name now appears in the first available column in the design grid (the second column in this case). This is a very convenient way to move field names into a grid. Notice that Access has again checked the Show box.

4. Add the **First Name** and **Pay Rate** fields, respectively, to the Field cells of the third and fourth columns in the design grid. (You may need to scroll through the field list to find the Pay Rate field name.) Your grid should resemble Figure 5.5.

Figure 5.5   **The query design after adding four fields**

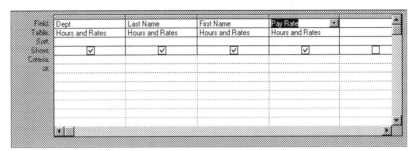

5. Click on the **Run** button to run the query and switch to the Datasheet view. You can run a query by clicking on this button, by choosing the *Query, Run* command, or simply by switching to the Datasheet view for the query.

6. Examine the query's resulting datasheet. Only the four fields you specified appear, and they are in the order in which you specified them: Dept, Last Name, First Name, and Pay Rate. The resulting datasheet includes information from every record in the Hours and Rates table. The records are in the same order in which they appear in the table.

SORTING RECORDS IN A QUERY

By default, Access displays records in a resulting datasheet in the order in which they appear in the query's underlying table. You can sort your queries, however, to make the records appear in any order you like. You sort records in the resulting datasheet by selecting options in the design grid's Sort row. To do so:

- Place the insertion point in the Sort cell of the field by which you want to sort records. (For example, if you want to sort by last name, place the insertion point in the Sort cell for the Last Name field.)

- Click on the cell's drop-down arrow to display a list of possible sort orders.

- Select the desired sort order, either Ascending or Descending.

You also may want to sort by more than one field. In a telephone book, for example, the records are sorted by last name and then by first name. To instruct Access to sort records in this manner, select sort options in each field by which you wish to sort. Access will sort records by the leftmost field for which you specify a sort order, and will then work its way to the right through the remaining fields for which there is a sort order. In a query, you can sort by up to ten fields.

Let's sort our query first by last name, and then by first name:

1. Click on the **Design View** button to return to the Design view (or choose **View, Query Design**).

2. In the design grid, click in the Sort cell for the Last Name column to display the cell's drop-down arrow. (The Sort cells are in the third row of the grid.)

3. Click on the **drop-down arrow** and then choose **Ascending** to instruct the query to sort records in ascending order by last name. In a text field, *ascending order* means the same thing as alphabetical order.

4. Click in the Sort cell for the First Name column, click on its **drop-down arrow**, and then choose **Ascending** (see Figure 5.6). Any records that have the same value in the Last Name field will appear in alphabetical order by first name.

Figure 5.6   **Setting sort options in the design grid**

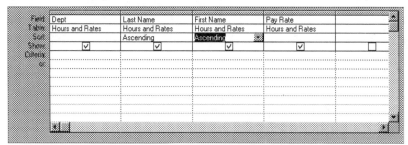

5. Click on the **Datasheet View** button to run the query, and then observe its resulting datasheet. (As we mentioned, there are many ways to run a query.) Now the records appear in order by last name, and then by first name (see Figure 5.7). Notice that the Bingas, who appear together, are sorted alphabetically by first name (Alice, then Dennis, then Sam).

Figure 5.7   **The sorted datasheet**

Dept	Last Name	First Name	Pay Rate
CE	Abel	Marie	$6.75
MK	Abot	Robert	$21.24
SS	Beaton	Robert	$12.50
MK	Bell	William	$22.50
MK	Binder	Julia	$25.00
EE	Binga	Alice	$15.75
MK	Binga	Dennis	$28.00
SS	Binga	Sam	$13.30
EE	Carter	Andrea	$16.00
SS	Chase	Wilma	$15.50
CE	Conner	Bill	$6.30
ES	DeMarco	Alice	$8.90
MS	Desoto	Frank	$16.00
EE	Donaldson	Roger	$12.00
EE	Evans	Nancy	$15.00
ES	Harper	Harry	$10.00
SS	Haslam	David	$13.50
ES	Henley	Albert	$10.75
MK	James	Ted	$23.65

SAVING AND NAMING THE QUERY

You might remember us saying that a form's Filter window, like a query, allows you to sort records. One advantage of queries over filtering, however, is that you can save a query as a database object. Then, the next time you want to see that information in that order, you simply run the query again by double-clicking on the query object name. On the other hand, you must perform a filter manually each time you use it.

To save the design of a query, you follow these steps:

● Choose *File, Save As/Export* to open the Save As dialog box.

● Type a name for the query. Query names are subject to the same rules as table and field names, and can't have the same name as an existing table.

● Click on *OK*.

Your query name then will appear in the list of query object names in the Queries tab of the Database window.

Let's save our query design:

1. Choose **File, Save As/Export** to open the Save As dialog box.

2. In the Save As dialog box, type **My Pay Rates**, and then click on **OK** to name and save the query. The title bar now displays your new query name.

3. Close the Query window and then observe the Database window. *My Pay Rates* now appears in the list of query object names.

REARRANGING THE FIELDS IN A DESIGN GRID

You can change the order of fields in a resulting datasheet by changing the order of columns in the query's design grid. To move a column in the design grid:

• Click on the column's field selector to select the column.

• Drag the field selector for the column to the desired location. (As you drag, Access will display a dark line to indicate the new location of the selected column.)

When you save the query design, the new order of the columns will become a permanent part of the design.

Let's add three new fields to the design grid of an existing query, and then rearrange the order of the fields:

1. In the Database window, select the **Employee List** query object name, and then click on the **Design** button to open the query in Design view. The field list in the Query window's upper pane tells you this query is based upon the Employee Rates table.

2. In the field list, double-click on **First Name** to add it to the fourth column of the design grid.

3. In the field list, double-click on **Hours** and then on **Pay Rate** to add these two fields to the design grid. (You will need to scroll down in the field list to see these fields.)

4. Run the query and observe the resulting datasheet. Fields appear in the datasheet in the order in which we arranged them in the design grid. It might be easier to have the First Name field appear before the Last Name field.

5. Return to the Design View window for the query.

6. Point to the **field selector** for the First Name column until the mouse pointer changes to a downward-pointing arrow (the field selector is the very thin button directly above the Field cell), and then click to select the field column. The field selectors work just as they do in a table's Design view, but are in a different location.

7. Point to the field selector for the selected column (First Name), and then drag it to just left of the Last Name column (see Figure 5.8). As you drag, a black line appears showing you where Access will insert the column when you release the mouse button.

Figure 5.8   **Moving a field column by dragging**

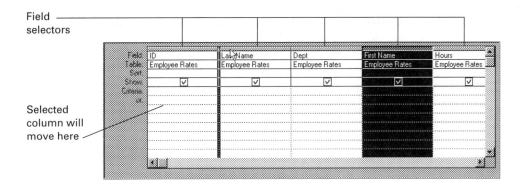

Field selectors

Selected column will move here

8. Run the query again, and then observe the resulting datasheet. The First Name field now appears just before the Last Name field.

SETTING CRITERIA IN A QUERY

So far, we've created queries that limit visible fields and sort records. Another important feature of queries, however, is their ability to select only those records that meet certain conditions, or *criteria*. For example, the MK Staff and Rates query selects only the records of Marketing department employees.

Criteria can require an exact match for a specific value—say, only records for employees who work exactly 40 hours per week—or a more general match, such as only the records of those employees whose last names begin with *B*, or those who make more than $10 per hour.

SETTING A CRITERION FOR A QUERY

To set a criterion for a query, type the criterion in the Criteria cell for the appropriate field in the design grid. The MK Staff and Rates query, for example, selects only records for Marketing department employees because the criterion "MK" was set in the Dept column's Criteria cell.

When you move the insertion point out of a Criteria cell in which you've entered a value, Access might adjust the format of the criterion. When you enter text as criteria, Access adds double quotation marks around that text; when you enter a date, Access adds pound signs (#) around the date. You can add this punctuation yourself when you type the criteria, but it's usually easier to let Access do the job for you.

Let's add a criterion to your query so that it will select only the records of Chemical Engineering department employees:

1. Return to Design view.

2. In the design grid, click in the Criteria cell for the Dept column. No drop-down arrow appears this time; we'll have to enter criteria by typing.

3. Type **CE** to specify that the query select only those records in which the value in the Dept field is *CE* (the department code for Chemical Engineering).

4. Press **Tab**, and then observe the Criteria cell. Access has changed the value you entered (*CE*) to include double quotation marks (*"CE"*).

5. Run the query, and then observe the resulting datasheet (see Figure 5.9). It displays only the records for the four Chemical Engineering (CE) department employees.

Figure 5.9   **Viewing only CE department employees**

ID	First Name	Last Name	Dept	Hours	Pay Rate
0012	Marie	Abel	CE	35.5	$6.75
0009	Bill	Conner	CE	40	$6.30
0022	Homer	Jones	CE	40	$17.25
0014	Joseph	Zambito	CE	40	$15.50

6. Save the modified query as **My CE Employee List** (use the *File, Save As/Export* command).

SETTING CRITERIA WITH A WILDCARD CHARACTER

You can use wildcard characters to create criteria that look for values that are not exact matches. For example, you might want to see records for employees whose names begin with *B*, or whose department codes contain an *E* as the second character. You can use the asterisk (*) to represent any number of characters. For example, the criterion *c** would specify any text beginning with *c*, including *cat, cowabunga,* or *CNN*. You can use the question mark (?) to represent any single character. For example, the criterion *B???* could match Buzz or Bean, but would exclude Bon and Binga.

When you use a wildcard character in a criterion, Access adjusts the criterion in two ways. First, it places double quotation marks around what you typed. Second, Access adds the Like operator and a space before the first quotation mark. The *Like operator* instructs Access to search for values that follow a certain pattern (things that are *like* other things), rather than searching for exact matches. Criteria that use wildcard characters are not case sensitive.

Let's delete your current criterion for the Dept field and set a criterion that instructs your query to select the records of every employee whose last name begins with *B*:

1. Return to Design view, select **"CE"** in the Dept column's Criteria cell, and then press **Delete** to delete the criterion.

2. In the Last Name column's Criteria cell, type **b*** ; then press **Tab** and observe the screen. Access has changed the criterion to *Like "b*"*.

3. Run the query, and then compare the dynaset with Figure 5.10. The query selected records only for employees whose last names begin with *B*. Notice that the criterion is not case sensitive. In other words, although you entered a lowercase *b* in the Criteria cell, Access still found names that begin with an uppercase *B*.

Figure 5.10   **People whose last names begin with B**

ID	First Name	Last Name	Dept	Hours	Pay Rate
0030	Robert	Beaton	SS	35	$12.50
0028	William	Bell	MK	40	$22.50
0004	Julia	Binder	MK	25	$25.00
0008	Alice	Binga	EE	15.5	$15.75
0020	Dennis	Binga	MK	40	$28.00
0007	Jane	Binga	EE	40	$17.00
0011	Sam	Binga	SS	35.5	$13.30

 SETTING CRITERIA WITH COMPARISON OPERATORS

You can use comparison operators in several ways:

- Exact criteria (for example, every employee who works *exactly* 40 hours per week)

- Criteria that exclude certain values (for example, every employee who *does not* work exactly 40 hours per week)

- Criteria for a range of values (for example, every employee who works *less than* 40 hours per week)

Table 5.1 lists Access's comparison operators and their meanings.

Table 5.1   **Comparison Operators**

Operator	Meaning
<	Less than
>	Greater than
=	Equal to
<=	Less than or equal to
>=	Greater than or equal to
<>	Not equal to

Let's use a comparison operator to select the records of employees who make more than $15 per hour.

1. Return to Design view, and then delete the criterion in the Last Name column.

2. In the Pay Rate column's Criteria cell, type **>15**. (You might need to scroll to see the Pay Rate column.)

3. Run the query, and then observe the resulting datasheet (see Figure 5.11). The query selected only the records of employees with a pay rate higher than $15 per hour.

Figure 5.11   **Employees who make more than $15 per hour**

ID	First Name	Last Name	Dept	Hours	Pay Rate
0013	Robert	Abot	MK	40	$21.24
0028	William	Bell	MK	40	$22.50
0004	Julia	Binder	MK	25	$25.00
0008	Alice	Binga	EE	15.5	$15.75
0020	Dennis	Binga	MK	40	$28.00
0007	Jane	Binga	EE	40	$17.00
0029	Andrea	Carter	EE	40	$16.00
0016	Wilma	Chase	SS	40	$15.50
0018	Frank	Desoto	MS	40	$16.00
0001	Ted	James	MK	38	$23.65
0022	Homer	Jones	CE	40	$17.25
0026	Ruth	Naylor	MK	40	$27.00
0010	Dominick	Osowski	MK	40	$22.00
0003	Penny	Packer	MK	35	$24.00
0005	Maria	Sanders	ES	29.5	$17.00
0025	Barbara	Stira	MK	40	$26.00
0014	Joseph	Zambito	CE	40	$15.50

COMBINING CRITERIA TO CREATE AND CONDITIONS

You can combine criteria to force records to meet more than one criterion. For example, you can select employees who make more than $10 per hour *and* who work 40 hours per week. There are a couple of ways in which you can create such criteria:

• Enter criteria in more than one column of the design grid. For example, to specify only those records for employees who both work in the Marketing department *and* were hired in 1988, you could type *MK* as the criterion in the department column and **/*/88* as the criterion in the hired-date column.

• Use the *And operator* to set multiple criteria within a single field. For example, to specify the records for employees who make more than $10 *and* less than $20 per hour, you could type *>10 And <20* as the criterion in the Pay Rate column.

There is practically no limit to the number of criteria you can set at one time. You even can combine the two methods just described to specify records that meet more than one condition both across and within fields. For example, you can specify records for employees who work in the Marketing department, *and* were hired in 1988, *and* make more than $10 *and* less than $20 per hour by entering all of those criteria on the Criteria row.

Let's create some And conditions in our query:

1. Return to Design view, and then enter **MK** in the Dept column's Criteria cell. (Do *not* delete the criterion in the Pay Rate cell.) There are now criteria for both the Pay Rate *and* the Dept fields of the design grid (see Figure 5.12; if you have moved out of its cell, you will see quotation marks around the MK criterion).

Figure 5.12   **Creating an And condition**

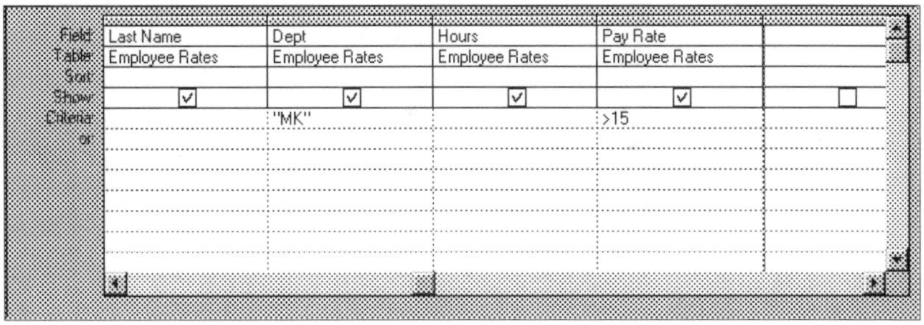

2. Run the query, and then observe the resulting datasheet. It shows records only for employees who work in the Marketing department *and* earn more than $15 per hour.

3. Return to Design view, and then place the insertion point to the right of *>15* in the Pay Rate column's Criteria cell. We will add on to this criterion by using the And operator.

4. Press the spacebar, type **and <25**, and then press **Tab**. Access changes your *and* to *And*, so the criterion now reads *>15 And <25* (see Figure 5.13).

5. Run the query and observe the resulting datasheet. The query selected only the five records for employees who work in the Marketing department *and* who earn more than $15 an hour *and* less than $25 per hour.

Figure 5.13   **Setting an And condition within a field**

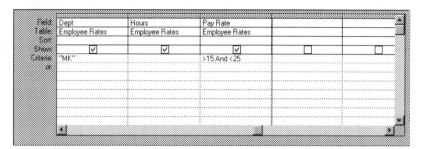

COMBINING CRITERIA TO CREATE OR CONDITIONS

In contrast to And conditions, *Or* conditions let you specify records that meet any one of two or more criteria. For example, you can specify the records of employees who work in either the Marketing department *or* the Chemical Engineering department.

As with And conditions, there are a couple of ways to create Or conditions:

- Set one criterion on the Criteria row and another on the Or row (located just below the Criteria row). For example, to specify records for employees who either work in the Chemical Engineering department *or* who make more than $20 per hour, you would type *CE* in the Dept column's Criteria cell, and then enter *>20* in the Pay Rate column's Or cell.

- You also can create an Or condition within a single field by using the Or operator in its Criteria cell. For example, to specify the records for employees who work less than 25 hours *or* more than 40 hours per week, you would type *<25 Or >40* in the Hours column's Criteria cell.

As is true of And conditions, you can combine the two methods just described. You also can use both the And and Or operators in the same query; Access will select any record that meets all the criteria on the Criteria row, *or* meets all the conditions on any Or row. (Although not labeled, every row that follows the first Or row is also an Or row.)

Let's create some Or conditions in our criteria:

1. Return to the Design view, and then delete the criteria in the Pay Rate column.

2. In the Hours column's Or cell, type **<30**, and then observe the Dept and Hours columns. The criteria (*"MK"* for Dept and *<30* for Hours) are on separate rows (see Figure 5.14).

Figure 5.14   **Creating Or conditions in the design grid**

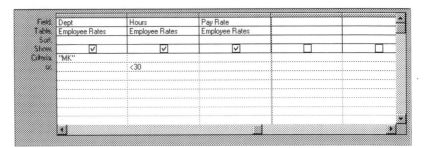

3. Run the query and observe the resulting datasheet. The query selected those records for employees who work in the MK department *or* who work fewer than 30 hours per week. Or conditions *increase* the number of records that meet the criteria by allowing records into the resulting datasheet if they meet either condition, rather than both. And conditions *restrict* the number of records that meet the criteria by requiring that they meet more than one condition.

4. Return to Design view, and then place the insertion point to the right of the text *"MK"* in the Dept column's Criteria cell.

5. Press the **spacebar**, type **or CE**, and then press **Tab**. Access changes your *or* to *Or* and places double quotation marks around *CE*.

6. Run the query, and then observe the resulting datasheet. The query selected records for employees who work in either the MK *or* the CE department, *or* who work fewer than 30 hours per week. Again, adding another Or condition increased the number of records that meet the criteria.

SETTING CRITERIA TO FIND EMPTY FIELDS

When you are responsible for managing a database, it is often useful to find records that have no data in certain fields. For example, when a number of new employees are hired, you might create incomplete records for them, and then fill in the rest of the data as it becomes available.

To select records with empty fields, you can use the *Is Null* expression as a criterion. (To find records that don't have empty fields, you can use the *Is Not Null* expression.)

Let's use the Is Null expression to find records with empty ID fields:

1. Return to Design view, and then delete the criteria in the Dept and Hours columns. There should now be no criteria in the design grid.

2. In the ID column's Criteria cell, type **is null**, and then press **Tab**. Access changes *is null* to *Is Null*.

3. Run the query, and then observe the resulting datasheet (see Figure 5.15). The query selected the three records with empty ID fields.

Figure 5.15 **Records with null ID fields**

ID	First Name	Last Name	Dept	Hours	Pay Rate
	Alice	DeMarco	ES	25.5	$8.90
	Roger	Donaldson	EE	40	$12.00
	John	Ward	ES	25	$8.50

4. Save the query as **My Missing IDs**.

EDITING RECORDS IN THE RESULTING DATASHEET

Earlier in this chapter, you learned that a datasheet resulting from a query is dynamic because it changes as the data in your tables changes. This also works the other way: Changes you make in a resulting datasheet can change data in the underlying tables.

This feature makes queries even more useful because you can use them not only to view data, but also to change it. For example, in the last activity you used a datasheet resulting from a query to find employee records that have empty ID fields. Now, you can add ID numbers to the datasheet to update the underlying table.

It's no coincidence that datasheets resulting from queries look just like tables; you can edit records in them just as you would in a table.

Let's use the datasheet resulting from the My Missing IDs query to fill in some missing IDs, and then take a look at the underlying table, Employee Rates:

1. In the ID field for Alice DeMarco's record, type **0027**. Notice as you type that the record selector displays a pencil indicator, just as it does when you're editing a record in a table.

2. In the ID field for Roger Donaldson's record, type **0017**.

3. Close the Query window.

4. Open the Employee Rates table, and observe the records for Alice DeMarco and Roger Donaldson. The ID numbers you entered in the datasheet resulting from the My Missing IDs query appear in this table.

5. Close the Table window.

PERFORMING CALCULATIONS IN QUERIES

In addition to allowing you to see subsets of the data in a query, you also can use queries to perform calculations on your data. For example, you could use a query to see what everyone's pay rate would be if you raised the rates by 7 percent. Or you could use a query to calculate employees' gross pay by multiplying their hourly rates by their hours worked.

CREATING A CALCULATED FIELD

You can perform a calculation involving fields within the same record by adding a *calculated field* to the design grid. To create a calculated field, you would enter a calculation expression in a blank Field cell.

To specify field names within a calculation expression, you must type square brackets around each field name. For example, to calculate an employee's gross pay (by multiplying the Hours and Pay Rate fields), you would type *[Hours]*[Pay Rate]* in a blank Field cell.

Table 5.2 lists some of the arithmetic operators you can use in calculated fields, and some sample expressions for those operators.

When you enter a calculation expression in a Field cell, Access supplies a default field name (Expr1, Expr2, and so on) to head the column in the resulting datasheet. For example, Access might

Table 5.2   **Arithmetic Operators**

Operator	Expression	Action
+	[Hired Date]+30	Add 30 days to value in Hired Date field
-	[Price]-[Discount]	Subtract value in Discount field from value in Price field
•	[Hours]*[Pay Rate]	Multiply value in Hours field by value in Pay Rate field
/	[Gross Pay]/[Hours]	Divide value in Gross Pay field by value in Hours field

change the *[Hours]*[Pay Rate]* expression to *Expr1:[Hours]*[Pay Rate]*. It would then display the results of that calculation in the resulting datasheet under the heading *Expr1*. To replace this default name with something more meaningful, simply replace the text *Expr1* in the field cell of the design grid (but leave the rest of the expression intact).

Let's create a calculated field so that we can see employees' gross pay in our query:

1. Open a new Query window in Design view. (Display the list of query object names in the Database window, click on **New**, click on **Design View**, and then click on **OK**.) Access displays the Add Table dialog box.

2. Double-click on **Hours and Rates** to add that table's field list to the Query window, and then click on **Close** to close the dialog box.

3. In the field list, double-click on **Dept**, **Hours**, and **Pay Rate** to add those fields to the design grid. (You will need to scroll to see all the field names.)

4. Place the insertion point in the fourth Field cell, and then type **[hours]*[pay rate]** to create an expression that will calculate gross pay. (You must enclose field names within square brackets, but you can type them in any case.)

5. Press **Tab**, and then observe the design grid. Access has changed the calculated field to include the text *Expr1:*, but

you cannot see the entire expression. Often when you create expressions, you will have this problem. Fortunately, there's a good solution.

6. Point to the expression in the fourth Field cell, click the *right* mouse button to display a shortcut menu, and then choose **Zoom** to display the Zoom dialog box for the expression (see Figure 5.16); you now can see the entire expression.

Figure 5.16   **Zooming a field expression**

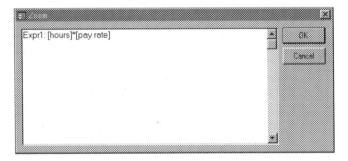

7. Click on **OK** to close the dialog box, then run the query and observe the resulting datasheet. The query has calculated the gross pay for each record and now displays this data in the Expr1 field. (Don't be concerned about the uneven number of decimal places that appear in this field; you'll learn how to format calculated fields in Chapter 10.)

8. Return to Design view, select the text *Expr1* (don't select the colon separating Expr1 from the calculation, or the calculation itself), and then type **Gross Pay** to replace Expr1. (**Hint:** If you have trouble editing the expression in the design grid, why not zoom it? Just point to the expression, click the right mouse button, and choose **Zoom**. When you're done editing, click on **OK**.)

9. Run the query, and then observe the resulting datasheet. The calculated field now has the more meaningful title *Gross Pay* (see Figure 5.17).

10. Save the query as **My Gross Pay**.

Figure 5.17 **The Gross Pay calculated field**

Dept	Hours	Pay Rate	Gross Pay
MK	38	$23.65	898.7
ES	40	$10.00	400
MK	35	$24.00	840
MK	25	$25.00	625
ES	29.5	$17.00	501.5
EE	40	$15.00	600
EE	40	$17.00	680
EE	15.5	$15.75	244.125
CE	40	$6.30	252
MK	40	$22.00	880
SS	35.5	$13.30	472.15
CE	35.5	$6.75	239.625
MK	40	$21.24	849.6
CE	40	$15.50	620
EE	40	$12.00	480
SS	40	$15.50	620
ES	25.5	$8.90	226.95
MS	40	$16.00	640
ES	40	$10.75	430

Record: |◄|◄| 1 |►|►|►►| of 30

USING THE EXPRESSION BUILDER

You can use the Expression Builder to help you build expressions when you are not entirely sure of their proper syntax. To use this very handy tool:

- Point to a Field cell (or anywhere you would like to enter an expression) and click the right mouse button to display the shortcut menu.

- Choose *Build* to display the Expression Builder dialog box.

- Select fields, functions, and operators and paste them into the expression.

- Click on *OK*.

The Expression Builder is an extremely valuable tool, and we're only touching upon its capabilities here. But let's use it to create a field that calculates employees' benefits cost as a function of gross pay:

1. Switch to Design view, and then click the right mouse button in the first blank Field cell in the design grid. A shortcut menu appears.

2. Choose **Build** to display the Expression Builder dialog box, which in certain ways resembles a calculator. The first list

contains folder icons. The My Gross Pay folder is open right now, so the second list shows the field names for our query.

3. In the second list, select **Gross Pay** and then click on **Paste** to paste the field name into the expression.

4. Click on the ***** button to enter the multiplication operator (*), and then type **.33**. (We will calculate the benefits cost as a third of gross pay.) So far, the expression should be *[Gross Pay]*.33*.

5. Press **Home** to move to the beginning of the expression, and then type **Benefits Cost:** to name it (see Figure 5.18). In this example, it would have been easy to simply type the expression, but for more complex expressions, the Builder is extremely useful.

Figure 5.18   **Using the Expression Builder to create a calculated field**

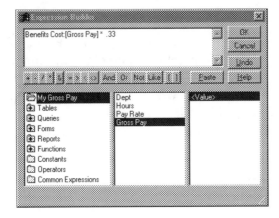

6. Click on **OK** to enter the expression, and then run the query. The new field appears in the resulting datasheet.

CALCULATING A TOTAL FOR A GROUP OF RECORDS

In addition to performing calculations within records, you also can use queries to perform calculations involving groups of records. This allows you to calculate summary information, or totals. With Access, you can calculate totals for every record in a resulting datasheet (for example, the average employee pay rate for the entire company), or totals for groups of records within a resulting datasheet (for example, the average employee pay rates for each department).

To create totals for groups of records, you would

- Choose *View, Totals* from the Design view of the Query window to display a Total row in the design grid (or click on the *Totals* button). Access places the text *Group By* in the Total cell for each field.

- Verify that the text Group By appears only in the Total cell of the field by which you wish to group records. For example, if you want to see each department as one line in the resulting datasheet, only the Dept field should contain the text *Group By* in the Total row. Every other field should either contain an expression (so a total can be calculated for all the records in each department), or be removed from the grid.

- In the Total cell of the field for which you wish to see calculated data, select the appropriate aggregate function from the drop-down list(s). *Aggregate functions* let you calculate aggregate values, such as sums and averages, for a group of values.

- Run the query.

Table 5.3 shows Access's aggregate functions and their purposes.

It's important that you include in the design grid only those fields either by which you are grouping records or upon which you are calculating a total. For example, if you want to calculate the average hours worked by department, include only the hours-worked and department fields in the grid. If the design grid contains any other fields, you should delete them.

Access calculates totals based upon all the records in a resulting datasheet, not in the underlying table. Therefore, if you set criteria to select only certain records, Access will use only values from those records in the calculation.

Let's use Access's totals feature to calculate the total gross-pay costs by department:

1. Return to Design view, and then observe the design grid. The grid does not contain a row for totaling values for groups of records.

Table 5.3   **Aggregate Functions**

Function	Use to Calculate
Sum	Total of values within a field
Avg	Average of values within a field
Min	Lowest value within a field
Max	Highest value within a field
Count	Number of values within a field (excluding fields with null values)
StDev	Standard deviation of values within a field
Var	Variance of values within a field
First	First value within a field
Last	Last value within a field

2. Click on the **Totals** button and then observe the design grid again. Access has added a Total row to the grid. The text *Group By* appears under each field.

3. Click on the Hours column's **field selector** to select the column, and then press **Delete** to delete the column.

4. Select and delete the **Pay Rate** and **Benefits Cost** fields. The design grid should now contain only the Dept and Gross Pay columns.

5. Click in the Gross Pay column's Total cell, and then click on its **drop-down arrow** to display a list of aggregate functions. You can total groups in many ways.

6. Select **Sum** to indicate that you wish to see the total gross pay for each department (see Figure 5.19).

7. Run the query, observe the resulting datasheet, and compare it to the design grid in Figure 5.19. In the query design,

Figure 5.19   **Selecting an aggregate function**

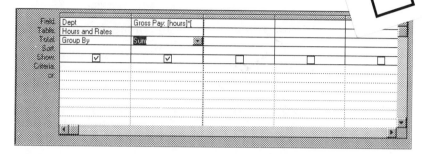

the Group By operator in the Dept column says you want to see one row for each department. The Sum function in the Gross Pay column tells Access to calculate the total gross pay for all the records in each department.

8. Save the query as **My Dept Gross Pay Totals**.

9. Close the Query window.

SUMMARY

In this chapter, you learned how to create and use select queries to limit the number of visible fields, sort records, select only those records that meet certain criteria, edit values, and perform calculations.

Here's a quick reference guide to the Access features introduced in this chapter:

Desired Result	How to Do It
View query design	From Database window, choose Query tab and click on **Design**; from Datasheet view, choose **View, Query Design** (or click on **Design View** button)
Create query	Display query object names, click on **New**, click on **Design View**, click on **OK**, select table upon which to base query, click on **Add**, and click on **Close**

Desired Result	How to Do It
Add field to query design	Open Field cell's drop-down list and select field name; or, double-click on field name in field list
Run query	Choose **Query, Run** (or click on **Run** button); or, click on **Datasheet View** button
Sort records in query	Display Sort cell's drop-down list, select sort order (Ascending or Descending), and then run query
Save and name new query (or rename existing query)	From Query window, choose **File, Save As/Export**; type query name; click on **OK**
Save modified query design	From Query window, choose **File, Save As/Export** or **File, Save**
Move column in design grid	Select column (click on **field selector**) and drag to new location
Set an exact query criterion	Type value in Criteria cell
Add And condition to criteria	Type criteria in more than one Criteria cell; or type **And** between criteria within Criteria cell
Add Or condition to criteria	Type criteria in Criteria cell and in Or cell; or type **Or** between criteria within one Criteria cell
Set criterion to find empty field	Type **Is Null** in Criteria cell
Create calculated field	Type calculation expression in empty Field cell, or use Expression Builder (right-click on field and choose **Build**)
Rename calculated field	Replace default field name in Field cell of design grid
Calculate totals	Choose **View, Totals** (or click on **Totals** button); select **Group By** for field(s) by which to group records; select aggregate function(s) for field(s) on which to calculate; run query

In Chapter 6, you'll learn how to create and customize a form to help you enter and view data.

CHAPTER 6: FORM BASICS

Viewing Data in
Forms

Using Form View

Creating a From
Using a Form
Wizard

Sorting and
Filtering Records
While in a Form

In Chapter 5, you learned how to use queries to ask questions about your data. In this chapter, you'll learn how to create, modify, and use forms to control and customize the way you view and edit data.

When you're done working through this chapter, you will know

- How to use a form to view records

- How to use a Form Wizard to create a form

- How to modify the design of a form

- How to preview a form

- How to sort and filter records through a form

- How to edit and add records through a form

VIEWING DATA IN FORMS

Forms let you see data however you want, rather than just in rows and columns. Many people use forms to view only certain fields, or to display only one record at a time. If you were editing home-address data in an employee information table, you could use a form

- To view and edit only the fields that are relevant to that task

- To display one record at a time so that you can focus on each individual employee

- To match a paper form you have been using to enter data; this makes the transition from paperwork to working in Access that much easier

USING FORM VIEW

Every form offers you two ways to view your data: Form view and Datasheet view. In Form view, you see data in a custom layout, often only one record at a time. To switch to Form view from any other view, you can either choose View, Form, or click on the Form View button.

If you do not have both the Access application and Employee Database windows opened and maximized, please do so now.

Let's take a look at a form:

1. Open and examine the Addresses and Extensions table. The table contains seven fields: Last Name, First Name, Adr, City, St, Zip, and Ext. There is only one way to view the data in a table: through the Datasheet view. This is useful in some

situations, but often presents you with more data than you want to see at any time.

2. Close the Table window.

3. Click on the **Forms** tab to display the list of form object names.

4. Double-click on **Address** to open the Address form (see Figure 6.1). This form is based upon data in the Addresses and Extensions table, at which we were just looking. The form displays six of the seven fields from Jane Martin's record. It is much easier to get a sense for Jane Martin as an employee in this view than in the Datasheet view of the table.

Figure 6.1   **The Address form**

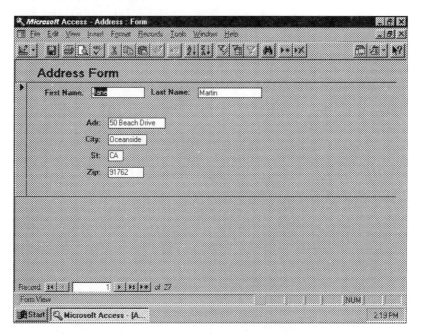

5. Press **Page Down** several times to view the next several records (you also can click on the **Next Record** navigation button). For each record, the form displays the same six fields, but with different values.

EXAMINING THE DATASHEET VIEW OF A FORM

Forms have a Datasheet view as well as a Form view. This view shows data in rows and columns, and may appear quite similar to the form's underlying table. A form's Datasheet view, however, will display only the fields that are visible in Form view. To switch to Datasheet view, choose View, Datasheet, or click on the Datasheet View button.

Let's take a look at the Datasheet view of the Address form:

1. Move to Maria Sanders's record (Record 6). The status bar indicates that this is Form view.

2. Click on the **Datasheet View** button to switch to Datasheet view. (To display the Datasheet View button, click on the drop-down arrow next to the Design View button.) The Datasheet view of the form looks very similar to the Addresses and Extensions table, except that it shows only six of the table's seven fields. Notice that Maria Sanders's record is still current, and that the status bar now displays *Datasheet View* (see Figure 6.2).

Figure 6.2   **The Datasheet view of the Address form**

First Name	Last Name	Adr.	City	St.	Zip
Jane	Martin	50 Beach Drive	Oceanside	CA	91762
Ted	James	34 Fields Street	Fort Worth	TX	76116
Marie	Abel	127 Ford Avenue	Shackelford	TX	76430
Julia	Binder	10 Cory Drive	Trenton	NJ	08753
Sam	Binga	50 Dallas Street	Pasadena	CA	91106
Maria	Sanders	12 East Avenue	Denton	TX	76201
Harry	Harper	82 East Avenue	Long Beach	CA	90745
Bill	Conner	32 Ash Lane	Allentown	NJ	08501
Roger	Donaldson	8165 Main Street	Trenton	NJ	08618
Penny	Packer	9929 Clearview	Vienna	VA	22181
Robert	Abot	99 Stonecreek Rd.	Trenton	NJ	08618
Nancy	Evans	21 Stonecreek Rd.	Trenton	NJ	08618
Joseph	Zambito	81 Pleasing Lane	Alhambra	CA	91801
Dominick	Osowski	23 Lakeside Ave.	S Granbury	TX	76048
Wilma	Chase	52 Pempleton Dr.	Albany	NY	12205
Alice	DeMarco	34 Sable Ave.	Bentwood	IL	61820
Dennis	Kyler	273 Fireside Dr.	Great Neck	NY	11023
Frank	Desoto	P.O. Box 7234	Trenton	NJ	07092
Albert	Henley	12 Divine Drive	San Pueblo	CO	80403
Robert	Beaton	391 State Street	West Seneca	NY	14224
Joe	Stira	200 Nester Street	Bath	NY	14708
Homer	Jones	466 Fairhaven St.	Los Alamos	MI	84104
William	Bell	66 Big Hill Rd.	Troy	NY	12182
David	Haslam	453 Lakeshore Dr.	Evans Mills	ND	58352

Record: 6 of 27

Datasheet view

3. Click on the **Form View** button to return to Form view. (To display the Form view button, you will again need to click on the drop-down arrow next to the Design View button.)

4. Close the Form window.

CREATING A FORM USING A FORM WIZARD

To help you create your own forms, Access provides you with Form Wizards. Whenever you start to create a new form, Access gives you the option of using one of the following types of Form Wizards:

- The *Form Wizard* builds forms, allowing you to select the fields (from one or more tables or queries), the layout (columnar, tabular, or Datasheet), and the background style.

- If you pre-select the table or query that the data will come from, you can choose one of the *AutoForm Wizards.* The advantage of these wizards over the Form Wizard is that you don't have to answer any questions; Access simply creates the form in the specified layout. There are three types of AutoForm Wizards:

  - The *AutoForm: Columnar Wizard* builds forms that display one record at a time. The fields appear in a single column.

  - The *AutoForm: Tabular Wizard* builds forms that display fields from many records in a row-and-column format.

  - The *AutoForm: Datasheet Wizard* builds forms that look very much like a table in Datasheet view.

- The *Chart Wizard* builds forms that display data from fields as charts.

- The *PivotTable Wizard* creates a control on a form that allows you to summarize large amounts of data on one form.

 SELECTING A DATA SOURCE

To create a new form using the Form Wizard, you follow these steps:

- In the Database window, click on the *Forms* tab to display the list of form object names.

- Click on *New* to display the New Form dialog box. You have the option of creating a form from scratch in Design view or using one of the Wizards.

- Click on *Form Wizard*, then click on *OK*. Access displays a series of panes that allow you to choose various features for your form.

Let's begin to create a form that eventually will resemble the Address form you just saw:

1. Be sure you're looking at the list of form object names, and then click on **New** to display the New Form dialog box.

2. Click on **Form Wizard**, then click on OK. Examine the first Form Wizard pane. You use this pane to select a table or query on which to base your new form, and to select the fields that you want to appear on the form, as well as the order in which the fields appear (more on selecting fields in the next section).

3. Click on the **drop-down arrow** next to the Tables/Queries box, and choose **Table:Addresses and Extensions** to base your new form upon the Addresses and Extensions table. (The Addresses and Extensions table happens to be the first table in the list, so it was already selected.) Your screen should resemble Figure 6.3.

Figure 6.3   **The first Form Wizard pane**

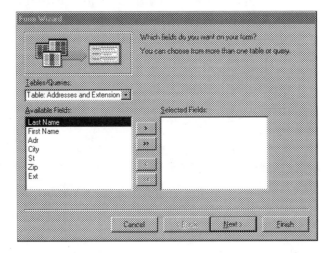

SPECIFYING FIELDS AND LAYOUT

You can choose which fields you want to see on a form. This can help you focus on pertinent information, or conceal certain data from other users. For example, if you create a home-address entry form based on an employee information table that contains salary information, you could choose not to include that information on the form.

After you start the Form Wizard, Access prompts you to specify the fields you want on the form, and the order in which to place them. To add a field to the form, select the field name in the Available Fields box and then click on the > button. To add all the fields, click on the >> button. (To remove field selections, click on < or <<.) The Form Wizard will place fields on the form in the order in which you select them.

After you finish answering one set of Form Wizard questions, click on the *Next* button to proceed to the next pane. (To change a previous answer, click on the *Back* button to return to previous panes.)

Let's choose the fields for our form:

1. In the Available Fields box, select **First Name**, and then click on > to move the First Name field to the Selected Fields box.

2. Click on < to remove the First Name field from the Selected Fields box.

3. Click on >> to move all the fields to the Selected Fields box (see Figure 6.4).

4. Click on **Next** to move to the next Form Wizard pane.

5. Examine the Form Wizard pane. You use this pane to select the layout you would like for your form. A preview of the layout is displayed. Click on the Tabular and Datasheet choices and examine the preview (see Figure 6.5).

6. Click on the **Columnar** choice, then click on **Next** to proceed to the next pane.

SELECTING A FORM STYLE AND ADDING A TITLE

The Form Wizard offers eight *styles* for forms. The style affects only the appearance, not the function, of forms. When you select

Figure 6.4   **Choosing fields for the form**

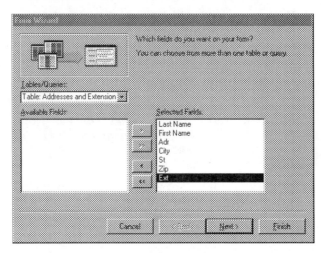

Figure 6.5   **Choosing a layout for your form**

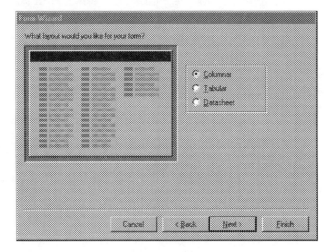

a style, the Form Wizard will show you a sample of what the form will look like.

After you select a style and click on Next, the Form Wizard will ask you to specify a title for your form. The title is the form's object name. This name will be displayed on the Database window's Forms tab.

Let's select a style and specify a title for your form:

1. Examine the Form Wizard pane. Access gives you eight choices of styles for the form. The preview on the left displays an example of the selected style.

2. Select **International** and examine the pane. The preview now shows an example of the International style.

3. Select each of the remaining styles, noting the examples in the preview, and then select **Standard**. This is the look we'll use for our form.

4. Click on **Next** to move to the next Form Wizard pane. Here you can enter a title that will appear on the Forms tab. By default, Access places the name of the table upon which the form is based in the Form Title box (in this case, Addresses and Extensions).

5. Type **My Address Form** to replace the selected text and specify a different title for the form (see Figure 6.6).

Figure 6.6 **The final Form Wizard pane**

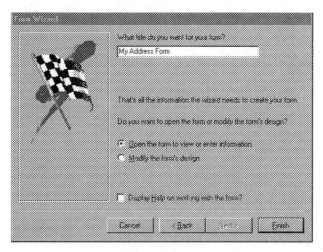

OPENING THE FORM

In the final Form Wizard pane, you can choose either to open the form with data in it, or to open its Design view. Simply select the desired option and then click on the *Finish* button. If you're not sure about any of the answers you've given in the previous panes, you can click on the Back button to return to them.

Let's open your new form:

1. Observe the final Form Wizard pane. You can choose either to modify the design of the form or to view the form with data in it. The default choice is to open the form to view or enter information, and we'll stick with that.

2. Click on **Finish** to open the form with data, and then maximize the Form window, if necessary (see Figure 6.7). The form contains data only from Jane Martin's record, and the fields appear in a column in the order in which you selected them. Each field has a label to its left.

Figure 6.7   **The new form**

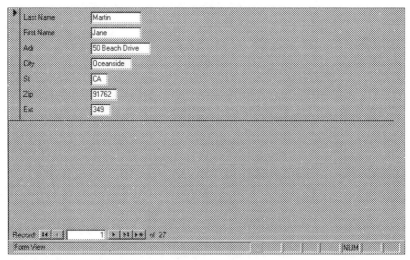

3. Press **Page Down** to view the next record. This form functions very much like the Address form you saw earlier in this chapter. Now we're looking at Ted James's record. As you move from record to record, the field names remain the same, while the data in the fields change.

UNDERSTANDING THE FORM DESIGN

Using a Form Wizard is often just the first step in creating a form. By working in a form's Design view, you can modify the design to suit your needs and taste. In Design view, you can view and manipulate the elements that determine how you see data in the form. Access divides the Design view of a form into three sections:

- A *Form Header* section, which determines what will appear at the top of every form (such as a title or instructions for using the form)

- A *Detail* section, which usually displays field and record information, and can change from record to record

- A *Form Footer* section, which determines what will appear at the bottom of every form

The elements you use to compose each section of a form are called *controls*. Access provides three types of controls:

- A *bound control* is linked to a field in a table or query. In Form view, a bound control will display a particular field value for a particular record.

- An *unbound control* displays information that does not change from record to record. Examples would be a form's title, a field label, or a line or shape.

- As the name suggests, you use a *calculated control* to calculate values based on one or more fields. A calculated control also can display such information as the current date or page number.

Let's take a look at the design of the form we just created:

1. Click on the **Design View** button to switch to the form's Design view.

2. Click on **View** to display the View menu; if there is a check mark next to the *Toolbox* command, choose **Toolbox** to hide the tool box. If the tool box is not open, click on **View** again to close the menu. (You will learn about the tool box in Chapter 10.) Your screen should resemble Figure 6.8.

3. Observe the Form window's three sections. The Form Header section is empty. The Detail section contains the fields and their labels. The Form Footer section is empty.

Figure 6.8   **Examining the form's design**

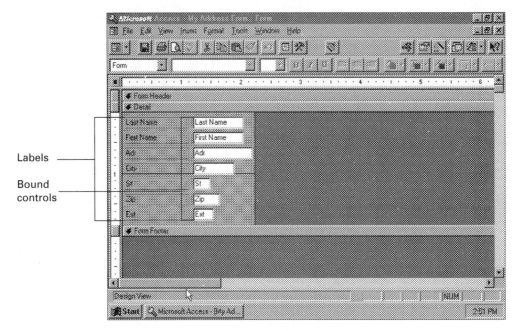

Labels

Bound
controls

4. Observe the controls in the Detail section. The boxes on the
left are labels, or unbound controls; the boxes on the right
are bound controls. In creating the form, the Form Wizard
used the name of each field as the text for each label.

SELECTING, DELETING, AND MOVING FORM ELEMENTS

You can select, delete, and move the elements that make up a
form. Here are some ways to manipulate bound controls and labels:

- To select a bound control *and* its label, click on the bound control. When you do, Access will show several small handles
  and one larger handle around the bound control. One large
  handle also will appear in the upper-left corner of the control's
  label. You use the smaller handles to change the size of a control, and the larger handles to move it.

- To delete a bound control and its label, select them and then
  press the *Delete* key.

- To move a bound control (but not its label):
  - Select the control.
  - Point to the large handle until the pointer takes the shape of a pointing finger.
  - Drag the control where you want it.
- To move a bound control *and* its label:
  - Select the control (and its label).
  - Point to an edge of the bound control; the mouse pointer will take the shape of an open hand.
  - Drag the control and label where you want them.

Let's experiment with these techniques.

1. Click on the **Ext** bound control to select both the bound control and its label (the bound control is the box on the right). Access should now display several smaller handles and one large one around the bound control, as well as a single large handle in the upper-left corner of the label (see Figure 6.9). You use the larger handles to move controls, and the smaller ones to change size.

2. Press **Delete** to delete the Ext bound control and its label.

3. Select the **Last Name** bound control and its label. (Click on the Last Name bound control; remember, that's the box on the right.) We'll move the two name fields so that they both appear on the first line of the form.

4. Point to the large handle in the upper-left corner of the Last Name bound control; this is the *move handle* for the control. If you're pointing to the correct handle, the pointer should look like a single pointing finger.

5. While pointing to the move handle, drag the bound control about 1 inch to the right (use the ruler at the top of the screen to gauge distance); then observe the Form window. This technique moves only the bound control, and not its label.

6. Click on the **Undo** button to return the Last Name bound control to its original position (or choose **Edit, Undo Move**).

7. Point to an edge of the Last Name bound control, away from any handles. The pointer should take the shape of an open hand.

Figure 6.9 **Selecting a control**

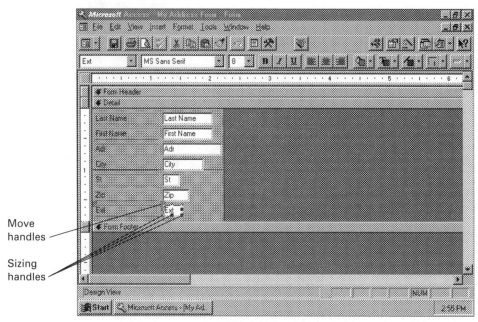

Move
handles

Sizing
handles

8. Use the open-hand pointer to drag the Last Name bound control about 3 inches to the right, and then observe the Form window. The open-hand pointer moves the Last Name bound control *and* its label. Also notice that Access expands the form's width to accommodate the new field placement.

9. Select the **First Name** bound control and its label. We'll move these controls up to the first line of the form.

10. Point to an edge of the bound control, then use the open-hand pointer to drag it and its label to the upper-left corner of the Detail section.

RESIZING AND ALIGNING FORM ELEMENTS

You can change the size of a control, and you also can align two or more controls to make your forms look neater. Here are some more techniques for working with a form's design:

• To resize a selected bound control or label, point to one of the *smaller* handles (the pointer will take the shape of a two-headed arrow), then drag to change the control's size.

- To select more than one control, select one, press and hold down *Shift*, and then select each other control.

- To align two or more controls:

  - Select the controls you wish to align.

  - Choose *Format, Align* to display the Align submenu.

  - Choose the desired alignment: *Left, Right, Top, Bottom,* or *To Grid.*

Let's change the size of the First Name bound control, and align it with the Last Name controls:

1. Point to the small handle in the bottom-right corner of the First Name bound control; this is a *sizing handle.* The pointer should take the shape of a two-headed arrow.

2. Use the arrow pointer to drag the sizing handle about $1/2$ inch to the right to enlarge the control.

3. Move the **Last Name** bound control, and its label, to about $1/4$ inch to the right of the First Name bound control.

4. Select the **Last Name** bound control (if necessary), press and hold the **Shift** key, and click on the **Last Name** label. Now sizing handles appear around the label as well as the bound control. We want to align the First Name and Last Name bound controls *and* their labels. To do this, we first must select all four.

5. While holding down the **Shift** key, click on the **First Name** bound control *and* its label; then release Shift. Now the First Name and Last Name controls, as well as their labels, are selected.

6. Choose **Format, Align, Bottom** to align the bottom edges of the selected bound controls and labels.

7. Choose **File, Save** to save the modified form design. (If the Save As dialog box appears, click on **OK**.)

8. Switch to Form view, and then observe the Form window (see Figure 6.10). Access no longer displays the Ext field or its label, and the First Name and Last Name fields appear in their new locations.

Figure 6.10   **The modified form**

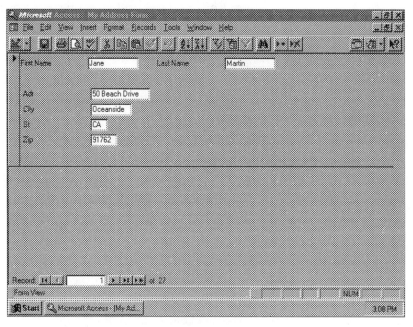

 PREVIEWING AND PRINTING THE FORM

Just as you can preview and print tables, queries, and reports, you can preview and print forms. When you preview or print a form, Access displays a separate copy of the form for each record in the underlying table or datasheet resulting from a query. Access also will try to fit as many forms as it can on one sheet of paper.

You also might want to print a blank record in a form to use as a paper data-collection form. This will make data entry easier because the paper form will match your electronic form.

To preview a form, choose File, Print Preview or click on the Print Preview button. To print from the preview screen, click on the Print button in the tool150bar.

Let's preview our form:

1. Click on the **Print Preview** button to preview the printed form. When printing forms, Access will fit as many records as it can on a single page.

2. Click on the **Zoom** button to enlarge the preview. Each copy of the form displays data from a different record (see Figure 6.11).

Figure 6.11   **Previewing the form**

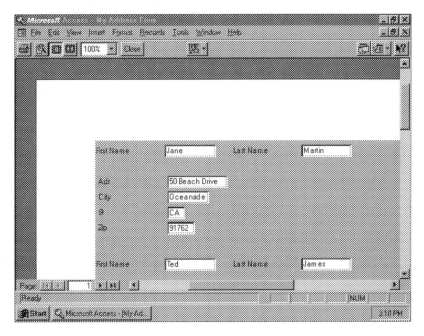

3. Click on the **Close** button in the toolbar to close the preview.

SORTING AND FILTERING RECORDS WHILE IN A FORM

You can sort records through a form's Filter window. You also can use a Filter window to display only records that meet certain criteria.

A form's Filter window is similar to the Design view of a query. Both windows have an upper pane containing a field list and a lower pane containing a grid. A Filter window, however, is more limited than a Query window, and you cannot save its design. However, for on-the-spot sorting and filtering, a Filter window is a valuable tool.

SORTING RECORDS IN A FORM

To sort records in a form by one field at a time (for instance by last name), while in Form view you simply click in the field and click on the Sort Ascending button. However, to perform a two-level sort (such as by last name, then by first name), you need to use the Filter/Sort window (or run a query).

To perform a multiple-level sort on records in a form, you would follow these steps:

- Choose *Records, Filter, Advanced Filter/Sort* to open the Filter window.

- Create a column in the filter grid for each field by which you want to sort. To do this, enter a field name in one of the filter grid's Field cells, and then select a sort order (just as you do in a design grid). As it does in a query, Access will sort by fields from left to right. Unlike a query, the form always will display the same set of fields, regardless of which fields you place in the filter grid.

- Click on the *Apply Filter* button to apply the sort.

Let's use the Filter window to sort your records by last and then first name:

1. Press **Page Down** several times and observe the records (you should be in Form view). The records appear in the order in which they appear in the underlying table.

2. Choose **Records, Filter, Advanced Filter/Sort** to open the form's Filter window. The Filter window includes a field list for the underlying table, and a filter grid.

3. In the field list, double-click on **Last Name** and then on **First Name** to enter them in the filter grid's first two columns.

4. In the Sort cells for both the Last Name and First Name columns, select **Ascending** (see Figure 6.12). This should be quite familiar from the last chapter, when we did the same thing in a design grid.

5. Click on the **Apply Filter** button to perform the sort and return to the Form window.

Figure 6.12   **Setting sort order in a filter grid**

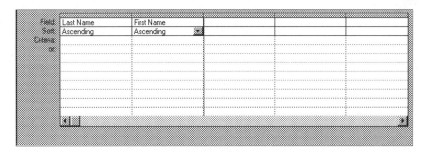

6. Press **Page Down** several times to view the next several records; they are now in order by last and then first name.

SETTING CRITERIA USING FILTER BUTTONS

When you are looking at a form in either Form or Datasheet view, three Filter buttons appear on the toolbar (see Figure 6.13).

Button	Use
Filter By Selection	Filters records based on data currently selected
Filter By Form	Displays blank version of active form or data sheet so you can set up a filter by selecting specific values in one or more fields
Apply Filter/ Remove Filter	Applies or removes Filter window settings

Figure 6.13   **Filter buttons**

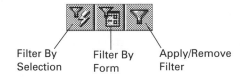

Filter By Selection   Filter By Form   Apply/Remove Filter

These buttons are extremely handy when you want to perform a simple filter. For instance, while in Form view, to display only the records with the last name "Binga," display one record with this last name, select the text "Binga," then click on the Filter By Selection button.

Another way to display only the records with the last name of "Binga" is to click on the Filter By Form button, and in the blank form, type "Binga" into the Last Name field (or select Binga from the drop-down list in the Last Name field), then click on the Apply Filter button.

We will now use the Filter window to perform more complicated filters, such as filters with And and Or conditions.

 ## SETTING CRITERIA IN A FORM'S FILTER WINDOW

Just as you can set criteria in a query, you can set criteria in a Filter window. This allows you to display only those records that you want to see.

To set criteria for records in a form:

- Choose *Records, Filter, Advanced Filter/Sort* to open the Filter window.

- Create a column in the filter grid for each field for which you want to set criteria. To do this, enter a field name in one of the filter grid's Field cells, and then enter a criterion in the Criteria row. (Again, this works just as it does in a design grid.)

- Click on the *Apply Filter* button to apply the filter.

Access will keep the filters and sorts you set in effect until you close the Form window or click on the Remove Filter button.

Let's add a criterion to our filter so that only records for employees who live in New York State appear; then we'll remove the filter/ sort to view all the records again:

1. Choose **Records, Filter, Advanced Filter/Sort** to switch to the Filter window. Notice that Access still displays the sort options you set.

2. Add the **St** field to the third Field cell in the filter grid (in the field list, double-click on the field name).

3. In the St column's Criteria cell, type **NY**. This is exactly the same as setting a criterion in a design grid.

4. Click on the **Apply Filter** button to apply your settings and return to Form view.

5. Press **Page Down** several times and observe the records. The form still displays records in order by last and then first name. Because of the criterion, however, only records for New York State employees appear.

6. Switch to Datasheet view. You can now see the effect of the filter/sort more easily (see Figure 6.14).

Figure 6.14   **The filtered records in Datasheet view**

Last Name	First Name	Adr	City	St	Zip
Beaton	Robert	391 State Stree	West Sen	NY	14224
Bell	William	66 Big Hill Rd.	Troy	NY	12182
Chase	Wilma	52 Pempleton D	Albany	NY	12205
Kyler	Dennis	273 Fireside Dr	Great Nec	NY	11023
Stira	Joe	200 Nester Stre	Bath	NY	14708

7. Click on **Remove Filter** to remove the filter/sort. Access now displays all the records.

8. Return to Form view.

EDITING AND ADDING RECORDS THROUGH A FORM

You can edit or add records in a table by using a form. Many of the selection and record-saving techniques you learned for tables in Chapter 2 also apply to forms. One nice shortcut in forms, though, is that you can select a field by clicking on its label.

Let's use our new form to edit and add a record:

1. Click on the **First Record** navigation button to move to Marie Abel's record.

2. Click on the **Adr** field label to select the contents of the Adr field. Often, this is easier than dragging over the text in a field.

3. Type **140 Oak Street** to replace the selected text.

4. Click on the **New Record** navigation button to move to the blank record at the end of the underlying table.

5. Click on the **Last Name** field label to place the insertion point in the Last Name field; then type your last name.

6. Press **Tab** to move to the First Name field, and then type your first name. (**Note:** The order in which the Tab key moves through the fields might seem strange here. It is based upon the order in which the fields were placed on the form.)

PRACTICE YOUR SKILLS

1. Complete the current record with your address information.

2. Close the Form window, saving the changes prompted.

3. Open your form's underlying table, Addresses and Extensions, and observe that the changes you made in the form appear in the table as well.

4. Close the Table and Database windows.

PRACTICE YOUR SKILLS

In Chapter 5, you learned how to create and use queries to view limited fields and records, to edit records, and to perform calculations. In this chapter, you learned how to create a form using a Form Wizard, and how to apply sorts and filters to a form. The following two activities give you an opportunity to practice these techniques.

In this activity, you will create a number of queries by specifying fields, setting sort orders and criteria, and creating calculated fields:

1. Open the **Practice** database file and then maximize the Database window (Chapter 2).

2. Create and run a new select query based on the Parking table. The resulting datasheet should display the ID, Park Lot, and Park Rate fields in descending order by Park Rate (there should be 52 records) (Chapter 5).

3. Return to Design view, set a criterion to select only those records in which the value of the Park Rate field is $55 or less, and then run the query (there should be 15 records) (Chapter 5).

4. Save the query design as **My Lowest Rates**; then close the Query window (Chapter 5).

5. Create and run another new select query based on the Parking table. The resulting datasheet should display all fields in records for employees who park in either the SE or NE lot (there should be 24 records) (Chapter 5).

6. Return to Design view, change the criteria to select only records for employees who park in the NE lot *and* who pay a rate greater than $65, and then run the query (there should be five records) (Chapter 5).

7. Return to Design view, change the criteria to select only records for employees who are not assigned to a parking lot, and then run the query (there should be four records) (Chapter 5).

8. Save the query design as **My Unassigned Parking** (Chapter 5).

9. Return to Design view, delete the current criterion, and then create a calculated field to display a 5-percent rate increase for employees who park in the NW lot (multiply the value of the Park Rate field by 1.05).

10. Name the calculated field **New NW Rate**, set a criterion to select records only for employees who park in the NW lot, and then run the query (there should be 14 records) (Chapter 5).

11. Save the query design as **My NW Parking Increase**; then close the Query window (Chapter 5).

In this activity, you will use the Form Wizard to create a new form, and then modify the form's design and apply a filter/sort:

1. Use the Form Wizard to create a new form based on the Parking table. Include the **Last Name**, **First Name**, and **Park Lot** fields on the form.

2. Give the form the **Columnar** layout, and the **Standard** style; then entitle it **Lot Assignments**.

3. Open the Form window in Design view; then maximize the window.

4. Modify the form's design by putting the Last Name and First Name bound controls and labels on the same line.

5. Save the form design as **My Parking Lot Assignments**.

6. Switch to Form view; then open the Filter window and specify a two-level, ascending sort by Last Name and then First Name.

7. Apply the filter/sort; then navigate through and observe the records (there should be 52).

8. Modify the filter/sort to specify only records for employees who park in the SW lot, apply the filter/sort, and then navigate through and observe the records (there should be ten).

9. Switch to Datasheet view and observe the records again.

10. Remove the filter.

11. Close the Form window (if you are prompted to save the changes to the form, click on **No**); then close the Database window.

SUMMARY

In this chapter, you learned how to use a form's different views, create a form with a Form Wizard, modify a form, preview a form, apply filter/sorts, and edit and add records through a form.

Here's a quick reference guide to the Access features introduced in this chapter:

Desired Result	How to Do It
View form in Form view	Choose **View, Form** or click on **Form View** button
View form in Datasheet view	Choose **View, Datasheet** or click on **Datasheet View** button
Create new form using Form Wizard	Display list of form object names in Database window, click on **New**, select **Form Wizard**, click on **OK**, and then answer Form Wizard's questions
Save and name new form	Choose **File**; type form name; click on **OK**
View form in Design view	Choose **View, Form Design** or click on **Design View** button

Desired Result	How to Do It
Select bound control and label	Click on bound control
Delete selected bound control and label	Press **Delete**
Move selected bound control	Point to control's move handle (pointer takes shape of pointing finger) and drag control to new location
Move selected control and label	Point to edge of control (pointer takes shape of open hand) and drag control and label to new location
Resize selected bound control	Point to sizing handle (pointer takes shape of double-headed arrow) and drag until control is desired size
Select more than one control	Select one control, press and hold **Shift**, select other controls, release **Shift**
Align selected controls	Choose **Format, Align**; then choose **Left**, **Right**, **Top**, **Bottom**, or **To Grid**
Save modified form design	Choose **File, Save As/Export**
Preview form	Choose **File, Print Preview** or click on **Print Preview** button
Sort records in form	Choose **Records, Filter, Advanced Filter/ Sort**, use filter grid to specify fields and sort options, and click on **Apply Filter** button
Show only certain records in form	Choose **Records, Filter, Advanced Filter/ Sort**, use filter grid to specify criteria, and click on **Apply Filter** button, or use **Filter By Selection** or **Filter By Form** buttons
Remove filter/sort	Click on **Remove Filter** button

In the next chapter, you'll learn how to create and use reports to present your data well on paper.

CHAPTER 7: REPORT BASICS

An Orientation to
Reports

Creating a Report

Creating a Report
with Groups

In Chapter 6, you learned how to use forms to customize the way you see data on the computer screen. In this chapter, you'll learn how to create and modify reports to customize the way you print data. You also will learn how to use reports to group and summarize your data.

When you're done working through this chapter, you will know

- About the design of a report
- How to create reports using a Report Wizard
- How to preview a report
- How to total fields and group records within a report
- How to modify a report's design

AN ORIENTATION TO REPORTS

In Chapter 2, you learned that reports are the best way to present your data on paper. Although you can print your data directly from tables, datasheets resulting from queries, and forms, reports give you greater control over how your data will print.

Among other things, reports let you

- Specify which fields to print
- Sort records
- Group records
- Calculate summary information
- Control the overall layout and appearance of your report

 PREVIEWING A BASIC REPORT

In Chapter 2, you previewed two reports: a basic report and a report in which the records were in groups. In this chapter, we'll take another look at those reports, and then learn how to create them ourselves.

If you do not have the Access application and the Employee Database windows open and maximized, please open and maximize them now.

Let's take another look at the basic report we saw in Chapter 2, and the table upon which the report is based:

1. Open and examine the Pay Rates table. This is our familiar employee payroll information. There are eight fields in the table.

2. Close the Table window.

3. In the Database window, click on the **Reports** tab to display the list of report object names, and then double-click on **Employee Hours and Rates** to preview the report (see Figure 7.1). The report shows hours and pay-rate information, and lists employees alphabetically. It also includes the title *Employee Hours and Rates* and the current date (your date will differ from the figure).

Figure 7.1   **The Employee Hours and Rates report**

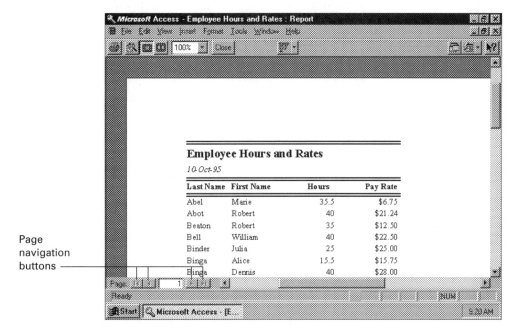

4. Observe the navigation buttons, then observe the Specific Page Number box. (In a preview screen, the record navigation buttons become page navigation buttons.) Because this is a single-page report, the navigation buttons are grayed out.

5. Use the vertical scroll bar to scroll to and observe the bottom of the page. Here, the report displays grand totals for hours and pay rates. There is a page number in the lower-right corner of the page.

6. Click on the **Close** button to close the preview screen.

UNDERSTANDING BASIC REPORT DESIGN

Like tables, queries, and forms, reports have a Design view in which you can modify their design. As with a form's Design view, Access divides a report's Design view into sections that contain controls. The number and type of these sections can vary depending upon the particular report, but they often include

- A *Report Header section*, which contains information that will appear only once, at the beginning of the report (such as the report title and date).

- A *Page Header section*, which contains information that will appear at the top of each page of the report (such as column-heading labels).

- A *Detail section*, which contains information that will appear once for each record in the report's underlying table or query. This information often makes up the bulk of a report.

- A *Page Footer section*, which contains information that will appear at the bottom of each page of the report (such as page numbers).

- A *Report Footer section*, which contains information that will appear only once, at the end of the report (such as sums or averages that summarize the information in the rest of the report).

You control record sorting and grouping by using the *Sorting and Grouping* window. To open this window, choose View, Sorting and Grouping, or click on the Sorting and Grouping button. This window contains a grid, in which you choose the fields by which to sort or group, and the manner in which to do so.

Let's take a look at the design of the Employee Hours and Rates report:

1. In the Database window, select **Employee Hours and Rates** (if necessary), and then click on the **Design** button to open the report's Design view.

2. If there is a small window called *Toolbox* showing, click once on its **Close** button to close it.

3. Examine the design of the report (see Figure 7.2). Access divides this window into five sections: Report Header, Page Header, Detail, Page Footer, and Report Footer.

Figure 7.2   **The design of a report**

Sorting and
Grouping
button

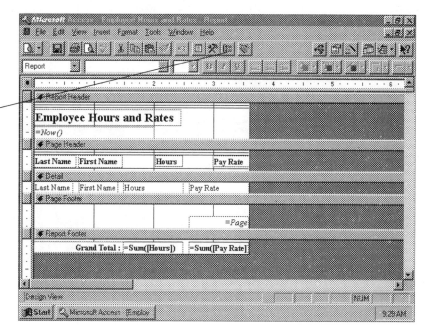

- The Report Header section contains a label that serves as the report title. It also contains the expression =*Now()*, which displays the current date. (You'll learn how to create calculated controls like this one in Chapter 10.)

- The Page Header section contains column headings.

- The Detail section contains bound controls that show field information for each record in the report's underlying table.

- The Page Footer section contains the expression =*Page*, which displays the current page number.

- Finally, The Report Footer section contains expressions that show the grand total for the Hours and Pay Rate fields.

  4. Compare the design to the report shown in Figure 7.1. Access prints the information in the Report Header, Page Header, Page Footer, and Report Footer sections once. (If this report had more than one page, the Page Header and Page Footer information would appear once on each page.) However, Access shows the Detail information once for each record in the report's underlying table.

5. Click on the **Sorting and Grouping** button to open the Sorting and Grouping window (this button is labeled in Figure 7.2). Access will sort the report's records first by last name, and then by first name (see Figure 7.3).

Figure 7.3 **The Sorting and Grouping window**

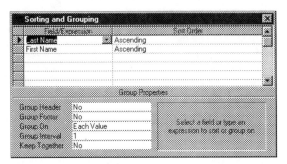

6. Click on the **Sorting and Grouping** button again to close the window; then close the report.

EXAMINING THE DESIGN OF A REPORT WITH GROUPS

The report you previewed at the beginning of this chapter printed one line for every record. The end of the report included grand totals that summarized data from all the records as a group.

There may be times, however, when you want to create smaller groups of records within a report, providing summary information for each of those groups. For example, if you create a report summarizing gross pay information for your employees, you might want to see subtotals for each department. To accomplish this, you would instruct Access to *group* the records by the data in the department field.

You can include up to ten levels of grouping in a report. For each level of grouping within a report, Access adds two new sections to the report's design:

• A *group header* section, which contains information that will appear at the beginning of each group (such as the name of the group)

- A *group footer* section, which contains information that will appear at the end of each group (such as a subtotal for the group)

In Design view, group header and footer sections will bear the name of the field or the expression upon which you base the groups. For example, in a report grouped by the Dept field, the name of the group header section will be *Dept Header*.

Let's preview a report in which the records are in groups, and then examine its design:

1. Preview the **Dept Gross Pay** report (double-click on the object name). In this report, the records appear in groups by department. Each department name appears at the beginning of a group of records, and a subtotal appears at the end of each group (see Figure 7.4).

Figure 7.4   **Previewing a grouped report**

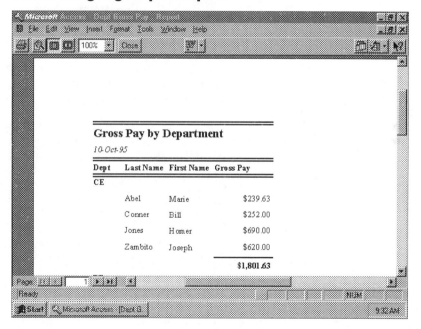

2. Click on the **Last Page** navigation button to move to the last page of the report (page 2), and then scroll to and observe the bottom of the page. The report includes a grand total and a page number.

3. Click on the **Close** button to close the preview screen and return to the Database window.

4. Open the **Dept Gross Pay** report in Design view (select the object name, and then click on **Design**). In addition to the sections you saw in the other report, this report includes Dept Header and Dept Footer sections that control information that appears once for each group of records. The control in the Dept Header section displays the department name for the group, and the expression in the Dept Footer section calculates the gross pay for each department.

5. Close the Report window.

CREATING A REPORT

You can avoid most of the difficult work involved in creating reports by using *Report Wizards*. Much like Form and Query Wizards, Report Wizards ask you questions about the report you want to create, and then build a new report based on your answers.

Access provides different types of Report Wizards:

- The *Report Wizard* builds a report, allowing you to select the fields (from one or more table or query), the grouping levels, sort order, the layout (vertical or tabular), and the style.

- If you preselect the table or query that the data will come from, you can choose one of the AutoReport Wizards. The advantage of these Wizards over the Report Wizard is that you don't have to answer any questions; Access simply creates the report in the specified layout. There are two types of AutoReport Wizards:

  - The *AutoReport: Columnar Wizard* builds reports that display one record at a time. The fields appear in a single column.

  - The *AutoReport: Tabular Wizard* builds reports that display the data in a table format, without groups and totals.

- The *Label Wizard* creates mailing and other types of labels.

SELECTING THE DATA SOURCE AND THE REPORT WIZARD

To start a Report Wizard, you would follow these steps:

- Display the list of report object names in the Database window.

- Click on *New* to open the New Report dialog box.

- Click on the *Report Wizard*, then click on *OK* to display the first Report Wizard dialog box.

Let's begin to create a simple report that will look much like the Employee Hours and Rates report:

1. In the Database window, click on **New** to display the New Report dialog box. Click on **Report Wizard**, then click on **OK**. You can base a report upon a table or a query.

2. In the Tables/Queries drop-down list, select **Table: Pay Rates** to base your new report upon the Pay Rates table.

SPECIFYING FIELDS AND SORT ORDER

In reports, you can choose to include only certain fields from the underlying table or query (just as you can in a form or query). For example, if you want to create a report on employees' gross pay, you probably don't need to include each employee's home address.

After you start the Report Wizard, Access asks you to specify the fields you want to include on the report. Selecting fields in this dialog box works exactly as it does in the Form Wizard: You add a field either by double-clicking on it, or by selecting it and then clicking on the > button. To add all the fields, click on >>. As with a Form Wizard, the Report Wizard will place fields on your report in the order in which you select them here.

When you finish selecting fields, click on Next two times to display a dialog box that asks you to specify up to four fields by which to sort records. To specify fields for sorting, you select the fields from drop-down lists, and then select ascending (A–Z) sort or descending (Z–A).

Let's add four fields to our report and specify that Access sort the records by last name, and then first name:

1. Observe the Report Wizard dialog box. You use this dialog box to specify the fields you want to include in the report, and the order in which you want them to appear.

2. In the Available Fields list box, double-click on **Last Name** to add the field to the report. (You also can select the field name and then click on **>**.)

3. Add the **First Name**, **Hours**, and **Pay Rate** fields to the report, in that order (see Figure 7.5).

Figure 7.5   **Selecting fields for a report**

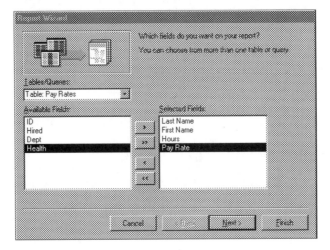

4. Click on **Next** to advance to the next dialog box.

5. This dialog box lets you add grouping levels. We will add these to our report later in this chapter. Click on **Next** to advance to the next dialog box.

6. Select **Last Name** from the first drop-down list, and **First Name** from the second drop-down list. (See Figure 7.6). The button next to the text box indicates whether the field will be sorted in ascending or descending order. The sort order is ascending by default, but if you wanted to change it, you would click on the Sort Ascending button next to the corresponding field name and it would turn into a Sort Descending button.

7. Click on **Next** to advance to the next dialog box.

Figure 7.6   **Specifying a sort order for a report**

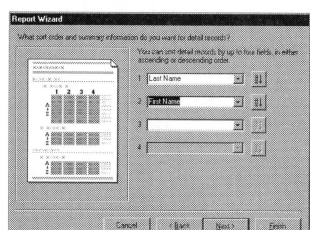

 SELECTING A LAYOUT FOR YOUR REPORT

There are two layout choices available. *Vertical* displays the records in one long column, with the field names along the left column of the page. *Tabular* displays the records much like a table, with the field names along the top of the page.

Another aspect of the report that can be changed is the orientation. *Portrait* means that the report will print on tall pages, and *Landscape* means that it will print on wide pages.

Let's examine the types of layouts, and then choose Tabular:

1. In the Layout box, select **Vertical**. Examine the sample that is displayed.

2. In the Layout box, select **Tabular**. We will use the Tabular layout for our report. Notice also that the option *Adjust the field width so all fields fit on a page* is checked. This will adjust the size of the text so that the fields fit on one page.

3. In the Orientation area, click on **Portrait** (if necessary).

4. Click on **Next** to advance to the next dialog box.

SELECTING A STYLE AND ADDING A TITLE

After selecting a sort order, you have the option of selecting a style for your report. The Report Wizard offers three styles: *Executive*, *Presentation*, and *Ledger*. As with forms, styles are purely cosmetic, and don't affect the contents of a report.

The final Report Wizard dialog box asks you to specify a title for your report. This title is used as the report's object name, and it also appears in the Report Header section of the report. You then can choose either to preview the report with data, or to modify its design.

Let's finish up our report by specifying a style and a title:

1. Examine the dialog box. You can choose among six styles. The sample on the left of the dialog box displays the selected style.

2. Select each style and examine how the sample changes to reflect what the report will look like.

3. Select the **Formal** style; then click on **Next** to advance to the final step of the Report Wizard. Here, you can enter a report title. (By default, Access suggests the name of the table upon which you based the report: *Pay Rates*.)

4. Type **My Hours and Rates** to replace the selected text in the Report Title box (see Figure 7.7). You can choose either to preview the report, or to modify the report's design. The default choice is to preview the report.

5. Click on the **Finish** button to create and preview the report. This report is similar to the Employee Hours and Rates report.

EXAMINING THE REPORT DESIGN

Let's take a look at the design of our new report:

1. Click on the **Zoom** button to display a preview of the whole report. Point to the lower right corner of the report (the mouse pointer is a magnifying glass) and click. This displays the footer, which contains the current page number and the total number of pages. Click the mouse button to display the whole document once again.

Figure 7.7   **Adding a title to the report**

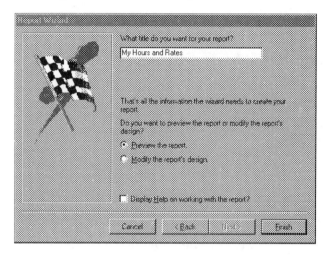

2. Examine other portions of the report, such as the date in the lower-left corner.

3. Click on the **Close** button to cancel the preview. Open the **My Hours and Rates** report in Design view. The design of this report is similar to that of the Employee Hours and Rates report.

4. Click on the **Sorting and Grouping** button to display the Sorting and Grouping window (see Figure 7.8). Access shows here how it created the sort you specified through the Report Wizard.

Figure 7.8   **The Sorting and Grouping window**

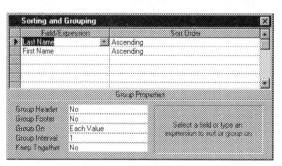

5. Close the Sorting and Grouping window.

6. Close the Report window.

CREATING A REPORT WITH GROUPS

You've just learned how to create a simple report using the Report Wizard. Now we'll use the Report Wizard to create a report that presents records in groups, and this time we'll base the report on a query instead of a table.

This report will provide gross pay information for employee records in groups by department. Because you need a gross pay field for this report—a field that is not available in the Pay Rates table—you will base the report upon the Concatenated Gross Pay query, which contains a calculated field for gross pay.

In many cases, you might prefer to base your reports upon queries. Here are some advantages of doing so:

- You can create calculated fields in the query, and then use those fields when creating the report.

- By setting criteria in a query, you can limit not only the fields, but also the records that appear in your report.

- You can create reports that use data from more than one table. (You'll learn how to create multiple-table queries in Chapter 8.)

- You can modify an existing report by changing its underlying query.

 STARTING A REPORT WIZARD AND SPECIFYING FIELDS

The first steps in creating this report are quite similar to those you followed to create your first report. Let's start by examining the query upon which we'll base the report; then we'll begin to create the report itself:

1. Run the **Concatenated Gross Pay** query and observe its resulting datasheet.

2. Switch to and examine the query's Design view. This query is based on the Pay Rates table, but only one of the query's fields, Dept, comes directly from that table. The Name and Gross Pay fields are calculated.

3. Point to the **Name** field expression, click the right mouse button to display the shortcut menu, and then choose **Zoom** to display the Zoom dialog box for the expression. The field expression combines—or *concatenates*—the First Name and Last Name fields. (You'll learn more about concatenated fields in Chapter 8.)

4. Click on **Cancel** to close the Zoom dialog box, and then close the Query window.

5. Display the list of report object names and click on **New** to display the New Report dialog box.

6. Click on **Report Wizard**, then click on **OK** to display the first Report Wizard dialog box.

7. Use the **Tables/Queries drop-down list** to select **Query: Concatenated Gross Pay**. We'll base this report on the query we just saw.

8. Click on **>>** to add all the fields to the report (see Figure 7.9).

Figure 7.9   **Selecting fields for the report**

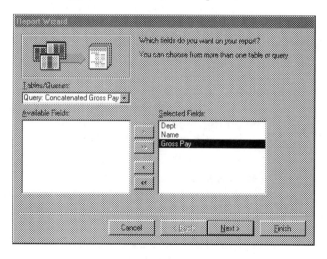

9. Click on **Next** to advance to the next dialog box.

DEFINING GROUPS

As you learned earlier in this chapter, you can include up to ten levels of grouping in a report. However, because most reports need far fewer than this, the Report Wizard lets you group by as few as four fields. (To group by more than four fields, you can use the Sorting and Grouping window.)

After you specify the field(s) by which to group records, you can specify the grouping interval by clicking on the *Grouping Options* button. In *Normal* grouping, Access groups records by the entire value within the field or fields. You also can choose to group by the first one to five characters within a field. For example, if your company uses product codes in which the first character of the code identifies a category, you could select *1st Character* to group those products by category. This would save you the trouble of creating a separate field for product category.

Because we want to group records by the entire value in our Dept field, we'll stick with the normal grouping method. Let's do it:

1. Examine the dialog box. You can select up to four fields by which to group records.

2. Double-click on **Dept** to instruct Access to group records in your new report by department (see Figure 7.10). This means that all the records in which the value in the Dept field is *CE* will appear together, as will the records in which the value in the Dept field is *MK*, and so on.

3. Click on the **Grouping Options** button. The default Group Interval is *Normal*, which causes Access to group records by the entire value within the field. You also can choose to group by a certain number of leading characters within the field. Click on **Cancel** to close the Grouping Intervals dialog box.

4. Click on **Next** to move to the next dialog box. Here, you define the sort order for your report.

5. Select the **Name** field for the first sort field.

6. Click on the **Summary Options** button. The Summary Options dialog box is used to specify how the grouped data will be calculated. For the Gross Pay field, select **Sum** as the calculation choice. Verify that in the Show box, **Detail and Summary** is selected (see Figure 7.11). Click on **OK** to close the Summary Options dialog box.

Figure 7.10   **Defining the groups for a report**

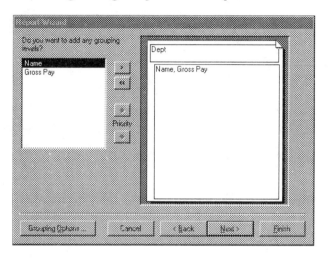

Figure 7.11   **The Summary Options dialog box**

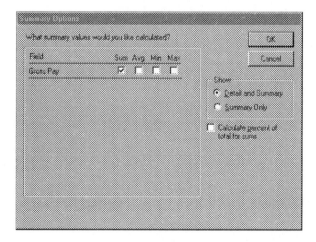

7. Click on **Next** to move to the next dialog box.

SPECIFYING A LAYOUT, STYLE, AND A TITLE

After you determine how to group and sort records in a report, the only tasks that remain are to select a layout and a style, and to specify a report title.

1. Examine the dialog box. The layout choices are different from the last time we used the Report Wizard. This is because we have chosen to group the data in this report.

2. Verify that **Stepped** is selected, select **Portrait** in the Orientation box (if necessary), and then click on **Next** to advance to the next Report Wizard dialog box.

3. Verify that **Formal** is selected, and then click on **Next** to advance to the final Report Wizard dialog box.

4. In the Report Title box, type **My Gross Pay by Department** to name the report object and supply a heading for the report.

5. Click on **Finish** to complete the report and preview it. Then, if necessary, maximize the Report window (see Figure 7.12). Records are in groups by department, and there is a gross-pay subtotal for each group (you might need to scroll to see this).

6. Click on the **Last Page** navigation button and then use the vertical scroll bar to scroll to the bottom of the page. There is a gross-pay grand total at the end of the report.

7. Click on the **Close** button in the Preview toolbar to cancel the preview and switch to the report's Design view. Like the groups and totals report design we saw earlier, this design includes Dept Header and Dept Footer sections for grouping records by the Dept field. The Dept Header section displays each department name. The Dept Footer section contains an expression that calculates the gross pay for each department.

MODIFYING THE REPORT DESIGN

If a Report Wizard does not build a report that is exactly what you want, you can modify its design through the report's Design view. To modify a report's design, you can use many of the techniques you learned in the last chapter for working with forms.

You also can modify a report's design by changing the properties of the controls that make up the design. (Control properties are

Figure 7.12   **Previewing the finished report**

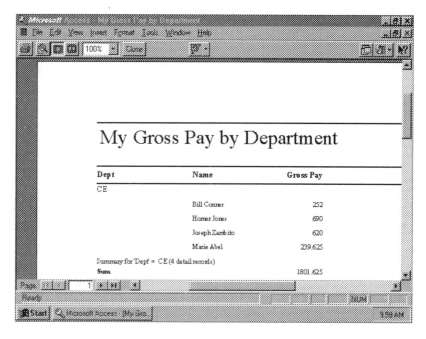

akin to properties for other Access elements; they determine the appearance and behavior of each control.)

Figure 7.13 shows some buttons that become available when you select a control in a Report's design view. Table 7.1 describes these buttons.

Figure 7.13   **Design buttons on the toolbar**

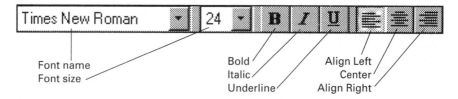

In Chapter 10, you'll learn some other methods for changing control properties.

Table 7.1   **Design Buttons**

Button	Use
Font name	Change *font*, or shape and appearance, of text
Font-size box	Specify size of text
Bold button	Boldface, or darken, text (**this text is bold**)
Italic button	Italicize, or slant, text (*this text is italic*)
Align Left button	Align text on left side of control
Center button	Center text within control
Align Right button	Align text on right side of control

Let's use some of these toolbar boxes and buttons to change the appearance of our report:

1. Click on the **Print Preview** button to preview the report; then, if necessary, scroll to the top of the report by using the vertical scroll bar.

2. Compare your report to the finished report pictured in Figure 7.14. In the figure, the report title and column headings have different fonts. Also, the header is centered at the top of the report.

3. Press **Esc** to close the preview window and return to the Design view. (You might find this easier than clicking on the Close button.)

4. In the Report Header section, select the **My Gross Pay by Department** label (click on it once). When you select a control, many toolbar options become available. The Font Name box shows that the title's font is *Times New Roman* (it may instead be *Tms Rmn* or *Times*).

5. Open the **Font** drop-down list, and then select **Arial** to change the title's font (refer to Figure 7.13, if necessary). If Arial is not a choice in your list of fonts, choose Helv or Helvetica (or any font that suits your fancy). Notice that the Font-size box tells you that the selected label's size is 24.

Figure 7.14 **The report after making some changes**

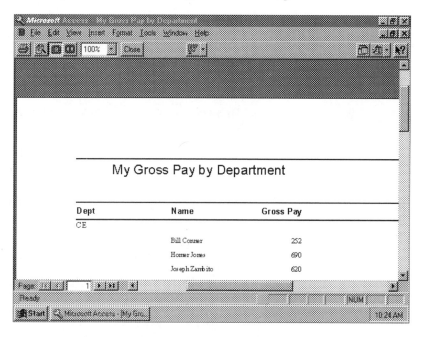

6. Open the **Font-size** drop-down list, and then select **16** to decrease the title's font size (refer to Figure 7.13, if necessary).

7. Verify that the Report Header label is selected.

8. Click on the **Center** button to center the heading within its control (refer to Figure 7.13).

PRACTICE YOUR SKILLS

1. Change the font for each heading in the Page Header section to **Arial** (or **Helv** or **Helvetica**).

2. Preview the report and compare it to Figure 7.14.

3. Use the **File, Save** command to save the changes to the report design.

4. Close the Report and Database windows.

SUMMARY

In this chapter, you learned how to view and modify a report's design, preview a report, and create a report using the Report Wizard.

Here's a quick reference guide to the Access features introduced in this chapter:

Desired Result	How to Do It
Preview report	Select report object name and click on **Preview** (or double-click on report object name)
Move through pages of pre-viewed report	Use page navigation buttons
Open report's Design view	Select report object name and click on **Design**
Open (or close) Sorting and Grouping window	Choose **View, Sorting and Grouping** (or click on **Sorting and Grouping** button)
Create new report using Report Wizard	Display report object names, click on **New**, click on **Report Wizard**, click on **OK**, select table or query upon which to base report, answer Report Wizard's questions
Save modified report	Choose **File, Save**
Change control's font	Select control and then select new font from Font Name box
Change control's font size	Select control and then select new font size from Font-size box
Change control's alignment	Select control and click on desired Alignment button

In Chapter 8, you'll learn how to create more specialized queries.

CHAPTER 8: ENHANCED QUERY DESIGN

Back in Chapter 5, you learned how to create and run single-table select queries. In this chapter, you will first review and then expand on that knowledge in order to construct queries more efficiently and to create more advanced single-table select queries. Then, we'll go on to devise some additional types of queries, including parameter, action, and multiple-table queries.

When you are done working through this chapter you will know

- How to create a query with a single click
- How to concatenate (that is, combine) values from two fields into a single field
- How to work more easily with lengthy expressions in the design grid
- How to specify records with unique values
- How to create and run a parameter query in order to specify criteria conveniently
- How to create and run an update query in order to change values in multiple records
- How to create and run an append query in order to copy records from one table to another
- How to create and run a delete query in order to delete multiple records
- How to create a crosstab query in order to group data by combination of values from different fields
- How to create a multiple-table query in order to combine data from multiple tables
- How to create a make-table query in order to create a new table

REVIEWING SELECT QUERIES

Throughout Chapter 5, you learned the basics of creating, running, and using select queries to view data. Because that was three chapters ago, let's take the time now to work with some select queries again as a review.

We'll also demonstrate how to create and work with queries more efficiently. Access offers a lot of shortcuts that become useful once you are comfortable working with the program. While we can't possibly show you all of these shortcuts, we will try to reveal some of the best ones.

CREATING AND RUNNING A SELECT QUERY

In Chapter 5, we created new queries from the Database window through the Show Table dialog box. However, you can create a new query more quickly—directly from a Table or Query window—by clicking on the New Object drop-down list, then clicking on the New Query button. When you use the New Query button, Access creates a new query based on the current table or query. You can also create a new query from the Database window by selecting the table or query object name upon which you want to base the new query, and then clicking on the New Query button.

When you click on the New Query button, the New Query dialog box is displayed. This dialog box offers you the options of using a Query Wizard to create a query or of simply starting the new query from scratch.

In this chapter, we'll use a new database file, Company. Rather than containing just employee data, this file contains companywide data.

If you do not have the Access application window opened and maximized, please open and maximize it now. If you have a Database window open, please close it.

Let's open our new database and create a select query using the New Query button:

1. Open the Company database file (located in the Access Work directory), and maximize the Company Database window.

2. From the Database window, open and examine the Payroll Data table (see Figure 8.1). Notice that the table contains 11 fields and 51 records, and the records are sorted in order by ID (ID is the table's primary-key field).

3. Click on the arrow next to the New Object button on the toolbar.

4. Click on **New Query** to open the New Query dialog box.

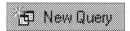

5. Verify that **Design View** is selected, then click on **OK**. This will open a new Query window in Design view and automatically add the current table to the query design. (We've opted not to use a Query Wizard so that we can build our query from scratch.)

Figure 8.1 **The Payroll Data table**

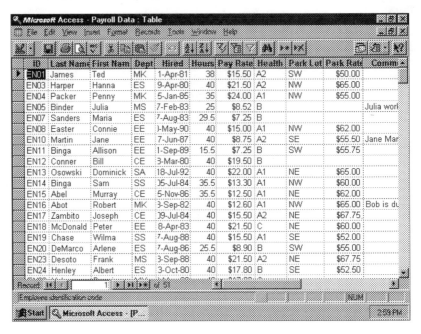

6. Add the field names **Last Name**, **First Name**, **Dept**, and **Pay Rate**, respectively, to the first four Field cells of the design grid (see Chapter 5).

7. In the Last Name column's Sort cell, select **Ascending** from the drop-down list.

8. Open and examine the Query menu. Notice that the *Select* option is checked. Access makes all new queries select queries by default. Close the Query menu.

9. Run the query (click on the **Run** or **Datasheet View** button), and observe the resulting datasheet (see Figure 8.2). It displays only 4 of the table's 11 fields (Last Name, First Name, Dept, and Pay Rate), it has sorted records not by ID (as in the underlying Payroll Data table) but by last name, and it has included all 51 records (because you set no criteria).

Figure 8.2   **The new query's resulting datasheet**

Last Name	First Name	Dept	Pay Rate
Abel	Gary	EE	$25.00
Abel	Murray	CE	$12.50
Abot	Robert	MK	$12.60
Beasley	Ken	CE	$22.50
Beaton	Robert	SS	$12.50
Bell	William	MK	$22.50
Berry	Sharon	MK	$19.25
Binder	Julia	MS	$8.52
Binga	Sam	SS	$13.30
Binga	Allison	EE	$7.25
Carter	Ben	EE	$26.50
Cassada	Bruce	CE	$21.50
Castile	Abraham	MK	$18.00
Chase	Wilma	SS	$15.50
Clark	Thomas	MK	$22.50
Cline	Darren	SS	$7.50
Conner	Bill	CE	$19.50
Davis	Eugene	ES	$14.50
DeMarco	Arlene	ES	$8.90

CREATING A CALCULATED FIELD

In Chapter 5, when we created a calculated field in a query to calculate gross pay, Access automatically named the field *Expr1*. Later, we changed Expr1 to a more meaningful name: *Gross Pay*. You can avoid this two-step process, however, simply by naming the calculated field as you create it. To do so, first type the calculated field's name followed by a colon (:), and then type your calculation expression. (Do *not* type any spaces before or after the colon.) For example, if you wanted to create a calculated field named *Gross Pay* by multiplying the Hours and Pay Rate fields, you would type *Gross Pay:[hours]*[pay rate]* in an empty Field cell.

As you start using longer expressions in the design grid, you may find that the grid's default column widths are not wide enough to display your entire expression at once. However, you can manually widen or narrow design-grid columns using the column-boundary-dragging technique that you used in Chapter 3 to resize a column in a Table window's Datasheet view.

Note: Unlike a Table window, in a Query window you cannot save your customized design-grid column widths. Once you close a Query window and then reopen it, Access sets all of your columns to the default width.

Let's create a calculated field, New Pay Rate, that calculates a 7-percent increase over the current pay rate, and then widen the calculated field's design-grid column to view the entire field:

1. Return to the Query window's Design view (click on the **Design View** button).

2. In the design grid's fifth Field cell, type **New Pay Rate:[pay rate]*1.07** to both create a calculated field and provide a custom name for that calculated field. (Remember that you must enclose field names within square brackets.) Notice that you cannot view the entire calculated field.

3. To change the field size, place the mouse pointer on the right edge of the calculated field's **field selector** until the pointer changes to a cross with a horizontal two-headed arrow. Then drag the column boundary about half a column width to the right. This should widen the column enough so that you can view the entire field.

4. Run the query and observe the resulting datasheet. It includes a New Pay Rate field, which calculates a 7-percent increase over the Pay Rate field (see Figure 8.3).

Figure 8.3   **The resulting datasheet with the New Pay Rate field**

Last Name	First Name	Dept	Pay Rate	New Pay Rate
Abel	Gary	EE	$25.00	26.75
Abel	Murray	CE	$12.50	13.375
Abot	Robert	MK	$12.60	13.482
Beasley	Ken	CE	$22.50	24.075
Beaton	Robert	SS	$12.50	13.375
Bell	William	MK	$22.50	24.075
Berry	Sharon	MK	$19.25	20.5975
Binder	Julia	MS	$8.52	9.1164
Binga	Sam	SS	$13.30	14.231
Binga	Allison	EE	$7.25	7.7575
Carter	Ben	EE	$26.50	28.355
Cassada	Bruce	CE	$21.50	23.005
Castile	Abraham	MK	$18.00	19.26
Chase	Wilma	SS	$15.50	16.585
Clark	Thomas	MK	$22.50	24.075
Cline	Darren	SS	$7.50	8.025
Conner	Bill	CE	$19.50	20.865
Davis	Eugene	ES	$14.50	15.515
DeMarco	Arlene	ES	$8.90	9.523

DELETING FIELDS FROM THE DESIGN GRID

Let's review how to delete a field from the design grid:

1. Return to Design view.

2. Click on the Last Name column's **field selector** (you'll need to scroll to the left on the design grid) to select the column.

3. Press **Delete** (or choose **Edit, Delete**) to delete the Last Name column from the design grid.

PRACTICE YOUR SKILLS

1. Delete the First Name column from the design grid.

2. Run the query, and then view the resulting three-column datasheet.

CREATING ADVANCED SELECT QUERIES

By the time you completed Chapter 5, you were using some fairly advanced techniques with select queries. We're now going to review two of those advanced techniques: calculating totals for groups of records and using a criterion with wildcard characters. Then we'll take a look at two new techniques: concatenating fields and specifying records with unique values.

GROUPING RECORDS AND CALCULATING AVERAGES

At the end of Chapter 5, we used Access's totals feature to group employee records by department and calculate the total employee gross-pay cost for each department (using the Sum aggregate function).

Let's use Access's totals feature this time to group employee records by department and calculate averages (using the Avg aggregate function) for both the current pay rate and the new pay rate:

1. Return to Design view.

2. Click on the **Totals** button to add a Total row to the design grid. Note that Access automatically adds the Group By operator under each field.

3. In the Pay Rate column's Total cell, click on the cell's **drop-down** list to change the operator from Group By to **Avg**.

4. In the New Pay Rate column's Total cell, change the operator to **Avg**. Your query will now also average the *new* pay rates by department. Because the Group By operator remains only under the Dept field, this instructs the query to average pay rates by department.

5. Run the query and observe the resulting datasheet. It displays only seven records, one for each department, and has calculated averages for both the Pay Rate and the New Pay Rate fields (see Figure 8.4).

Figure 8.4   **The resulting datasheet that groups records and averages pay rates**

Dept	AvgOfPay Rate	New Pay Rate
CE	$18.08	3491666666667
EE	$21.10	22.577
ES	$12.64	5202142857143
MK	$18.40	19.688
MS	$14.38	15.3866
SA	$22.00	23.54
SS	$13.31	2428888888889

6. Close the Query window (click on the Query window's **Close box**). Because you have not yet saved the query, Access asks if you want to save the query now.

7. Click on **No** to close the Query window without saving the query and return to the Payroll Data table.

CREATING A CONCATENATION EXPRESSION

When you store people's names in a table, it is usually best for sorting purposes to store first and last names in separate fields. If you then want to combine the first and last names temporarily for items such as mailing labels and form letters, you can use a query to concatenate (combine) values from two text fields into one by using a *concatenation expression*. You can create a concatenation expression by using the concatenation operator, **&**, to separate the field names within a design-grid Field cell. For example, if you wanted to create a new field to concatenate the First Name and Last Name fields, you could type *[First Name]&[Last Name]*.

When you create a concatenated field, Access runs together the values from the two fields with no space between them. For example, if a record's First Name field contains *Alice* and the Last Name field contains *Binga*, its concatenated field will contain *AliceBinga*.

You can add a space to your concatenation expression by enclosing the space within double quotation marks (") and separating the quotation marks and space from other elements in the expression with concatenation operators. For example, to concatenate the First Name and Last Name fields with a space in between, you could use the expression [First Name]&" "&[Last Name].

Another potential problem is that Access sorts concatenated fields by the fields' combined values. Using the above example, Access will sort records primarily by first name. But what if you want to sort by last name? To concatenate fields but still sort by only one of those fields:

- Place the field by which you want to sort (in this case, the Last Name field) in a separate Field cell in the design grid.

- Select a sort order in the Sort cell.

- Uncheck that field's Show box.

That way, the query will sort records by the separate field, but will not display the otherwise redundant field in its resulting datasheet. (Remember from Chapter 5 that the Show box tells a query whether or not to display the field in the resulting datasheet.)

Let's create a calculated field that concatenates the First Name and Last Name fields, and instruct the query to sort records only by last name:

1. Create a new query based on the Payroll Data table. (From the Payroll Data table, click on the New Object button, click on **New Query**, then click on **OK** in the New Query dialog box.)

2. Add the field names **Last Name**, **First Name**, and **Hired** to the first three Field cells of the design grid, in that order.

3. Run the query and then observe the resulting datasheet. The query displays last and first names in two separate fields. Notice also that the resulting datasheet displays the records in the order in which they are stored in the underlying table (by ID).

4. Return to Design view.

5. In the First Name field cell, select **First Name** (do *not* select the entire column).

6. Type **[first name]&" "&[last name]** to replace *First Name*. Then press **Tab**.

7. Widen the calculated field's column and observe the field. Access automatically named this field *Expr1* (see Figure 8.5).

Figure 8.5   **The concatenated field**

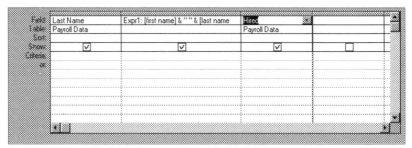

8. In the Last Name column's Sort cell, select **Ascending** from the drop-down list to instruct the query to sort records in ascending order by last name.

9. Run the query and observe the resulting datasheet. The query has sorted records by last name, and has successfully concatenated first and last names into a single field. However, the calculated field is titled *Expr1*, and the information in the Last Name field is redundant.

10. Return to Design view.

11. Uncheck the Last Name column's Show box.

12. Change the calculated field's name to **Name** (double-click on **Expr1** to select the default name, and type **Name**).

13. Run the query and observe the resulting datasheet. The calculated field is now titled *Name*, and the records remain sorted by last name, even though the resulting datasheet does not display the Last Name field (see Figure 8.6).

SETTING CRITERIA WITH WILDCARD CHARACTERS

You learned in Chapter 5 that you can use the wildcard characters
* and ? to set criteria for values that match a certain pattern rather
than for exact values. In that chapter, you set a criterion to search
for records of employees whose last names began with the letter
B. This time, let's set a criterion to search for records of employees who were hired in 1988:

1. Return to Design view.

2. In the Hired column's Criteria cell, type ***/*/88**, and then
   press **Tab**. Access automatically changes your criterion to
   Like "*/*/88".

3. Run the query and observe the resulting datasheet. It displays records only for the six employees hired in 1988 (see Figure 8.7).

Figure 8.6   **The final resulting datasheet**

Name	Hired
Gary Abel	1-Jun-91
Murray Abel	5-Nov-86
Robert Abot	3-Sep-82
Ken Beasley	1-Apr-93
Robert Beaton	3-Nov-87
William Bell	4-Apr-88
Sharon Berry	01-Jul-84
Julia Binder	7-Feb-83
Sam Binga	05-Jul-84
Allison Binga	1-Sep-89
Ben Carter	3-Aug-88
Bruce Cassada	5-Mar-89
Abraham Castill	1-Nov-82
Wilma Chase	7-Aug-88
Thomas Clark	1-Jan-89
Darren Cline	0-Jun-83
Bill Conner	3-Mar-80
Eugene Davis	2-Jun-87
Arlene DeMarco	7-Aug-86

Figure 8.7   **The resulting datasheet displaying only 1988 hires**

Name	Hired
William Bell	4-Apr-88
Ben Carter	3-Aug-88
Wilma Chase	7-Aug-88
Frank Desoto	3-Sep-88
Dennis Kyler	2-May-88
Andrew Weinste	4-Apr-88

4. Save the query as **My 1988 Hires**, and then close the Query window.

SPECIFYING RECORDS WITH UNIQUE VALUES

When you run queries that use only one or very few fields, the resulting datasheet may display the exact same value or set of values for multiple records. For example, if you generate a list of department codes from an employee information table that contains a department code for each record, you will probably get long lists of duplicate department codes. You can, however, instruct your query to omit redundancies by specifying that your resulting datasheet include unique values only.

To specify that a query include unique values only:

- From the Query window's Design view, click on the *Properties* button in the toolbar.

- In the Unique Values drop-down list, select *Yes*.

- Close the Query Properties box.

Let's create a resulting datasheet that displays unique values only:

1. Create a new query based on the Payroll Data table.

2. Add **Dept** to the design grid's first Field cell.

3. In the Dept column's Sort cell, select **Ascending** from the drop-down list.

4. Run the query and observe the resulting datasheet. It displays all 51 records from the underlying table, with many repetitions of each department code.

5. Return to Design view, and make sure that no cell contents are selected in the design grid. (Click on the gray area of the screen.)

6. Click on the **Properties** button in the toolbar to open the Query Properties box, and select **Yes** from the Unique Values drop-down list. Compare your screen to Figure 8.8.

Figure 8.8   **Specifying the display of unique values**

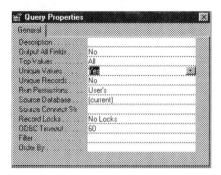

7. Close the Query Properties box and run the query. The result-ing datasheet displays the seven department codes only once each (see Figure 8.9).

Figure 8.9   **The resulting datasheet displaying unique values only**

8. Close the Query window without saving the query.

CREATING PARAMETER QUERIES

As you work with your data, you may need to run certain queries on a regular basis, but with different criteria each time you run them. Or, perhaps more importantly, you may need to design a query with changing criteria for another person who isn't familiar with query design. For example, you may need to design a query to show current sales figures for any given salesperson.

To meet this need, you could use one of the following strategies:

- Manually change the salesperson criterion before running the query each time (this won't help someone else, though).

- Design and save a separate query for every salesperson (which could clutter up your Database window, waste space on your computer's hard drive, and require additional work every time a new salesperson is hired).

- Create a parameter query that, when run, automatically opens a dialog box asking for the salesperson's name, and then displays that salesperson's data.

CREATING A SINGLE-PARAMETER QUERY

As its name implies, a *single-parameter query* asks for only one criterion. To create a single-parameter query from an existing query, you first need to determine two things:

- For which field do you want to set a parameter?

- What dialog-box text, or parameter name, do you want Access to use when it requests the criterion for that parameter's field?

Parameters are a specialized type of criterion expression, so you enter parameter names in the design grid's Criteria row. To set a parameter, type your parameter name in the appropriate Criteria cell, enclosing it within square brackets to allow Access to distinguish it from simple criteria. You can use any name for a parameter except the name of an existing field.

Let's create and run a parameter query that asks for a department code and then lists that department's employees:

1. Create a new query based on the Payroll Data table.

2. Add the field names **Last Name**, **First Name**, and **Dept**, respectively, to the first three Field cells of the design grid.

3. In the Dept column's Criteria cell, type **[Enter a Dept Code]**, making sure to include the brackets.

4. Attempt to run the query. Instead of displaying a resulting datasheet, the Enter Parameter Value dialog box is displayed, prompting you with the parameter you typed in the Dept column's Criteria cell in step 3 (see Figure 8.10).

5. In the dialog box, type **mk**, and click on **OK** to finish running the query. Notice that the resulting datasheet displays only records for Marketing (MK) department employees (see Figure 8.11). (Remember that, by default, criteria are not case sensitive.)

Figure 8.10   **The Enter Parameter Value dialog box**

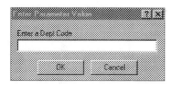

Figure 8.11   **The resulting datasheet of Marketing department employees**

Last Name	First Name	Dept
James	Ted	MK
Packer	Penny	MK
Abot	Robert	MK
Kyler	Dennis	MK
Castile	Abraham	MK
Wilson	Judy	MK
Bell	William	MK
Berry	Sharon	MK
Clark	Thomas	MK
Nelson	Luke	MK
Gardner	Gayle	MK

PRACTICE YOUR SKILLS

1. Return to Design view.

2. Run the query, specifying the records of Chemical Engineering (CE) department employees, and observe the resulting datasheet.

CREATING A MULTIPLE-PARAMETER QUERY

You can also create parameter queries that request multiple criteria. In a multiple-parameter query, you can set multiple parameters within a single field, separate parameters for separate fields, or a combination of the two. For example, you might want to design a query that asks both for a salesperson's name and for a given time period, and then displays that salesperson's sales figures for that period. To accomplish this, you could set three parameters: one in the Last Name field to ask for the salesperson's last name, and two in the Sales Date field to ask for the beginning and ending dates.

For each parameter you set, Access will open a separate Enter Parameter Value dialog box. Therefore, you need to provide an appropriate parameter name for each dialog box.

Remember that parameters are a type of criteria expression; therefore, you can set multiple parameters using any of the techniques for setting multiple criteria you learned in Chapter 5, including setting multiple parameters within a single field using the And and Or comparison operators.

Let's change our single-parameter query to a multiple-parameter query that asks for a department code and a hired-date time period, and then displays the records for every employee in that department who was hired during that time period:

1. Return to Design view.

2. Add **Hired** to the design grid's fourth Field cell.

3. Place the insertion point in the Hired column's Criteria cell, and then press **Shift+F2** to open the cell's Zoom box (or click the right mouse button and choose **Zoom**).

4. In the Zoom box, type **>=[Enter a Beginning Date] and <=[Enter an Ending Date]** (see Figure 8.12); then click on **OK** to close the Zoom box. When comparing dates, Access assigns lower mathematical values to earlier dates than to later dates. Thus, >= finds dates from that date forward, while <= finds dates from that date back. Notice that the Hired column's Criteria cell now contains the entire expression you typed in the Zoom box (even though you can see only part of the expression). There are now three parameters set in the design grid: one in the Dept column and two in the Hired column.

Figure 8.12   **Entering multiple parameters through the Zoom box**

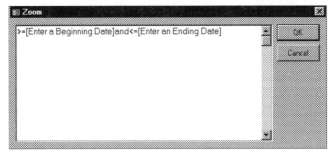

5. Attempt to run the query. The Enter Parameter Value dialog box prompts you for a department code.

6. Type **mk**, and click on **OK**. A second Enter Parameter Value dialog box prompts you for a beginning hire date.

7. Type **1/1/88**, and click on **OK**. A third Enter Parameter Value dialog box prompts you for an ending hire date.

8. Type **12/31/88**, and click on **OK**. Notice that the resulting datasheet contains the only two records that meet the three parameters you specified: Marketing (MK) department employees hired from January 1 through December 31, 1988 (see Figure 8.13).

Figure 8.13   **The resulting datasheet from a multiple-parameter query**

Last Name	First Name	Dept	Hired
Kyler	Dennis	MK	2-May-88
Bell	William	MK	4-Apr-88

9. Save the query as **My Parameter Query**, close the Query window, and return to the Payroll Data table.

CREATING ACTION QUERIES

So far, you have created only select queries—that is, queries that select and display records in a resulting datasheet, but do not change the records themselves in any way. To actually change the records themselves, you must use an action query.

Action queries are most useful for making similar changes to a group of records. For example, if you want to raise every Marketing department employee's salary by 7 percent, you can use an action query to calculate the raises and change the pay-rate fields. This way, you needn't open your employee information table and change each employee's pay-rate field manually.

You can also incorporate parameters into action queries in order to make them more flexible. Using the pay-raise example, you could use parameters to ask for the department and pay-raise percentage, thus enabling you to raise the pay by a different rate in each department.

Action queries change data instead of displaying datasheets, and you cannot use the Edit, Undo command to undo these changes. For this reason, it's a good idea to first review a resulting datasheet by designing and running the query as a select query, and then convert and run the query as an action query. Also, you may want to make a backup copy of your database file before running any action queries.

Action queries can be both helpful and destructive, so Access provides three types of warnings to prevent you from inadvertently changing data:

- In the Database window, Access displays an exclamation point before each action query's object name to indicate that the query will change data rather than just show it.

- Because action queries do not display datasheets, Access disables the Query window's Datasheet View button. To run an action query, you must click on the *Run* button (or choose *Query, Run* from the menu).

- After you start to run the query, Access displays a dialog box to inform you of how many records will be affected by the query, and to ask you to confirm the action. At this point, you can stop the query by clicking on *Cancel*; if you want Access to proceed, click on *OK*.

When you work with an action query, you may find it useful to check the query's underlying table both before and after running the query. As you may have already discovered, Access enables you to have more than one window open at a time. (In fact, when you are working in any Access database, the Database window is always open somewhere in Access's application window.) So, rather than closing and reopening Table and Query windows, you can keep all of the related windows open and simply switch between windows. You can do so through the Window menu, which displays the name of every open window and places a check mark next to the current (active) window. To switch to another window, select that window's name.

One disadvantage of switching between open windows, however, is that Access does not always automatically display the latest changes to data, even though it has already made those changes. To refresh the contents of an open window and ensure that you are viewing the latest data, press Shift+F9. (Alternatively, you can close and reopen the window.)

Access enables you to create four types of action queries:

- Update queries, which can update values in multiple records

- Append queries, which can copy records from one table to another

- Delete queries, which can delete multiple records

- Make-table queries, which can create new tables

 CREATING AN UPDATE QUERY

Update queries enable you to change values in multiple records. For example, you can use an update query to raise the parking rate for every employee who uses the SE or SW parking lot.

To create and run an update query:

- Create a select query based on the table that contains the records you want to update.

- Add any regular fields that will help you identify your records, and set any criteria that you need to specify the correct records to update.

- For each field that you want to update, add that field and create a calculated field that will supply the updated value.

- Run the query to make sure that the resulting datasheet displays the correct records and that your calculated fields have produced the correct values.

- When your select query produces the correct resulting datasheet, return to Design view and choose *Query, Update* to convert the select query to an update query. When you do, Access removes the Sort and Show rows from the design grid (because they are irrelevant to update queries), and adds an Update To row, which allows you to define how to update what fields.

- In the Update To cells for the fields you want to update, copy the appropriate calculation expressions from the query's calculated fields. (Don't include the calculated fields' field names.)

- Because you no longer need the query's calculated fields, delete their columns from the design grid.

- Run the query and confirm the update.

Let's create an update query to increase by 3 percent the annual parking-rate fees for all employees who use the SE or SW lot:

1. In the Payroll Data table, observe the parking rates for employees who use the SE or SW parking lot. The rates range from $50.00 to $57.75.

2. Open and examine the Window menu. The bottom of the menu lists the two windows open within the Access application window: the Company Database window and the Payroll Data Table window. Because the latter window is currently the active one, its name is checked. Choose **1 Company: Database** to activate the Database window.

3. From the Database window, open the **SE and SW Parking Rate Increase** Query window in Design view (select the query object name and click on **Design**). Notice that the query includes the four regular fields Park Lot, Park Rate, Last Name, and First Name, as well as a fifth calculated field called New Park Rate. Records are set to be sorted in ascending order by Park Lot, and then Park Rate, and the criterion of *"SE" Or "SW"* is set in the Park Lot column.

4. Place the insertion point in the New Park Rate column's Field cell, and then open the Zoom box (press **Shift+F2**) to examine the entire calculated field. This field will calculate a 3-percent parking-rate increase by multiplying the current parking rate by 1.03. Click on **Cancel** to close the Zoom box. As you already know, the title bar tells you that this is a select query.

5. Run the query and observe the resulting datasheet. It displays only the records for the 20 employees who use the SE or SW parking lot, in ascending alphabetical order by parking lot, and then the current parking rates, and lists both the current and calculated parking rates.

6. Choose **Window, 2 Payroll Data: Table** to switch to the Payroll Data table. Notice that the query has not changed any of the table's parking rates.

7. Choose **Window, 3 SE and SW Parking Rate Increase: Select Query** to return to the Query window, and then switch to Design view.

8. Choose **Query, Update** to change the query from a select query to an update query. Notice that the title bar reflects this change. Notice also that the Sort and Show rows have

been removed from the design grid, and an Update To row has been added.

9. In the Park Rate column's Update To cell, type **[park rate]*1.03** to specify a 3-percent increase for the field (see Figure 8.14).

Figure 8.14   **Adding an expression to update the Park Rate field**

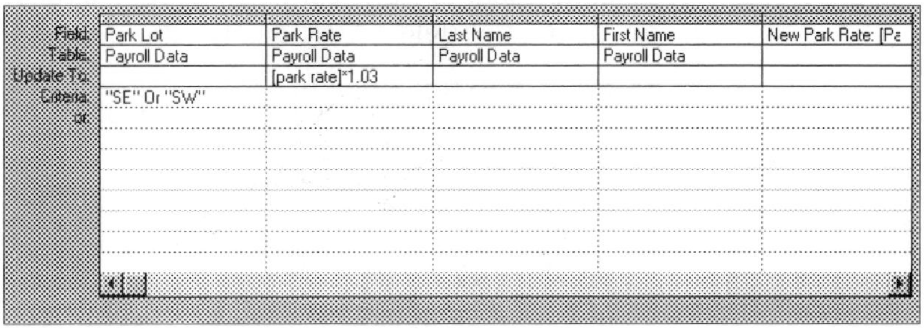

Field:	Park Lot	Park Rate	Last Name	First Name	New Park Rate: [Pa
Table:	Payroll Data	Payroll Data	Payroll Data	Payroll Data	
Update To:		[park rate]*1.03			
Criteria:	"SE" Or "SW"				
or:					

10. Delete the New Park Rate column from the design grid, because it is no longer needed.

11. Start running the query. (Remember that because this is an action query, you cannot use the Datasheet View button to run it.) A dialog box prompts you to confirm that your query should update 20 rows (that is, records).

12. Click on **YES** to update the records. Notice that because this is an action rather than a select query, Access does not display a datasheet after running the query.

13. Use the menu to switch to the Payroll Data table, and observe the updated table. The query has increased by 3 percent the park rates for all the employees who use the SE or SW parking lot.

14. Switch back to the Query window, save your modified query design under the query's original name (choose **File, Save**), and then close the Query window.

15. Switch to the Database window and observe the object name of the SE and SW Parking Rate Increase query. Because this is now an action query, an exclamation point and pencil precede its name.

CREATING A DELETE QUERY

When you want to delete multiple records from a table, you can use a delete query. For example, suppose that you were forced to lay off an entire department. The simplest way to delete the records of that department's employees would be to use a delete query.

Important Note: The effects of running a delete query are not reversible. Furthermore, when you run a delete query, you permanently alter the database. In order to avoid accidentally deleting records from your database, we recommend that you do not save your delete queries after running them.

To create and run a delete query:

- Create a select query based on the table from which you want to delete your records.

- Use the asterisk (*) in the design grid to specify all of the table's fields (a delete query will only delete entire records at a time).

- If you want to specify criteria, also add those fields to the design grid and then set your criteria.

- Run the query to make sure that your query will delete the correct records.

- When your select query produces the correct resulting datasheet, return to Design view and choose *Query, Delete* to convert your select query to a delete query. When you do so, Access removes the Sort and Show rows from the design grid, and adds a Delete row that enables you to specify the table from which you want to delete your records. In this Delete row, Access places a From operator under the asterisk to indicate that records will be deleted from that table, and a Where operator under any fields that you have used to set criteria.

- Run the query and confirm the deletion.

Let's create and run a delete query to delete the Systems Administration department employee records from the New Department Records table:

1. From the Database window, open and observe the **New Department Records** table. This table's design is identical to that of the Payroll Data table, but contains only ten records. The records are for the employees of the Systems Administration (SA) and Shipping and Receiving (SR) departments (see Figure 8.15).

Figure 8.15   **The New Department Records table**

ID	Last Name	First Name	Dept	Hired	Hours	Pay Rate	Health	Park Lot	Park Rate	Comment
EN88	Donohue	Jordan	SA	1-Sep-92	40	$22.00	B	NE	$65.00	
EN89	Fisher	Elyse	SA	1-Sep-92	40	$23.50	A1	NE	$65.00	
EN90	Latta	Jennifer	SA	4-Sep-92	40	$17.00	A1	SE	$55.00	
EN91	Jimenez	Pedro	SA	4-Sep-92	40	$17.00	B	SW	$55.00	
EN92	Rutkowski	Robert	SA	9-Oct-92	40	$18.00	A2	SW	$55.00	
EN93	Tobin	Linda	SA	9-Oct-92	40	$20.00	C	SE	$57.75	
EN94	Quincy	Mark	SR	1-Oct-92	40	$15.00	A1	SW	$55.00	
EN95	Potter	Hope	SR	1-Oct-92	35	$12.50	B	SE	$52.50	
EN96	Sharma	Kavita	SR	5-Aug-92	40	$16.00	A1	SE	$55.50	
EN97	Hart	Corey	SR	1-Sep-92	40	$16.00	A1	SE	$55.50	
*					40				$0.00	

2. Create a new query based on the New Department Records table.

3. In the Query window, drag the asterisk (*) from the New Department Records field list to the design grid's first Field cell to add all of the table's fields to the query.

4. Add **Dept** to the design grid's second Field cell.

5. In the Dept column's Criteria cell, type **SA** (for Systems Administration).

6. Run the query and observe the resulting datasheet. It displays records of the Systems Administration department employees only.

7. Return to Design view, and choose **Query, Delete** to change the select query to a delete query. Notice that the Sort and Show rows have been removed from the design grid, and a Delete row has been added. The *From* in the Delete cell of the New Department Records column instructs the query to delete records from only that table. The *Where* in the Dept column instructs the query to delete only those records that meet the criterion SA in the column's Criteria cell.

8. Start to run the query (click on the **Run** button). A dialog box prompts you to confirm that the query should delete six rows (records).

9. Click on **Yes** to delete the records. Then switch to and observe the New Department Records table. The table displays *#Deleted* in every field of the first six records (see Figure 8.16).

10. Press **Shift+F9**. The table now displays only the records of the four Shipping and Receiving (SR) department employees.

Figure 8.16   **The New Department Records table, indicating deleted records**

ID	Last Name	First Name	Dept	Hired	Hours	Pay Rate	Health	Park Lot	Park Rate	Commen
#Dele	#Deleted	#Deleted	#Dele	#Deleted	eleted	#Deleted	#Delete	#Deleted	#Deleted	#Deleted
#Dele	#Deleted	#Deleted	#Dele	#Deleted	eleted	#Deleted	#Delete	#Deleted	#Deleted	#Deleted
#Dele	#Deleted	#Deleted	#Dele	#Deleted	eleted	#Deleted	#Delete	#Deleted	#Deleted	#Deleted
#Dele	#Deleted	#Deleted	#Dele	#Deleted	eleted	#Deleted	#Delete	#Deleted	#Deleted	#Deleted
#Dele	#Deleted	#Deleted	#Dele	#Deleted	eleted	#Deleted	#Delete	#Deleted	#Deleted	#Deleted
#Dele	#Deleted	#Deleted	#Dele	#Deleted	eleted	#Deleted	#Delete	#Deleted	#Deleted	#Deleted
EN94	Quincy	Mark	SR	1-Oct-92	40	$15.00	A1	SW	$55.00	
EN95	Potter	Hope	SR	1-Oct-92	35	$12.50	B	SE	$52.50	
EN96	Sharma	Kavita	SR	5-Aug-92	40	$16.00	A1	SE	$55.50	
EN97	Hart	Corey	SR	1-Sep-92	40	$16.00	A1	SE	$55.50	
*					40				$0.00	

11. Close the New Department Records table; then close the Query window without saving your delete query.

USING A WIZARD TO CREATE A CROSSTAB QUERY

A *crosstab query* allows you to group data by combinations of values in different fields. For example, if you wanted to view a resulting datasheet that grouped employees by department and showed which parking lot they used, you could do so with a crosstab query. In this way, crosstab queries provide you with resulting datasheets containing unique data combinations that would not be readily available in the source table.

You can use Access's Query Wizard to guide you, step by step, through the process of creating a crosstab query:

- From the New Object drop-down list, click on the *New Query* button to open the New Query dialog box.

- Select *Crosstab Query Wizard*.

- Click on *OK*.

- In the upper portion of the Crosstab Query Wizard dialog box, select the table that contains the data you wish to use in your query, and then click on *Next*.

- Select the first field that you want to appear in the leftmost column (effectively, as row headings), and click on the > button. Continue in this manner until you have added all the desired fields. Then click on *Next*.

- Select the field that you want to appear as column headings, and click on *Next*.

- Select the field whose values you wish to calculate, and select the type of calculation. Then click on *Next*.

- Name the query (unless the default name provided is acceptable).

- Click on *Finish*.

Let's use the Payroll Data table to create a crosstab query that combines Dept data with Park Lot data:

1. In the Database window, click on the **New Object** button in the toolbar. The New Object button is now a New Query button, since it was the last New Object button selected. (When you're using a wizard to create a query, it's not necessary to do so from the source table's window; for that matter, it's not even necessary to open the source table.)

2. In the New Query dialog box, select **Crosstab Query Wizard**, then click on **OK**.

3. Examine the Crosstab Query Wizard dialog box (see Figure 8.17). As with other wizards, this dialog box will remain until we have completed our crosstab query; however, the contents of the dialog box will change as we specify each query component (in effect, a new pane will open). Notice the following features, which are common to all the panes (and, in general, are common to wizards):

   - The top pane of the dialog box is where you specify the query criteria. In this first pane, you are prompted to select the table upon which you want the crosstab query to be based.

   - The Sample box displays a sample of the resulting datasheet's structure. The Sample box will update as you answer each question that pops up in the dialog box.

   - Along the bottom of the dialog box are the commands that allow you to control where you are in the process of creating a crosstab query.

4. Select the **Payroll Data** table, and click on **Next**. The next pane opens in the top portion of the dialog box. Here you are prompted to specify the leftmost column in the table, ID (see Figure 8.18).

Figure 8.17   **The Crosstab Query Wizard dialog box**

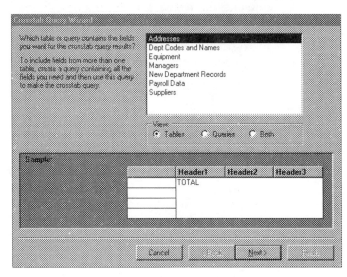

Figure 8.18   **Specifying the leftmost column**

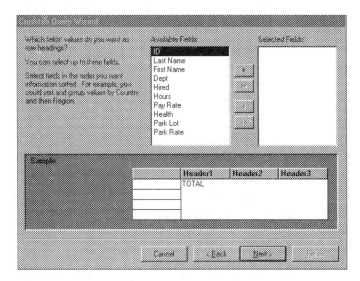

5. Select the **Dept** field, and click on the **>** button to place that field in the leftmost Columns box. In the Sample box, you can see that the various departments will appear down the first column. These will, in effect, function as row headings.

6. Click on **Next** to display the next pane. In this pane, you're asked to supply the field that will serve as the resulting datasheet's column headings.

7. Select the **Park Lot** field and take a look at the Sample box. The different parking lots will serve as column headings. Click on **Next** to display the next pane. Now we're prompted to select the field and type of calculation we want to appear at the intersections of the rows and columns. Notice that *ID* is the field selected by default, and *Count* is the default calculation type (see Figure 8.19). With these settings, the resulting datasheet will display a tally of the number of employees in each department who park in a given lot. (The ID field is selected by default because it serves as the primary key, and we know that every record in our table has a value in that field; therefore, there is no danger of any record being skipped.) Notice also that, by default, the query will calculate a grand total for each row.

Figure 8.19   **The selected default field and calculation type**

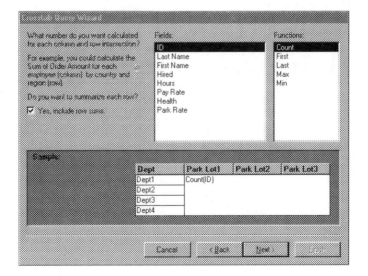

8. Click on **Next** to accept the default field and calculation type. The last pane is displayed, suggesting a name for the crosstab query. Notice that, with the current settings, the results of the query will be displayed.

9. Click on **Finish** to accept the default name and display the resulting datasheet (see Figure 8.20). Notice that the departments are displayed in the leftmost column. The Total Of ID column tells you how many employees are in each department. The next column tells you how many employees do not park in any of the lots. The remaining columns represent the four different lots.

Figure 8.20   **The crosstab-query resulting datasheet**

Dept	Total Of ID	<>	NE	NW	SE	SW
CE	9	1	3	2	3	
EE	10		4	4	1	1
ES	7	1	1	1	1	3
MK	11	2	1	5		3
MS	4	1	2		1	
SA	1		1			
SS	9			2	4	3

10. Switch to Design view to see the query's structure. Notice that *Crosstab* has its own row in the design grid. Return to Datasheet view.

11. Close the crosstab query. Notice that the crosstab query is listed as a query object in the Database window.

CREATING MULTIPLE-TABLE QUERIES

Through multiple-table queries, you can use data from more than one table at a time by combining that data into a single datasheet. For example, you can store employee names in one table and their addresses in another table, but combine that data when you need to generate an employee mailing list.

EXAMINING THE DESIGN OF A MULTIPLE-TABLE QUERY

Before you create your own multiple-table query, let's take a look at the design of an existing one:

1. Switch to the Payroll Data table. Notice that the table contains employee names, but no addresses.

2. Switch to the Database window; then open and observe the Addresses table. This table includes employee addresses, but no first or last names.

3. Close both tables; then open the **Home Addresses** query in Design view. You can see that the window's upper pane holds field lists from both the Addresses and Payroll Data tables. Notice that these field lists are joined by a line connecting their common ID fields. The design grid includes a Table row, which indicates from which table the query will obtain the values for each field. The First and Last fields are from the Payroll Data table; the Address, City, St, and Zip fields are from the Addresses table.

4. Run the query and observe the resulting datasheet. It displays data combined from both tables. Close the Query window.

JOINING TABLES

To obtain a meaningful resulting datasheet from a multiple-table query, you may need to join your tables—that is, to show Access which fields in each table share common values. For example, you could join an employee name table with an employee address table, using an employee ID field stored in each table. (It's a good idea to include in every table a field that relates to a field in at least one other table. We'll take a closer look at using fields to establish table relationships in Chapter 9.)

Before you can join tables, you need to add multiple field lists to the upper pane of the query window's Design view through the Show Table dialog box. To join tables:

- Open the *Show Table* dialog box. (If you create a new query from the Database window by clicking on the New button, Access opens the Show Table dialog box automatically; to open the Show Table dialog box from a query window, click on the *Show Table* button in the toolbar.)

- Click on the name of each table you wish to add, and click on *Add*.

- Once you've added all of the desired tables, click on *Close*.

Access automatically creates join lines between related fields in each of the tables' field lists (like the join line you viewed in the previous exercise). To create a join line manually, select and drag one field name over to its companion field name in another field list.

Once you've joined the tables in your query design, you can add fields to the design grid from any of the field lists. For example, if you wanted to create a mailing list, you could add first- and last-name fields from one table, and address fields from another.

Let's create a multiple-table select query based on the Payroll Data and Addresses tables in order to combine employee names, parking-lot data, and addresses into a single resulting datasheet:

1. In the Database window, click on **New** to start creating a new query. In the New Query dialog box, verify that **Design View** is selected, then click on **OK**. The Show Table dialog box opens.

2. Select **Payroll Data**, and click on **Add** to add the Payroll Data table's field list to the query design.

3. Select **Addresses**, and click on **Add** to add the Addresses table's field list to the query design.

4. Click on **Close**, and observe the Query window's upper pane. It holds both tables, and a join line connects the ID fields of the two tables.

5. From the Payroll Data field list, add **Last Name**, **First Name**, **Park Lot**, and **Park Rate**, respectively, to the design grid's first four Field cells.

6. From the Addresses field list, add **Address**, **City**, **St**, and **Zip**, respectively, to the design grid's next four Field cells. Notice that the Table row in the design grid allows you to see which fields belong to which table.

7. Run the query and observe the resulting datasheet. It displays data from both tables (see Figure 8.21).

Figure 8.21   **The resulting datasheet generated from joined tables**

Last Name	First Name	Park Lot	Pay Rate	Address	City	St	Zip
James	Ted	SW	$15.50	34 Fields Street	Walworth	NY	14568
Harper	Hanna	NW	$21.50	82 East Avenue	Adams Basin	NY	14410
Packer	Penny	NW	$24.00	450 N. Madison St.	Holley	NY	14470
Binder	Julia		$8.52	10 Cory Drive	Hulberton	NY	14473
Sanders	Maria		$7.25	12 East Avenue	Leicester	NY	14481
Easter	Connie	NW	$15.00	21 Stonecreek Rd.	Shortsville	NY	14548
Martin	Jane	SE	$8.75	50 Smart Drive	Knowlesville	NY	14479
Binga	Allison	SW	$7.25	50 Dallas Street	South Byron	NY	14557
Conner	Bill		$19.50	32 Ash Lane	Perkinsville	NY	14529
Osowski	Dominick	NE	$22.00	23 Lakeside Ave.	Pultneyville	NY	14538
Binga	Sam	NW	$13.30	50 Dallas Street	South Byron	NY	14557
Abel	Murray	NE	$12.50	127 Ford Avenue	Lakeville	NY	14480
Abot	Robert	NW	$12.60	99 Stonecreek Rd.	Gorham	NY	14461
Zambito	Joseph	NE	$15.50	81 Pleasing Lane	Rose	NY	14542
McDonald	Peter	NE	$21.50	8165 Main Street	Oaks Corners	NY	14518
Chase	Wilma	SE	$15.50	52 Pempleton Dr.	Wyoming	NY	14591
DeMarco	Arlene	SW	$8.90	34 Sable Ave.	Gorham	NY	14461
Desoto	Frank	NE	$21.50	P.O. Box 7234	Wayland	NY	14572
Henley	Albert	SE	$17.80	12 Divine Drive	Holley	NY	14470

CREATING A MAKE-TABLE QUERY

Once you've created a multiple-table select query (or any other type of select query, for that matter), you can create a new table that duplicates the query's resulting datasheet by converting and running that query as a make-table query. Creating a new table can be useful when you need to supply data to another user, but you want to supply only limited fields or records, or need to combine the data from multiple tables into a single table.

Once you've created a select query that produces the resulting datasheet that you want to save as your new table:

- Return to Design view and click on the arrow next to the *Query Type* button, then click on *Make Table* to open the Make Table dialog box.

- Enter a name for your table.

- Click on *OK*.

When you run the query, a dialog box indicates how many records the query will copy into your new table. Click on OK to confirm the copy.

Let's modify our query so that it finds records only for those employees who use the company parking lots; then we'll convert the query and use it to create a new table:

1. Observe the Query window. Notice that some of the records do not have values in the Park Lot and Park Rate fields.

2. Return to Design view. Then, in the Park Lot column's Criteria cell, type **is not null** to specify records that do not have an empty Park Lot field. (In Chapter 5, you'll remember that you used the *Is Null* expression to find records that did have empty fields; *Is Not Null* finds just the opposite.)

3. Press **Tab** to move to the next cell, and observe your criterion. The case of the expression has changed to *Is Not Null*.

4. In the Zip column's Sort cell, select **Ascending** from the drop-down list.

5. Run the query, and observe the resulting datasheet. It displays only those records that have values in the Park Lot field, and has sorted the records by zip code (see Figure 8.22).

Figure 8.22

The resulting datasheet displaying only employees who use the company parking lots

Last Name	First Nam	Park Lot	Pay Rate	Address	City	St	Zip
Harper	Hanna	NW	$21.50	82 East Avenue	Adams Basin	NY	14410
Pierce	Edward	SE	$12.50	23 Griswold St.	Bellona	NY	14415
Hartle	Susan	SW	$17.50	589 Westwood Blvd.	Branchport	NY	14418
Clark	Thomas	NW	$22.50	17 Larnic Lane	Byron	NY	14422
Beasley	Ken	NW	$22.50	67 Oxford St.	Byron	NY	14422
Cline	Darren	SW	$7.50	82 Brookdale Road	Caledonia	NY	14423
Murray	Nancy	NW	$23.00	762 Culver Road	Dresden	NY	14441
Abot	Robert	NW	$12.60	99 Stonecreek Rd.	Gorham	NY	14461
DeMarco	Arlene	SW	$8.90	34 Sable Ave.	Gorham	NY	14461
Vetch	Randall	SW	$14.00	45 Central Blvd.	Hall	NY	14463
Henley	Albert	SE	$17.80	12 Divine Drive	Holley	NY	14470
Packer	Penny	NW	$24.00	450 N. Madison St.	Holley	NY	14470
Castile	Abraham	NW	$18.00	67 Fargo Road	Ionia	NY	14475
Warfield	Cristin	NE	$17.50	57 Wayward Way	Kendall	NY	14476
Abel	Gary	NE	$25.00	14 Latta Road	Bluff Point	NY	14478
Cassada	Bruce	NW	$21.50	2 Highpoint Way	Bluff Point	NY	14478
Martin	Jane	SE	$8.75	50 Smart Drive	Knowlesville	NY	14479
Abel	Murray	NE	$12.50	127 Ford Avenue	Lakeville	NY	14480

Record: 1 of 46

6. Return to Design view, and click on the arrow next to the **Query Type** button to display a list of the types of queries you can create in the query design grid. Click on Make Table to open the Make Table dialog box. This is where you will specify a name for the table you wish to make.

7. In the Make Table box, type **My Parking and Addresses**; then click on **OK**.

8. Start to run the query. (Because this is an action query, click on the **Run** button.) A dialog box prompts you to confirm that the query should copy 46 records into a new table.

9. Click on **Yes** to create the new table.

10. Close the query without saving it.

11. From the Database window, open and observe the **My Parking and Addresses** table. The records in the table are identical to those in your query's resulting datasheet. (Compare Figure 8.23 with Figure 8.22.)

Figure 8.23   **The My Parking and Addresses Table**

Last Name	First Name	Park Lot	Pay Rate	Address	City	
Harper	Hanna	NW	$21.50	82 East Avenue	Adams Basin	NY
Pierce	Edward	SE	$12.50	23 Griswold St.	Bellona	NY
Hartle	Susan	SW	$17.50	589 Westwood	Branchport	NY
Clark	Thomas	NW	$22.50	17 Larnic Lane	Byron	NY
Beasley	Ken	NW	$22.50	67 Oxford St.	Byron	NY
Cline	Darren	SW	$7.50	82 Brookdale R	Caledonia	NY
Murray	Nancy	NW	$23.00	762 Culver Roac	Dresden	NY
Abot	Robert	NW	$12.60	99 Stonecreek I	Gorham	NY
DeMarco	Arlene	SW	$8.90	34 Sable Ave.	Gorham	NY
Vetch	Randall	SW	$14.00	45 Central Blvd.	Hall	NY
Henley	Albert	SE	$17.80	12 Divine Drive	Holley	NY
Packer	Penny	NW	$24.00	450 N. Madison	Holley	NY
Castile	Abraham	NW	$18.00	67 Fargo Road	Ionia	NY
Warfield	Cristin	NE	$17.50	57 Wayward W	Kendall	NY
Abel	Gary	NE	$25.00	14 Latta Road	Bluff Point	NY
Cassada	Bruce	NW	$21.50	2 Highpoint Wa	Bluff Point	NY
Martin	Jane	SE	$8.75	50 Smart Drive	Knowlesville	NY
Abel	Murray	NE	$12.50	127 Ford Avenu	Lakeville	NY

Record: ⏮ ◀   1   ▶ ⏭ ▶* of 46

12. Close the Table window.

SUMMARY

In this chapter, you learned how to create and run queries more efficiently, how to create advanced select queries, and how to create and run parameter, action, and multiple-table queries.

Here's a quick reference guide to the Access features introduced in this chapter:

Desired Result	How to Do It
Create a select query using the toolbar	From a Query window, click on the **Query Type** drop-down arrow, click on select
Widen a design-grid column	Place the mouse pointer on the right edge of the column's field selector until the pointer changes to a cross with a horizontal, two-headed arrow, drag the column boundary to the right, and then release the mouse button
Create a concatenation expression	In a design grid's Field cell, type field names within brackets and text within double quotation marks, separating each item with the concatenation operator **&**
Open the Zoom box	Click in a cell and then press **Shift+F2**; or click the right mouse button and choose **Zoom**
Specify records with unique values only	From a Query window's Design view, click on the **Properties** button; in the Unique Values Only list box, select **Yes**; click on **OK**
Create a parameter query	Within a design-grid Criteria cell, type a parameter name enclosed within square brackets
Run an action query	Click on the **Run** button
Refresh the contents of an open window	Press **Shift+F9**

Desired Result	How to Do It
Convert a select query to an update query	From the Query window's Design view, click on the arrow next to **Query Type** button, click on **Update**
Add all of a table's fields to the design grid	From the table's field list, drag the asterisk (*) to a design-grid Field cell
Convert a select query to a delete query	From the Query window's Design view, click on the arrow next to **Query Type** button, click on **Delete**
Create a crosstab query using a wizard	From the **New Object** drop-down list, click on the **New Query** button to open the New Query dialog box; select **Crosstab Query Wizard**, and click on **OK**; select the table that contains the data you wish to use in your query, and then click on **Next**; select the leftmost Column field, and click on the > button; continue in this manner until you have added all the desired fields; click on **Next**; select the field that you want to appear as column headings, and click on **Next**; select the field whose values you wish to calculate, select the type of calculation, and click on **Next**; name the query, and click on **Finish**
Convert a select query to a make-table query	From the Query window's Design view, click on the arrow next to **Query Type** button, click on **Make Table**
Create a multiple-table query	Use the query design's Add Table dialog box to add multiple tables to the query design
Specify fields that contain values	In a design-grid Criteria row, type **is not null** under the appropriate field names

In the next chapter, you'll learn how to use new methods of modifying a table's Datasheet-view layout, how to change field properties, how to work with keyed tables, and how to create table relationships.

CHAPTER 9: ENHANCED TABLE DESIGN

Changing Field
Properties

Working with
Keyed Tables

In Chapter 3, you learned the basics of creating a table and defining its fields. In this chapter, you will learn how to refine your table designs in order to make them easier to use and make your data more reliable and consistent. You'll also learn more about working with a table's primary key.

When you're done working through this chapter, you will know

- How to examine and modify field properties
- How to change the display formats of fields
- How to set default values
- How to set validation rules and validation text
- How to remove, add, and change a table's primary key

CHANGING FIELD PROPERTIES

Field properties determine the appearance and behavior of fields. More specifically, field properties can

- Determine how values are displayed in a field
- Limit the range of values or the number of characters in a field
- Establish a field's default value

You might remember that when you created text fields in Chapter 3, you changed the Field Size property to limit the number of characters allowed in that field. For example, when you created an ID field and set that field's Field Size property to 4, you limited the number of characters in that field to four. For all other fields and field properties, however, you accepted all of Access's field-property defaults.

When you create a form or report using a table's fields, those fields' properties are duplicated in those objects as *control properties*. However, if you change field properties in a table, you may not automatically affect existing control properties on forms and reports. Therefore, if you want to set field properties that will affect control properties in forms and reports, you should set those properties in your table before creating objects based on that table. (You will learn more about control properties and their relationships to field properties in Chapter 10.)

EXAMINING FIELD PROPERTIES

To view or modify a table's field properties:

- Open that table's window in Design view.
- Place the focus in the row of the field for which you want to change field properties.

- Make your desired changes in that field's property boxes (located on the left side of the Table window's lower pane).

Each field data type (Text, Number, Currency, Date/Time, and so on) has its own set of field properties, and each of those field properties has unique capabilities relative to the data type and to other field properties. For this reason, rather than trying to memorize all of the possible choices for every field property in every situation, you can turn to Access's Help system. The program often displays brief messages relevant to the task at hand in the status bar or somewhere in an object window. To get more detailed context-sensitive help, open Access's Help window using the F1 key. For example, if the text field's Field Size property is selected, you can press F1 to open the Help window that pertains to the Field Size property for text fields.

In the next exercise, we are going to examine field properties in an existing table. Some of these field properties are the same default field properties you saw in Chapter 3; others are custom properties that serve a specific purpose. One custom setting that we'll look at instructs Access to capitalize values automatically when you enter lowercase text; you'll use context-sensitive Help to view the other possible settings for that field property.

If you do not have both the Access application and the Company Database windows opened and maximized, please open and maximize them now.

Now let's start:

1. Open the Payroll Data table in Design view and observe the Table window's upper pane. The *ID* text field is selected. The left side of the Table window's lower pane displays the field properties for the ID field. In the right side of the window's lower pane, notice that, because the ID row's Field Name box is selected, Access displays a brief Help message on naming fields.

2. Select the ID field's Field Size property box (press **F6** or click in the property box); then observe the right side of the lower pane. It now displays a brief Help message on a text field's Field Size property (see Figure 9.1).

3. Move to the Format property box and observe the brief Help message for this property. The Format property determines how Access displays values in the ID field. Notice that the

Figure 9.1   **The property boxes and brief Help message in Design view**

Property
boxes

Brief Help
message

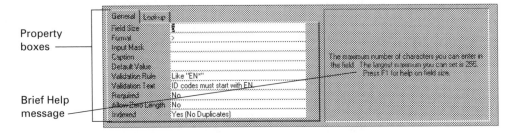

Format property box contains the format >, which is not explained in the brief Help message.

4. Press **F1** to open the Help window for the Format property, and then maximize the Help window.

5. Click on the bulleted item **Text and Memo Data Types** (because ID is a text field) to view Help on the Format property relative to text and memo fields. (You'll learn about memo fields later in this chapter.) The Help window informs us that the > Format property changes all characters to uppercase if they aren't already.

6. Close the Help window.

7. Switch to Datasheet view, and then observe the values in the ID field. All characters are displayed in uppercase.

8. Select **EN03** in the ID field for Hanna Harper (Record 2), and then type **en03** to replace the value.

9. Press **Tab** to move from the field, and observe the value you just entered. Because of the > Format property, Access displays the value as *EN03*.

 MODIFYING THE DISPLAY FORMAT OF A DATE/TIME FIELD

To help you determine possible settings for a field property, Access often supplies a list of settings right in the Table window. If there is a list for a particular field property, Access displays a drop-down arrow whenever that property's box is selected, enabling you to select a setting from that property box's drop-down list rather than enter it manually.

For the Format property of date/time fields, Access provides a list of seven possible settings:

- *General Date*, for example, 11/15/94 04:30 PM

- *Long Date*, for example, Monday, November 15, 1994

- *Medium Date*, for example, 14-Nov-94

- *Short Date*, for example, 11/14/94

- *Long Time*, for example, 4:30:00 PM

- *Medium Time*, for example, 04:30 PM

- *Short Time*, for example, 16:30

Note: For some date/time formats, Access depends on the settings in the Regional Settings of the Windows Control Panel. For more information on viewing or changing these settings, refer to your Microsoft Windows documentation.

You can enter dates and times in any of these formats; Access automatically displays the date or time in the format specified by that date/time field's Format property. For example, if you type 14–Nov–94 in a date/time field set with the Short Date Format property, Access displays your date as 11/14/94. One of the advantages of field properties is that they ensure data conformity while allowing for flexibility in data entry.

Let's change the Format property for the Hired date/time field from Medium Date to Short Date:

1. Return to Design view, move to the Hired row, and observe the properties for the Hired field (in the lower pane). The Format property is currently set to *Medium Date*.

2. Switch to Datasheet view and observe the values in the Hired field. Dates are displayed in the Medium Date format *dd-mmm-yy*.

3. Return to Design view; then move to the Hired field's Format property box to display the property box's drop-down arrow.

4. Open the Format property box's drop-down list and select **Short Date**. Then save your change to the table design (click on the **Save** button).

5. Switch to Datasheet view and observe the values in the Hired field. The dates are now displayed in the Short Date format *mm/dd/yy* (see Figure 9.2).

Figure 9.2   **Hired field values displayed in Short Date format**

ID	Last Name	First Name	Dept	Hired	Hours	Pay Rate	Health	Park Lot	Park Rate	Con
EN01	James	Ted	MK	4/1/81	38	$15.50	A2	SW	$51.50	
EN03	Harper	Hanna	ES	4/19/80	40	$21.50	A2	NW	$65.00	
EN04	Packer	Penny	MK	1/15/85	35	$24.00	A1	NW	$55.00	
EN05	Binder	Julia	MS	2/17/83	25	$8.52	B			Julia v
EN07	Sanders	Maria	ES	8/17/83	29.5	$7.25	B			
EN08	Easter	Connie	EE	5/20/90	40	$15.00	A1	NW	$62.00	
EN10	Martin	Jane	EE	6/7/87	40	$8.75	A2	SE	$57.17	Jane
EN11	Binga	Allison	EE	9/1/89	15.5	$7.25	B	SW	$57.42	
EN12	Conner	Bill	CE	3/8/80	40	$19.50	B			
EN13	Osowski	Dominick	SA	7/18/92	40	$22.00	A1	NE	$65.00	
EN14	Binga	Sam	SS	7/5/84	35.5	$13.30	A1	NW	$60.00	
EN15	Abel	Murray	CE	11/25/86	35.5	$12.50	A1	NE	$62.00	
EN16	Abot	Robert	MK	9/18/82	40	$12.60	A1	NW	$65.00	Bob is
EN17	Zambito	Joseph	CE	7/9/84	40	$15.50	A2	NE	$67.75	
EN18	McDonald	Peter	EE	4/8/83	40	$21.50	C	NE	$60.00	
EN19	Chase	Wilma	SS	8/17/88	40	$15.50	A1	SE	$53.56	
EN20	DeMarco	Arlene	ES	8/7/86	25.5	$8.90	B	SW	$56.65	
EN23	Desoto	Frank	MS	9/18/88	40	$21.50	A2	NE	$67.75	
EN24	Henley	Albert	ES	10/13/80	40	$17.80	B	SE	$54.08	

MODIFYING THE DISPLAY FORMAT OF A NUMBER FIELD

It is important to note that the Format property does not actually change the values that you enter in a field; it just changes the way Access displays those values. For example, when you typed *en03* earlier in this chapter and Access displayed the value as *EN03*, the underlying value was still en03.

This difference between what you type and what Access displays may seem minor for text values; however, it can be very significant for numbers that you use in calculations. For example, you could type *40.5* in a number field, only to have Access display that value as *40*. Because Access stored the value as you typed it (40.5), however, the program does use the entire number in any calculations.

Why would you want to display only part of a number's value? To make that number easier to read. For example, if you are creating a report that contains multimillion-dollar figures, displaying numbers to the second decimal place might be distracting. In this case, you might omit the decimal places in the number's display.

Because number and currency fields are similar, they have similar field properties and field-property settings. There are six standard settings for the Format property of number and currency fields:

- *General Number* displays values as entered, using as many or as few decimal places as necessary. An example is 5425.6.

- *Currency* precedes values with a dollar sign, includes thousand separators, as necessary, and always displays two decimal places. An example is $5,425.60. If the value is negative, Access encloses it in parentheses and displays it in red.

- *Fixed* displays values with a fixed number of decimal places from 0 to 15. The default number of decimal places is 2. An example is 5425.60.

- *Standard* displays values as entered, but adds thousand separators as needed. An example is 5,245.6.

- *Percent* displays values multiplied by 100 and followed by a percent sign. An example is 524560%.

- *Scientific* displays numbers in standard scientific notation. An example is 5.24E+03.

If the Format cell for a number field is blank, Access displays numbers using the General Number setting.

When you use any number format other than General Number, you can use the Decimal Places property to determine how many decimal places to display. When the Decimal Places property is set to Auto, Access uses the Format property setting's default to determine the number of decimal places. For example, if you set a field's format property to Fixed and its Decimal Places property to Auto, Access will display values with two decimal places, because the default number of decimal places for the Fixed format is two.

Let's change the Format property for the Hours field to Fixed, and then set the Decimal Places property so that every value in the Hours field displays one decimal place:

1. Observe the values in the Hours field. Decimal places are displayed only as needed (see Figure 9.2).

2. Switch to Design view, move to the Hours row, and then observe the Hours field's Format property box. It is empty.

3. Open and observe the Format property drop-down list. Access provides six formats for number fields.

4. Select **Fixed**, and then save the table design.

5. Return to Datasheet view and observe the values in the Hours field. Each value displays two decimal places.

6. Switch to Design view and observe the Hours field's Decimal Places property box. It is currently set to *Auto*.

7. Select the Decimal Places property box. The Help message on the right side of the lower pane tells you that this property determines the number of digits displayed to the right of the decimal point.

8. Open and observe the Decimal Places property drop-down list. You can use this list to specify any number of decimal places from 0 to 15.

9. Select **1**, and then save the table design.

10. Switch to Datasheet view and observe the values in the Hours field. Each value now displays one decimal place (see Figure 9.3).

Figure 9.3   **Hours displayed to one decimal place**

ID	Last Name	First Name	Dept	Hired	Hours	Pay Rate	Health	Park Lot	Park Rate	Con
EN01	James	Ted	MK	4/1/81	38.0	$15.50	A2	SW	$51.50	
EN03	Harper	Hanna	ES	4/19/80	40.0	$21.50	A2	NW	$65.00	
EN04	Packer	Penny	MK	1/15/85	35.0	$24.00	A1	NW	$55.00	
EN05	Binder	Julia	MS	2/17/83	25.0	$8.52	B			Julia v
EN07	Sanders	Maria	ES	8/17/83	29.5	$7.25	B			
EN08	Easter	Connie	EE	5/20/90	40.0	$15.00	A1	NW	$62.00	
EN10	Martin	Jane	EE	6/7/87	40.0	$8.75	A2	SE	$57.17	Jane
EN11	Binga	Allison	EE	9/1/89	15.5	$7.25	B	SW	$57.42	
EN12	Conner	Bill	CE	3/8/80	40.0	$19.50	B			
EN13	Osowski	Dominick	SA	7/18/92	40.0	$22.00	A1	NE	$65.00	
EN14	Binga	Sam	SS	7/5/84	35.5	$13.30	A1	NW	$60.00	
EN15	Abel	Murray	CE	11/25/86	35.5	$12.50	A1	NE	$62.00	
EN16	Abot	Robert	MK	9/18/82	40.0	$12.60	A1	NW	$65.00	Bob is
EN17	Zambito	Joseph	CE	7/9/84	40.0	$15.50	A2	NE	$67.75	
EN18	McDonald	Peter	EE	4/8/83	40.0	$21.50	C	NE	$60.00	
EN19	Chase	Wilma	SS	8/17/88	40.0	$15.50	A1	SE	$53.56	
EN20	DeMarco	Arlene	ES	8/7/86	25.5	$8.90	B	SW	$56.65	
EN23	Desoto	Frank	MS	9/18/88	40.0	$21.50	A2	NE	$67.75	
EN24	Henley	Albert	ES	10/13/80	40.0	$17.80	B	SE	$54.08	

SETTING DEFAULT VALUES

If you enter the same value in a field for a majority of records, you can speed up data entry by specifying that value as a default value. Once you do, Access enters that value automatically when you enter a new record. For example, if you expect that most new employees will work 40 hours per week, you can set a default value of 40 in the hours-worked field. For the infrequent employee who doesn't work 40 hours per week, you can simply replace the default value with another value as you enter that employee's record. Default values provide a convenient shortcut when you enter new records; however, setting a default value does not affect values in existing records.

In Chapter 3, you saw Access automatically set a default value of 0 for number and currency fields as you created those fields. In the next exercise, you'll see the same default value, which Access has already set in the Park Rate field, and then you'll set your own default value in the Hours field:

1. Move to and observe the blank record at the end of the table (click on the **New Record** navigation button). Access has already placed a default value of 0, displayed as $0.00, in the Park Rate field.

2. Switch to Design view; then display and observe the Park Rate field's properties (click in the Park Rate row). The Default Value property is set to 0.

3. Display and observe the Hours field's properties. The Default Value property box is empty.

4. Type **40** in the Default Value property box.

5. Save the table design, and return to Datasheet view. Observe the table's last blank record: The Hours field now displays the default value that you entered in step 4 (see Figure 9.4).

Figure 9.4   **The default value displayed in the Hours field**

EN87	Gardner	Gayle	MK	12/1/86	40.0	$16.75	B	SW	$59.48
					40.0				$0.00

SETTING VALIDATION RULES AND TEXT

Validation rules are field properties you can set to require or prevent certain values or patterns of values in a field. With validation rules you can require that an employee ID code begin with specific characters, or prohibit a pay rate from exceeding a certain dollar amount. Validation rules help to promote data conformity, and can help prevent data-entry errors. Like default values, though, validation rules do not affect existing records (unless you attempt to change existing values within those records).

Whenever you set a validation rule, you should also set *validation text* explaining that rule. Access displays this validation text in a dialog box that it opens whenever data entered into that field does not follow the validation rule. For example, if you set a validation rule preventing a value in an hours-worked field from exceeding 60, your validation text might be *Employees cannot be scheduled to work more than 60 hours per week.* When you then enter a value greater than 60 in that field, Access opens a dialog box containing your text to explain the validation rule, and prevents you from saving that record until the value adheres to the validation rule.

To set a validation rule and text in a Table window's Design view, display the field properties of the field for which you want to set the rule and text. Then type a validation expression in the Validation Rule property box, and type some validation text in the Validation Text property box.

You can use the same techniques for setting validation expressions as you have used for criteria expressions. For example, if you want to prevent hours-worked values from exceeding 60, type *<=60* in the hours-worked field's Validation Rule property box.

Let's look at a field that has a validation rule and text set already. Then we'll set and test a validation rule and text for a second field:

1. In the ID field of the table's last blank record, type **in99** and then press **Tab** to leave the field. A dialog box informs you that ID codes must start with the letters *EN*.

2. Click on **OK**, and replace *in99* with **en99**. Then press **Tab**. Access accepts your new ID code and displays it in uppercase. (Remember that the ID field employs the > Format property.)

3. Choose **Edit, Undo Current Field/Record** to clear the new record.

4. Switch to Design view; then display and observe the ID field's properties (see Figure 9.5). The Validation Rule property requires that ID numbers start with EN; the Validation Text property provides text for the dialog box that Access opens when the Validation Rule property is violated (as you saw in step 1).

5. Display and observe the Pay Rate field's properties. Both the Validation Rule and Validation Text property boxes are empty.

Figure 9.5   **The ID field's properties**

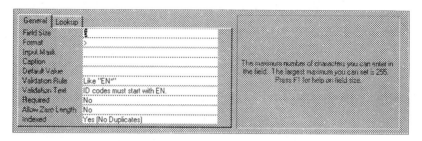

6. In the Validation Rule property box, type **<=45** to disallow new pay rates greater than $45.00.

7. In the Validation Text property box, type **You cannot enter a pay rate greater than $45.00.**

8. Save the table design. A message box is displayed, informing you that data integrity rules have been changed, and asking you if you want the existing data to be checked against the new rule.

9. Click on **Yes**. (Notice that, in this case, the data checking was not as lengthy a task as the message box might have led you to believe.) Now, switch to Datasheet view.

10. In the ID field for the new record, enter **EN94**.

11. In the Pay Rate field for the new record, type **47.5,** and then press **Tab**. Access opens a dialog box containing the validation text you typed, informing you that a pay rate cannot exceed $45.00.

12. Click on **OK**, replace *47.5* with **27.5**, and then press **Tab**. Access accepts the new pay rate.

13. Complete the record by entering the following data:

Last Name:	Osborn
First Name:	Lloyd
Dept:	ee
Hired:	5/14/93

Health: c

Park Lot: ne

Park Rate: 55

EXAMINING A MEMO FIELD

Text fields can hold up to 255 alphanumeric characters each. If you need more room than that (for example, to store notes on individual employee performance), you can use a memo field. Memo fields can hold up to 32,000 alphanumeric characters.

Depending on the amount of data stored in a record's memo field, you may not be able to see all of that data in Datasheet view. However, you can easily view and edit the contents of a memo field through the Zoom box. To open the Zoom box for a memo field in a Table window's Datasheet view, select the desired memo field and then press Shift+F2.

Forms offer other alternatives for viewing and editing memo fields. You'll learn about working with memo fields on forms in Chapter 10.

Let's look at a memo field in the Payroll Data table:

1. Press **Ctrl+Home** to return to the top of the table; then scroll to the right and observe the table's rightmost field, Comments. In some of the records, the Comments field contains text, but you can't see all of the text because the column is too narrow (it also doesn't fit in the window).

2. Move to the Comments field for Jane Martin's record (Record 7), and then open the field's Zoom box (press **Shift+F2**). Notice that its contents exceed the 255-character maximum for text fields (see Figure 9.6).

3. Click on **Cancel** to close the Zoom box, and switch to Design view.

4. Observe the Comments row. Comments is set to the Memo data type.

5. Close the Table window.

Figure 9.6   **Displaying the memo-field contents in the Zoom box**

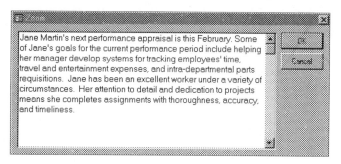

WORKING WITH KEYED TABLES

In Chapter 3, you learned that a table's primary key is a field or combination of fields that enables Access to uniquely identify each table record.

In addition, you learned that Access automatically sets a primary-key field's Indexed property to Yes (No Duplicates). This property setting instructs Access to

* Automatically sort records in a table by values in that field

* Automatically index records by those values in order to speed data retrieval

* Prevent you from entering duplicate values in the primary-key field(s)

In this section, you'll learn ways to remove, change, and work with primary keys.

REMOVING A PRIMARY KEY

As you learned in Chapter 3, it is relatively easy to set a primary key using the Primary Key button in the toolbar. To remove a table's primary key:

* Open the desired table in Design view.

* Click on the *Indexes* button (or choose *View, Indexes*) to open the Indexes window.

* Select the primary-key row in the Indexes window.

* Press *Delete*.

Let's remove the primary key from the Suppliers table:

1. Open and examine the Suppliers table. The table's records are in order by telephone number (not a very practical arrangement!).

2. Switch to Design view and examine the Phone row. The key indicator is displayed on the row's field selector, indicating that Phone is the table's primary-key field.

3. Click on the Indexes button to open the table's Indexes window (see Figure 9.7). Notice the window's name: *Indexes: Suppliers*. The Indexes window contains columns for Index Name, Field Name, and Sort Order.

Figure 9.7   **The Indexes: Suppliers window**

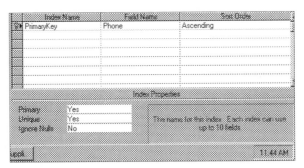

4. In the Indexes window, click on the primary key's **field selector** to select the entire row; then press **Delete**. In the background, you can see that the key icon has been removed from the Phone field selector. There is currently no primary key set in the Suppliers table.

5. Close the Indexes window. (Click on the **Indexes** button, or click on the **Close** button on the Indexes window.)

ADDING AN AUTONUMBER DATA TYPE PRIMARY-KEY FIELD

Access works much faster and more easily with tables that have primary keys. Although Access doesn't require you to set a primary key for every table, we strongly recommend that you do so.

To add an AutoNumber primary-key field:

- In Design view, move the focus to the row above which you wish to add the new field. Then click on the *Insert Row* button in the toolbar.

- In the new row, type the new field name; then press *Tab*.

- In the Data Type drop-down list box, select *AutoNumber*.

- In the Indexed property drop-down list box, select *Yes (No Duplicates)*.

- Click on the *Primary Key* button.

When entering data, you cannot enter values into a AutoNumber field; Access does so automatically. When entering and viewing data, you may find that values in an AutoNumber field look similar to record numbers. However, AutoNumber-field values and record numbers may not necessarily be the same for every record. To determine a record's number, select that record and then observe the Specific Record Number box.

Let's add an AutoNumber primary-key field. Then, we'll see how an AutoNumber field works in Datasheet view:

1. With the Company Name field selected, click on the **Insert Row** button in the toolbar. A blank row is inserted above the Company Name row.

2. In the blank row under Field Name, type **ID** and press **Tab** to move to the Data Type column. From the Data Type drop-down list, select **AutoNumber**.

3. In the Indexed property drop-down list (in the lower pane), select **Yes (No Duplicates)**. This assures us that the ID field values will not be duplicated.

4. Now select the ID field and click on the **Primary Key** button to make ID the primary-key field. Then compare your screen to Figure 9.8.

Figure 9.8   **The added primary-key field**

5. Attempt to switch to Datasheet view. A dialog box prompts you to save the table before switching to Datasheet view.

6. Click on **Yes** to save the table; then observe the ID field. Access automatically added consecutive numbers, beginning with 1, to the ID field.

7. Move to the last blank record's Company Name field, and type **Electrical Connections**.

8. Save the record (choose **Records, Save Record**). Notice the new record's ID field. Access automatically added the next consecutive value, *5*.

PRACTICE YOUR SKILLS

1. Enter the following values to complete the record:

Address:	20 Outlet Rd.
City:	Wyoming
St:	NY
Zip:	14591
Phone:	898–2100
Contact Person:	John McDonald

2. Press the **Tab** key, and compare your screen to Figure 9.9.

Figure 9.9   **The completed ID AutoNumber field in Datasheet view**

ID	Company Name	Address	City	St	Zip	Phone	Contact I
1	Phones and Faxes	1010 South Ave.	Piffard	NY	14533	855-4321	Barbara M
2	Office Options	33 West Ave.	Nunda	NY	14517	876-1992	Julie Wort
3	Desktop Organizers	747 Coldwater Rd.	Caledonia	NY	14423	887-0062	Tony LaD(
4	PC Pieces	431 Jay St.	Wyoming	NY	14591	898-8989	Ray Getzi
5	Electrical Connectior	20 Outlet Rd.	Wyoming	NY	14591	898-2100	John McD
(AutoNumber)							

CHANGING THE PRIMARY-KEY FIELD

Although you can always use an AutoNumber field as a primary-key field, you may prefer to minimize the number of fields in your tables by identifying an existing field or set of fields that will uniquely identify your records. To change a table's primary-key field, select and set the new field or fields as you would if the table did not already have a primary key. When you do, Access automatically reassigns the primary key to the new field or fields and removes the former primary-key assignment. Once you've reassigned a primary key to another field, you can delete Access's AutoNumber field.

Let's change the primary-key field from the ID field to the Phone field, and then delete the ID field:

1. Switch to Design view, and then open and observe the Indexes: Suppliers window (click on the **Indexes** button). Notice that ID is the primary-key field.

2. In the Table window, make the Phone row the primary key (select the **Phone** field and click on the **Primary Key** button). The key indicator moves from the ID row's field selector to the Phone row's field selector, indicating that Phone is now the primary-key field. Notice that the Indexes window also reflects the primary-key change. Notice that the Phone field's Indexed property is set to *Yes (No Duplicates)*.

3. Close the Indexes window.

4. Select the ID row and press **Delete**. Access opens a dialog box to inform you that deleting the ID field will also delete the data contained within the field.

5. Click on **Yes**. Yet another dialog box opens, informing you that any indexes pertaining to the ID field will also be deleted.

6. Click on **Yes** to delete the ID field and its data.

7. Save the table design and switch to Datasheet view. Notice that the record you added (Electrical Connections) is no longer displayed at the end of the table, but rather is sorted, along with the other records, by telephone number (see Figure 9.10). Notice also that the ID field is no longer a part of the table.

Figure 9.10 **The table after changing the primary key and deleting the ID field**

Company Name	Address	City	St	Zip	Phone	Contact Person
Phones and Faxes	1010 South Ave.	Piffard	NY	14533	855-4321	Barbara Mohr
Office Options	33 West Ave.	Nunda	NY	14517	876-1992	Julie Worth
Desktop Organizers	747 Coldwater Rd.	Caledonia	NY	14423	887-0062	Tony LaDuca
Electrical Connection	20 Outlet Rd.	Wyoming	NY	14591	898-2100	John McDonald
PC Pieces	431 Jay St.	Wyoming	NY	14591	898-8989	Ray Getzin

TESTING A DUPLICATE VALUE IN A PRIMARY-KEY FIELD

You've learned that Access sets the primary-key field's Indexed property to Yes (No Duplicates) to prevent duplicate values from being entered in that field.

Now, let's see what happens when we try to enter a duplicate value in a primary-key field:

1. Add the following values to the table's last blank record:

Company Name:	Commercial Decorators
Address:	440 Washington St.
City:	Nunda
St:	NY
Zip:	14517
Phone:	876–1992
Contact Person:	Valerie Hernandez

You'll notice that the phone number is the same as that of Office Options.

2. Attempt to save the record. (Choose **Records, Save Record**.) A dialog box opens, informing you that you can't have duplicate values in a primary-key field.

3. Click on **OK**. Change the telephone number for Commercial Decorators to **876-1002**, and then save the record.

4. Press **Shift+F9**. Access reorders the records according to the primary-key field, Phone. (You saw in Chapter 8 that the *Records, Refresh* command refreshes the contents of open windows.)

PRACTICE YOUR SKILLS

1. Add the following values to the table's last blank record:

Company Name:	Computer Solutions
Address:	310 Oxford St.
City:	Piffard
St:	NY
Zip:	14533
Phone:	887–0062
Contact Person:	Keesha Clark

2. Attempt to save the record.

3. Change the Phone field to **855–0062**.

4. Save the record, reorder the records according to the primary-key field, and then compare your screen to Figure 9.11.

5. Close the Table and Database windows.

PRACTICE YOUR SKILLS

In Chapter 8, you learned how to create different kinds of queries. In this chapter, you learned how to work with a variety of field properties, and how to remove and change primary keys. The

Figure 9.11   **The Suppliers table after adding the seventh record**

Company Name	Address	City	St.	Zip	Phone	Contact Person
Computer Solutions	310 Oxford St.	Piffard	NY	14533	855-0062	Keesha Clark
Phones and Faxes	1010 South Ave.	Piffard	NY	14533	855-4321	Barbara Mohr
Commercial Decorate	440 Washington S	Nunda	NY	14517	876-1002	Valerie Hernand
Office Options	33 West Ave.	Nunda	NY	14517	876-1992	Julie Worth
Desktop Organizers	747 Coldwater Rd.	Caledonia	NY	14423	887-0062	Tony LaDuca
Electrical Connection	20 Outlet Rd.	Wyoming	NY	14591	898-2100	John McDonald
PC Pieces	431 Jay St.	Wyoming	NY	14591	898-8989	Ray Getzin

following activities give you an opportunity to apply some of these techniques.

In this activity, you will create a parameter query to produce a datasheet of employees who park in the SW parking lot, as shown in Figure 9.12.

Figure 9.12   **The parameter query's resulting datasheet**

Employee Name	Park Lot
Sharon Berry	SW
Allison Binga	SW
Darren Cline	SW
Arlene DeMarco	SW
Gayle Gardner	SW
Susan Hartle	SW
Ted James	SW
Patricia Smith	SW
Randall Vetch	SW
Rodney Ward	SW

Follow these steps at your computer:

1. Open the Practice database file, and maximize the Database window, if necessary (Chapter 2).

2. Open and observe the Parking Lots and Rates table (Chapter 2).

3. From the Table window, create a new query based on the Parking Lots and Rates table (Chapter 8).

4. Add the Last Name field to the design grid's first Field cell (Chapter 5).

5. In the design grid's second Field cell, enter an expression to concatenate the First Name and Last Name fields with a space in between (Chapter 8).

6. Name the concatenated field **Employee Name** (Chapter 8).

7. Add the **Park Lot** field to the design grid's third Field cell (Chapter 5).

8. Specify that the records be sorted in ascending order by last name (Chapter 5).

9. Specify that the query not display the Last Name field in its resulting datasheet (Chapter 8).

10. In the Park Lot field's Criteria cell, set a parameter expression to ask for a parking-lot value (Chapter 8).

11. Run the query, providing **sw** as the value for the Park Lot field's parameter (Chapter 8).

12. Compare your resulting datasheet to Figure 9.12.

13. Save the query as **My Parameter Parking Lots** (Chapter 5).

14. Close the Query window, leaving the Parking Lots and Rates table open and active (Chapter 2).

In the next activity, you will modify and test some field properties in the Parking Lots and Rates table. You will also remove the table's primary key.

1. Switch to the Parking Lots and Rates table's Design view (Chapter 3).

2. For the Park Lot field, set a default value of **sw**.

3. For the Park Rate field, set a validation rule that requires a minimum parking rate of $50, and then set some appropriate validation text to accompany the rule.

4. Save the table design, then switch to Datasheet view. (When Access asks if you want the existing data to be checked against the new rule, click on **Yes**. When Access tells you that existing data violates the new settings, click on **Yes**. This message appears because the table has several records with no values in the Park Rate field.)

5. Move to and observe the default Park Lot value of *sw* in the table's last blank record (Chapter 3).

6. In the blank record's Park Rate field, type **45**, and then attempt to save the record (Chapter 3).

7. Close the dialog box, and change the Park Rate value to **55**.

8. Add the following values to the remainder of the record (Chapter 3):

Last: Bonski

First: Igor

Dept: EE

ID: EN88

Then compare your screen to Figure 9.13.

Figure 9.13   **The new record**

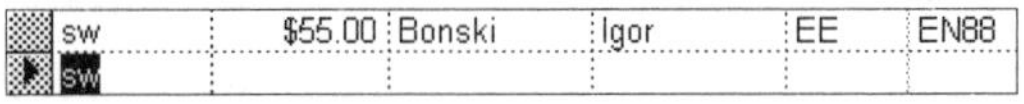

9. Return to Design view and remove the table's primary key (Chapter 7).

10. Close the Indexes window.

11. Set the primary key back to ID.

12. Save the table design. Then close the Table and Database windows (Chapter 3).

SUMMARY

In this chapter, you learned how to use field properties to enhance the performance of your tables, how to remove and reset a table's primary key, and how to create and use table relationships.

Here's a quick reference guide to the Access features introduced in this chapter:

Desired Result	How to Do It
Use context-sensitive Help	Press **F1**

Modify field properties	With a table open in Design view, select field's row, and use field's property boxes
Modify date/ time field's display format	Change field's Format property
Modify number field's display format	Change field's Format and/or Decimal Places property
Set default value for field	Type value in field's Default Value property box
Set validation rule for field	Type value or expression in field's Validation Rule property box
Set validation text for field	Type text in field's Validation Text property box
Remove table's primary key	In Design view, click on **Indexes** button, select primary-key row in Indexes window, and press **Delete**
Change primary key	In Design view, place focus in desired row, and click on **Primary Key** button

In Chapter 10, you'll learn how to use control properties and various control styles to create enhanced forms. You'll also learn how to use the Main/Subform Form Wizard to create two forms that enable you to view data from two tables and/or queries in a single Form window.

CHAPTER 10: ENHANCED FORM DESIGN

Editing a Memo
Field and
Enhancing Its
Control

Adding Controls
to Enhance an
Existing Form

Creating a Form
That Contains a
Subform

In Chapter 6, you learned how to use a Form Wizard to create a basic single-column form, and how to modify that form's design by deleting, moving, sizing, and aligning controls. In Chapter 7, you learned how to modify controls on a report by changing control properties through the toolbar. In this chapter, you will learn how to enhance the performance and appearance of your forms by modifying and adding control properties through a control's property sheet, and by adding controls to existing forms. You will also learn how to create and use a form that displays data from two related tables and/or queries at the same time.

When you're done working through this chapter, you will know

- How to use an enlarged control to view and edit a memo field

- How to use a control's property sheet to modify control properties

- How to add a control to an existing form

- How to add a calculated control to calculate values that are not available through the form's underlying table or query

- How to add a rectangle control to display a rectangle

- How to add a list-box control to enable you to select values from a list

- How to use the Form Wizard to create a form that displays data from two related tables and/or queries

EDITING A MEMO FIELD AND ENHANCING ITS CONTROL

Forms are more flexible for displaying data than are tables. For example, instead of using the Zoom button to view and edit lengthy values, you can use an enlarged control to provide a large area for viewing and editing the memo field. By changing control properties, you can also add scroll bars to a control, enabling you to scroll through lengthy values.

 ### EDITING A MEMO FIELD

You can view and edit a memo field much as you would any other field. An enlarged control on a form, however, makes the task a little easier. If a memo field's *bound control* (that is, the control that displays the contents of a memo field) still is not large enough to display the entire field, you can use your arrow keys to navigate through the field.

If you do not have both the Access application and the Company database windows opened and maximized, please open and maximize them now.

Let's use a form with an enlarged memo-field control to view and edit a memo field.

1. Open the Comments form. Notice that the form contains five fields and their labels, arranged vertically. Notice also that the Comments field is very large.

2. Move to Jane Martin's record (Record 7), and observe the text in the Comments field. Even though the field is large, you still cannot see all of the text.

3. Place the insertion point at the end of the Comments field's visible text, and then press the **Down Arrow** to move the insertion point to the end of the text.

4. Press the **spacebar**, and type **Jane's position is under review by management for possible reclassification.** As you type, notice that the text automatically wraps to the next line (see Figure 10.1).

Figure 10.1   Editing a memo field

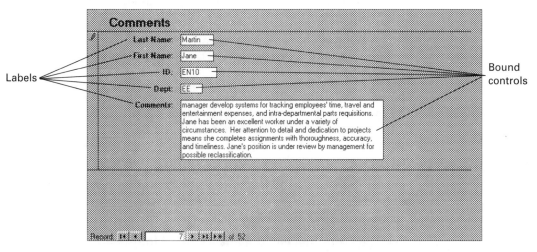

DISPLAYING AND MODIFYING CONTROL PROPERTIES

In Chapter 7, you learned how to modify some control properties—such as font, font size, and alignment—in a Report window's Design view by selecting the control and then using drop-down lists and toolbar buttons. Because controls work much the same way in form design, these drop-down lists and buttons are available for *some* control properties when you select a control in a form's design.

To view and modify *all* of a control's properties, you must work through a control's property sheet. Like the table property sheet you worked with in Chapter 9, a control's property sheet lists all of the properties that affect the appearance and behavior of a control.

To open a control's property sheet:

- Display the form in Design view.

- Select the control.

- Click on the *Properties* button.

If the property sheet is already open, simply click on the control to display that control's properties. When you click in blank areas of the form, the property sheet displays properties of each of the form's sections (Form Header, Detail, and Form Footer), as well as properties of the form itself. The property sheet's title bar always names the type of control or other object for which it is currently displaying properties.

Remember that you can get help on any specific property by first clicking on that property's box (in the property sheet), and then pressing F1.

The control property that we're going to change in the next exercise is the Scroll Bars property. Setting this property to Vertical instructs Access to display a vertical scroll bar for that field whenever you are in Form view and that field is selected. Scroll bars can make a lengthy field easier to move through.

Let's change the Scroll Bars property for the Comments bound control:

1. Switch to Design view and observe the form's sections. The Form Header contains a control for the form's title, *Comments;* the Detail contains five white bound controls and their labels; the Form Footer is currently empty. Notice also the toolbox displayed somewhere over the form. (The toolbox is normally displayed by default. However, if it is not visible, choose **View, Toolbox** to display it. We'll discuss the toolbox in the next section.)

2. Open the form's property sheet (click on the **Properties** button in the toolbar). If the sheet's title bar does not read *Form*,

click to the right of the form's border (past the 5-inch mark on the horizontal ruler) to display the form's properties. The first property on the list, Record Source, indicates that the Comments form is based on the Payroll Data table (see Figure 10.2).

Figure 10.2   **The Comments form's property sheet**

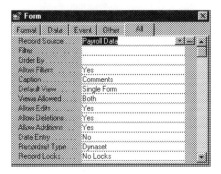

3. Select the **Last Name** label and observe the property sheet. It's now titled *Label* and displays the selected label's properties.

4. Select the **Last Name** bound control. The property sheet's title bar indicates that this bound control is a text-box control. *Text-box* controls and labels are two styles of controls. (You'll learn about other control styles later in this chapter.)

5. Select the **Comments** bound control. You can see that this bound control is also a text-box control.

6. In the property sheet, scroll down to observe the Scroll Bars property. It is currently set to *None*.

7. Open the Scroll Bars drop-down list, and select **Vertical** to insert a vertical scroll bar in the Comments bound control.

8. Close the property sheet and switch to Form view. Notice that no scroll bar is as yet visible in the Comments field.

9. Click in the Comments field. The vertical scroll bar is now displayed in the field (see Figure 10.3). Use the scroll bar to scroll through the field.

10. Save the form as **My Comments**, and then close it.

Figure 10.3   **The Comments field with a vertical scroll bar**

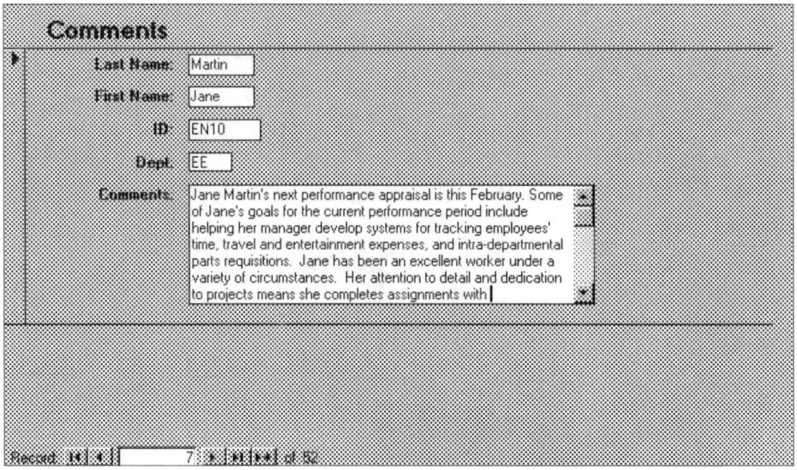

ADDING CONTROLS TO ENHANCE AN EXISTING FORM

In Chapter 6, you learned how to use a Form Wizard to create a basic form. Form Wizards are fast and convenient to use because they ask you key questions about your form design, and then do the detail work of creating the form for you.

If you rely solely on Form Wizards, however, you can only create forms that are designed by the Form Wizard, rather than by you. Knowing how to add controls to forms manually will significantly improve your ability to produce forms that work and look the way you want them to.

By knowing how to add controls manually, you can

- Create forms from scratch without using a Form Wizard

- Create controls to display values that are not available through the form's underlying table or query

- Use various control styles beyond the label and text-box controls you've seen in forms created by Form Wizards

EXAMINING AN ENHANCED FORM

Before we start creating our own enhanced form, let's take a look at an existing enhanced form that is based on the Form Data query:

1. From the Database window, open the Form Data query in Design view. Notice that the query is based on the Payroll Data table, and Gross Pay is a calculated field that multiplies the Hours and Pay Rate fields. (You'll need to scroll to the right to see the Gross Pay field.)

2. Switch to the Database window and open the Payroll form. Observe the form: The Form Header section contains a company logo, today's date, and a form title. In the form's Detail section, the Gross Pay field and its label are enclosed within a rectangle; department codes and full names are displayed in a list box; and the Monthly Parking Rate field exists only on this form, not in the form's underlying Form Data query.

3. As you click on the **Next Record** navigation button several times, observe the Dept list box. The highlighted department code and name change to reflect the appropriate department for each employee record.

4. Switch to Design view and observe the Gross Pay and Monthly Parking Rate controls. The Gross Pay control is a bound control based on the Form Data query's Gross Pay calculated field. The Monthly Parking Rate control is a calculated control based on the Form Data query's regular Park Rate field (see Figure 10.4).

EXAMINING THE TOOLBOX

You've already learned that Access provides three control types: bound, unbound, and calculated. For each of these control types, Access also provides a selection of control styles. (Your Access documentation makes no distinction between control types and control styles. For the purposes of this book, however, we have defined these two terms separately. A *control type* determines what information a control displays, while a *control style* determines how that information is displayed.)

Before this chapter, the only control styles you saw on forms were text boxes and labels. In Form view, the text-box control style

Figure 10.4   **The Payroll form in Design view**

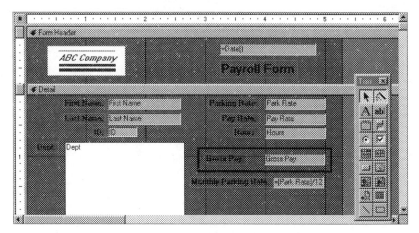

enables you to view, type, and delete values. The label control style displays information, but cannot be edited in Form view.

The Payroll form, however, contains some controls with other styles: The company logo is contained within an unbound object frame control, the rectangle enclosing the Gross Pay field and its label is a rectangle control, and the department codes and names are displayed in a list-box control. Other available control styles include combo boxes (also known as drop-down lists), check boxes, option buttons, toggle buttons, and lines.

Some of these control styles may seem familiar to you because you have seen similar elements in dialog boxes throughout Access. In fact, by using various control styles, you can design forms that look and work much like Access's own dialog boxes. For example, rather than having users type in a department code for an employee record, you can design a form that enables users to select a department from a drop-down list (combo box). Control styles enable you to create enhanced forms that are easy to use, promote data consistency, and look better than forms that use only a few control styles.

To add controls to a form manually, you must use the toolbox. Not to be confused with the toolbar, the toolbox contains specialized tools that enable you to specify the style of control you'd like to add to a form. The toolbox is displayed automatically when you display a form in Design view.

Before we start using the toolbox, let's use Access's Help system to learn more about it:

1. Click on the **Label** tool, then press **F1** to display a description of that tool; then, read the description. (See Figure 10.5 if you cannot locate the Label tool.)

Figure 10.5   **The toolbox**

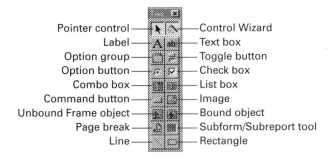

Pointer control —— Control Wizard
Label —— Text box
Option group —— Toggle button
Option button —— Check box
Combo box —— List box
Command button —— Image
Unbound Frame object —— Bound object
Page break —— Subform/Subreport tool
Line —— Rectangle

2. Click on the description window to close it. Click on the **Text Box** tool, then press **F1** and read the description of that tool.

PRACTICE YOUR SKILLS

1. Close the description window.

2. Click on the toolbox's other tools, then press **F1** to read their descriptions.

3. Close the description window and the Form window. (If a dialog box prompts you to save changes, click on **No**.)

ADDING A TEXT-BOX BOUND CONTROL

To add a text-box bound control to a form:

● Open the Form window in Design view.

● Click on the *Text Box* tool (in the toolbox).

● If it is not already open, open the field list by clicking on the *Field List* button (in the toolbar). The field list shows all of the regular and calculated fields from the form's underlying table or query.

- Drag the desired field name from the field list to the desired position on the form. By default, Access automatically adds a label with that field's name next to your new text-box control.

You can also create a bound text-box control without using the field list by clicking on the Text Box tool, clicking on the form to create an unbound text-box control, and then binding the control to a field by setting the control's Control Source property to that field's name. However, using the field list is simpler and enables Access to automatically provide text for the bound control's label.

A more significant advantage of using the field list when adding a bound control is that Access automatically copies the field's properties into the control's properties; this does not happen when you convert an unbound control to a bound control. For example, if you use the field list to add a pay-rate field that is formatted as currency in the form's underlying table or query, Access automatically sets your control's Format property to Currency as well. (All of this happens automatically when you use a Form Wizard.)

Let's add the Form Data query's calculated Gross Pay field to a form:

1. Open the New Payroll form. Like the Payroll form, this form is based on the Form Data query. However, you can see that it does not include a company logo or many of the Payroll form's bound controls and labels.

2. Switch to Design view, and then click on the **Field List** button to display the list of fields from the form's underlying query.

3. In the toolbox, click on the **Text Box** tool. Your mouse pointer changes to crosshairs with the tool's icon attached.

4. Use the pointer to drag **Gross Pay** from the field list to just below the Hours bound control. As you drag, notice that the mouse pointer changes to a field icon. Release the mouse button to place a Gross Pay bound text-box control and its label below the Hours bound text-box control and label.

5. Use the Gross Pay label's *move* handle (the large handle on the label's upper-left corner) to align the label under the Hours label (see Figure 10.6).

6. Close the field list and align the Gross Pay label horizontally, so that the colon (:) is aligned with those above it.

7. Save the form as **My New Payroll**.

Figure 10.6   **The form with the Gross Pay controls added**

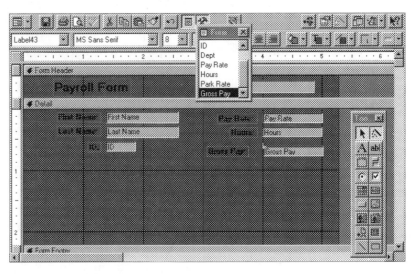

MODIFYING A BOUND CONTROL'S FORMAT PROPERTY

You've learned that if you use the field list when adding a bound control to a form, that control inherits its associated field's properties as control properties. However, Access does not maintain a link between field and control properties. If you change a field property, Access does not automatically change the properties of any existing controls bound to that field. Likewise, if you change a bound control's properties, you do not affect the properties of that control's associated field.

This ability to set control properties independently of field properties provides you with a great deal of freedom in designing forms. For example, suppose you need to design two forms based on the same table: one for top managers, another for line managers. The only difference between the two forms is that top managers can set an employee's pay rate at any level, but line managers cannot assign pay rates of greater than $20 per hour. If you set a validation rule for the pay-rate field in the forms' underlying table, both levels of managers would be bound by the same rule. The solution: Instead of setting the validation rule as a field property in the table, set the validation rule as a control property in the line managers' form, and set no validation rule in the top managers' form.

Another common need for control properties is in handling a query's calculated field. For example, as you've seen throughout this book, whenever you created a calculated gross-pay field by multiplying an hours-worked field and a pay-rate field, Access did not format the gross-pay field as currency. Access does provide a Format function that you can use in a query to control the format of a calculated field. (For more information on the Format function, see your Access documentation.) However, if you plan on using the calculated field on a form anyway, you may find it simpler just to add the calculated field as is to the form, and then change control properties.

Let's take a look at how Access displays the Gross Pay control you just added to your form; then we'll change that display by modifying the control's Format property:

1. Switch to Form view. Notice that the Gross Pay field is not formatted as currency.

2. Switch to the Form Data query, run the query, and observe the resulting datasheet. Here, the Gross Pay field is also not formatted as currency.

3. Switch back to the New Payroll Form window.

4. Now switch to Design view, select the Gross Pay bound control (if necessary), and then open the property sheet for that control.

5. Open the Format property's drop-down list, and select **Currency**. Close the property sheet.

6. Save the form design, and then switch to Form view. Notice that the Gross Pay field's values are now formatted as currency (see Figure 10.7).

7. Switch to the Form Data query and observe the Gross Pay field. You can see that changing the Gross Pay field's Format property in the form did not affect the Gross Pay field here.

ADDING A CALCULATED CONTROL

As you've seen in this and earlier chapters, you can use a query's calculated field to display values on your form that are not stored in any tables. However, to display values on your forms that are neither stored in tables nor calculated through queries, you can use calculated controls.

Figure 10.7   **The Gross Pay field, formatted as currency**

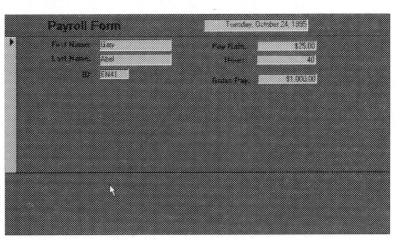

You have seen calculated controls a number of times already in this book: Access uses them to display the current date, page numbers, and summary information. You can create your own calculated controls for these same purposes. You can also use a calculated control in place of a query's calculated field to calculate values from existing fields in a form's underlying table or query.

Calculated controls provide you with a great deal of flexibility: They are not limited by the choice of fields from a form's underlying table or query, and you can modify calculated controls directly from a Form window's Design view rather than modifying the design of the form's underlying table or query.

Because calculated fields and calculated controls have similar names and can perform similar functions, it is easy to confuse the two. Keep in mind that you create calculated fields in a query and calculated controls in a form or report. Also, in a form's design, a calculated field's bound control looks just like a regular field's bound control; a calculated control, on the other hand, displays an expression.

To create a calculated text-box control:

● Display the form in Design view.

● In the toolbox, click on the *Text Box* tool.

- Click on the form where you want to add the control. By default, Access automatically adds a label next to your new control.

- Click in the new unbound text-box control, and type the desired expression to convert the unbound control to a calculated control. Alternatively, you can select the unbound control, open the property sheet (if it isn't already open), and then type the expression in the control's Control Source property box.

You can enter expressions for a calculated text-box control just as you would enter them for a calculated field in a design grid's Field cell. However, calculated-control expressions must begin with an equal sign (=). For example, to create a gross-pay calculated field, you might type *[hours]*[pay rate]*. For a calculated control, you would type this expression as *=[hours]*[pay rate]*. As you've already seen in forms and reports, you can also enter expressions such as *=Now()* and *=Page* to display the current date and page number.

Because Access cannot determine appropriate text for the labels of calculated and unbound controls as it can for bound controls, you might want to provide your own descriptive text.

To change a label's text in Design view:

- Select the label.

- Select the text within the label.

- Type your new text over the selected text.

Let's create a calculated text-box control to display each employee's monthly parking rate:

1. If necessary, switch to the Form Data query's resulting datasheet. Notice that it does not contain a monthly parking rate field. However, it does contain a Park Rate field for annual parking rates.

2. Close the query and return to the Form window. Switch to Design view.

3. In the toolbox, click on the **Text Box** tool; then click just below the Gross Pay bound control. Access places a default-size label and text-box control beneath the Gross Pay bound control and label.

4. Click in the new text-box control; then type **=[park rate]/12** to create a calculated control that calculates a monthly parking rate from the Form Data query's annual Park Rate field.

5. Press **Enter** to select the calculated control, and then open the control's property sheet. Notice that the calculated control's Control Source property contains the same expression you typed directly into the control.

6. Set the calculated control's Format property to **Currency**, and then close the property sheet.

7. Select the calculated control's label, double-click on the label's text to select all of the text except the colon, and then type **Monthly Parking Rate** to provide a more descriptive label for your calculated control. Access automatically expands the label's size to fit the new text.

8. Press **Enter** to select the Monthly Parking Rate label, and then align the label under the Gross Pay label. Compare your screen to Figure 10.8.

Figure 10.8   **The completed Monthly Parking Rate controls**

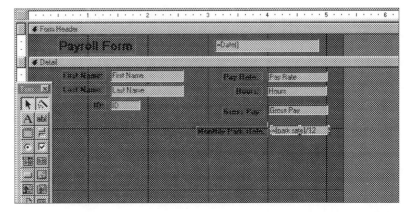

9. Save the form; then switch to Form view.

10. Use the form's navigation buttons to view several records. Access calculates the monthly parking rate for each record (except for records of employees who do not use the parking lots), and formats the result as currency.

ADDING A RECTANGLE CONTROL

You can use rectangle controls on your forms as a design feature, for example, to highlight certain controls or to bring related controls together visually.

To add a rectangle control to a form:

- Display the form in Design view.

- In the toolbox, click on the *Rectangle* tool.

- Position the mouse pointer on the form where you want one of the rectangle control's corners to be, drag to the diagonally opposite corner, and then release the mouse button.

Rectangle controls do not display values. Therefore, you cannot create rectangle controls as bound or calculated controls.

Let's draw a rectangle control around the Gross Pay bound control and label to highlight those controls:

1. Switch to Design view.

2. In the toolbox, click on the **Rectangle** tool. The mouse pointer changes to crosshairs with the tool's icon attached.

3. Position the center of the crosshairs just above and to the left of the Gross Pay label, drag to just below and to the right of the Gross Pay bound control, and then release the mouse button. As you drag, Access displays an outline of your rectangle around the two controls. When you release the button, Access inserts a rectangle control that outlines the Gross Pay bound control and label.

4. Save the form.

ADDING A LIST-BOX CONTROL

Text-box controls are a good way to enter a wide variety of values into fields. For example, you would probably want to use text-box controls for employee names and pay rates because these values vary widely. For a field such as a department field, however, which should contain one of a very limited set of values, you may instead want to use a list-box control.

A list-box control eliminates the need to remember a list of department codes or names, because it lists all of them for you. To set the department field for any employee record, you could then display that record in Form view and simply select the appropriate department.

List-box controls can also help to increase data-entry accuracy. For example, if you use short department codes such as EE, you could easily type DE instead of EE. Because a list-box control would enable you to choose only from a list of preset options, however, it would eliminate this type of error.

List-box controls can also quicken data entry. For example, if you use full department names instead of codes, you may find yourself typing Electrical Engineering or Chemical Engineering over and over. With a list box, you simply click.

When you create a list-box control, you must supply Access with a list of values for that control. One way to provide a source for list-box values is to specify the name of a table or query containing those values in the list-box control's Row Source property box. In Form view, the list box will then display all of the values contained, by default, in that table or query's first field. When you then select a value from the list box while entering records, Access copies that value from the Row Source property's table or query into the form's underlying table or query. For existing records, Access uses the value in the form's underlying table or query to select the matching value in the list box. You can accomplish this most easily by using the List Box Wizard.

To create a list-box control using the List Box Wizard:

- Display the form in Design view.

- With the *Control Wizards* button depressed in the toolbox, click on the *List Box* tool.

- If you want your list-box control to be bound to a field, drag that field's name from the field list to the form. If you want it to be unbound, click on the form. By default, Access adds a label next to your new control.

- Follow the prompts displayed in each pane of the List Box Wizard dialog box.

- After you have answered the prompt in the last pane, click on *Finish*.

Let's create a list-box control bound to the Dept field that displays values from the Dept Codes and Names table:

1. Click on the **List Box** tool.

2. Open the field list (click on the **Field List** button), and drag **Dept** from the field list to about half an inch below the ID bound control (use the on-screen rulers for scale). Because the Control Wizard's toolbox button was depressed before you clicked on the List Box tool, the List Box Wizard dialog box is displayed (see Figure 10.9). The first prompt asks you if you want the data drawn from an existing table or query.

Figure 10.9   **The List Box Wizard dialog box**

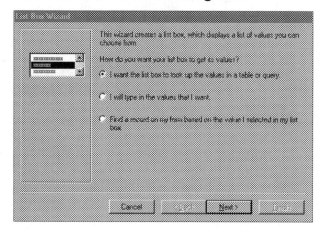

3. Click on **Next** to accept the default setting and open the next pane. You are prompted to select the table to which you want your list box to be tied.

4. Double-click on **Dept Codes and Names** to select the table and open the next pane. (You can see that under View, *Tables* is selected by default.) In the next pane, you are prompted to select the field(s) that contain the values you want to include in the list box.

5. Under *Available Fields*, double-click on **Deptcode** and **Dept-name**. As you double-click on each field name, it is automatically entered under the *Selected Fields box*.

6. Click on **Next** to open the next pane. You are now prompted to adjust the width of the columns. A sample of the list box is displayed. By default the Key column (Deptcode) is hidden. We will leave the Deptcode filed hidden to simplify the list box.

7. In the sample, double-click on the right edge of the Deptname column header. The column width is automatically adjusted for the best fit (see Figure 10.10).

Figure 10.10 **The adjusted column width**

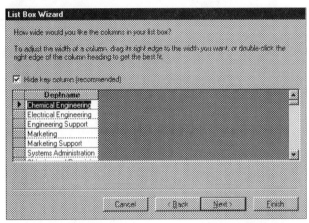

8. Click on **Next** to open the next pane. Now, you're asked to select the field that you want to store or use in your database.

9. Click on **Next** to instruct Access to store the data in the Dept field. The final pane is opened, prompting you to name the list box.

10. Click on **Finish** to accept the default name (Dept). The Dept bound control and label are displayed in the form.

11. Close the Form Data field list, then align the Dept label under the ID label. (You might need to move the toolbox out of the way first.) Then compare your screen to Figure 10.11. (If necessary, move the toolbox back to its original location.)

12. Save the form, and switch to Form view. The department names are displayed in the list box, and a vertical scroll bar has been added to the box (see Figure 10.12).

13. Close the form.

Figure 10.11   The added Dept list box and label

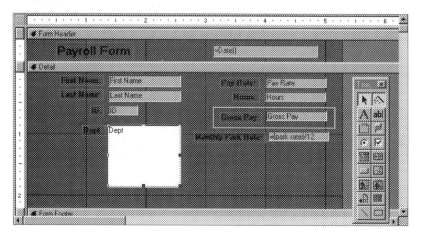

Figure 10.12   The Dept list box in Form view

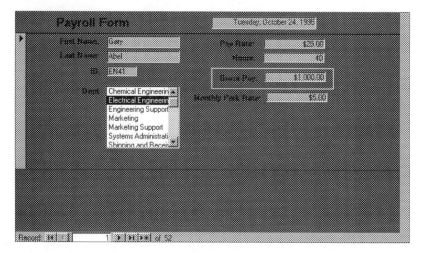

CREATING A FORM THAT CONTAINS A SUBFORM

If you have a one-to-many relationship between tables or queries, you can use a *main form* and a *subform* within a single form window to view both sides of that relationship. (See Chapter 9 for an explanation of one-to-many relationships.) For example, if you have a one-to-many relationship between a department information table and an equipment inventory table, you can use a main form to select a department (the *one* side), and then view that department's equipment inventory in the subform (the *many* side).

To display two forms within a single form window, Access uses a *subform control* on a main form. You can think of a subform control as an intelligent window through which you can view subform data. It's intelligent because, as you move from record to record in the main form, Access automatically applies a filter to the subform so that the latter only displays records relevant to the main form's current record. For example, when you move to the Chemical Engineering department's record in the main form, the equipment inventory subform displays only the Chemical Engineering department's equipment.

 ## EXAMINING A MAIN FORM AND SUBFORM

When Access displays a main form and subform within a single Form window, it provides two sets of record navigation buttons to enable you to scroll through both forms independently. The main form's navigation buttons are at the bottom of the Form window, and the subform's navigation buttons are at the bottom of the subform itself.

Let's take a look at an existing form that contains a subform:

1. Open the **Dept Equipment Purchased** form. The Form window contains two forms: a larger main form, which contains the form title, Department field, and Department label; and a smaller subform, which contains the department's equipment inventory with serial numbers and purchase dates (see Figure 10.13). Notice also the two sets of record navigation buttons. Access displays the main form's navigation buttons at the bottom of the Form window; the subform's navigation buttons are directly beneath the equipment list.

Figure 10.13   The Dept Equipment Purchased form

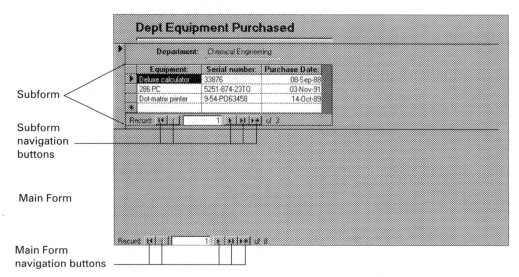

Subform

Subform navigation buttons

Main Form

Main Form navigation buttons

2. Observe the form as you click on the main form's **Next Record** navigation button several times. As the department name changes, the data in the subform also changes to display each department's equipment inventory.

3. Switch to Design view and observe the form design. You can now see more clearly the distinction between the shaded main form and the white Equipment subform control contained within it.

4. Close the Form window.

SETTING UP A ONE-TO-MANY RELATIONSHIP BETWEEN TWO TABLES

In order to create a form containing a subform, the two forms involved must have a relationship established. A one-to-many relationship is the most common type of relationship established among tables and queries. Basically, in a one-to-one relationship a record in one table (A) can have many matching records in another table (B), but a record in Table B has no more than one matching record in Table A.

Relationships are established between tables or queries in the Relationships window. In this window, you can drag a field that you want to relate from one table to another table. The related fields don't have to have the same names, but they must have the same data type and contain the same type of information.

When you close the Relationships window, a dialog box is displayed, asking if you want to save the layout (the way the tables are arranged in the window). The relationships you create are saved in the database, regardless of whether you save the layout or not. If this layout is saved, it will be displayed the next time you display the Relationships button.

Let's establish a relationship between the Dept Codes and Names table and the Equipment table:

1. Make sure that all Table windows are closed. You can't create or modify relationships between open tables.

2. Click on the **Relationship** button to display the Relationships window with the Show Table dialog box opened.

3. In the Show Table dialog box, double-click on **Dept Codes and Names** and **Equipment** to added these two tables to the Relationships window. Close the Show Table dialog box.

4. If a relationship had been established between these two tables, there would already be a line from a field name in one table to a field name in the other table. Since this is not the case, we will set up a relationship now.

5. Drag the **Deptcode** field from the Dept Codes and Names table to the **DeptCode** field in the Equipment table. The Relationships dialog box is displayed.

6. Click on Create to create the relationship. Compare your screen to Figure 10.14.

7. Close the Relationships window. When prompted to save changes to the layout of "Relationships," click on **Yes**.

USING A FORM WIZARD TO CREATE A MAIN FORM AND SUBFORM

The toolbox contains a Subform/Subreport tool, which enables you to add subform controls to a main form's design. However, if you want to create from scratch a main form and subform based

Figure 10.14   The Relationships window

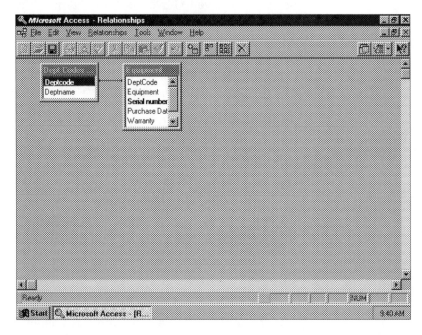

on related tables or queries, you can instead use the Form Wizard. If the table relationships were set up correctly, the Form Wizard handles the details of placing the appropriate controls on the forms and establishing the link between the two forms it creates.

When the Form Wizard completes your forms, it's a good idea to check the subform control's Link Master Fields and Link Child Fields properties. These two control properties determine the link between the two forms' underlying tables or queries. The Link Master Fields property specifies the linking field from the main form's underlying table or queries. The *Link Child Fields* property specifies the linking field from the subform's underlying table or query. If these property boxes are blank, the Form Wizard has not successfully linked the two forms, and your main form and sub-form most likely will not operate together correctly. In that case, you will need to establish the correct linking fields yourself. (For more information on how table relationships affect main forms and subforms, see Access's online Help.)

Let's use the Form Wizard to create a main form and subform to take advantage of the one-to-many relationship between the Dept Codes and Names table and the Equipment table:

1. Open and examine the Equipment table. This table contains information about each department's equipment inventory. Close the table after you have examined it.

2. Display the list of form objects, and click on **New** to begin creating a new form. The New Form dialog box is displayed.

3. Double-click on **Form Wizard** to select Form Wizard and proceed to the first pane of the Wizard dialog box.

4. In the Tables/Queries drop-down list, select **Table: Dept Codes and Names** as the data source for the main form.

5. Move **Deptname** to the Selected Fields list (double-click on **Deptname**). Now you will pick a data source for the subform, along with the fields you want to include.

6. In the Table/Queries drop-down list, select **Table: Equipment** as the data source for the subform.

7. Move **Equipment**, **Serial Number**, and **Purchase Date** to the Selected Fields list. Click on **Next** to advance to the next pane.

8. Because we set up the relationship between the Equipment and the Dept Codes and Names tables, the Wizard asks which table you want to view by. Verify that **by Dept Codes and Names** is selected. Also verify that **the Form with subform(s)** option is selected. Click on **Next** to advance to the next pane.

9. Verify that the Datasheet option is selected as the layout for your subform. Click on **Next** to advance to the next pane.

10. Select **Standard** as the style (if necessary), then click on **Next** to advance to the last **Wizard** pane.

11. Change the suggested Form title to **My Dept Equipment Purchased**, and the Subform title to **My Equipment Subform**. Click on **Finish**.

12. Observe the Form window. It contains a main form and a subform.

13. Switch to Design view. Then open and observe the My Equipment subform control's property sheet (select the control first). Move the property sheet next to the toolbox (at the right of the window). Notice that the Link Child Fields property is set

to the subform table's DeptCode field, and the Link Master Fields property is set to the main form table's Deptcode field, indicating that the Form Wizard has successfully linked the main form and subform (see Figure 10.15).

Figure 10.15   **Verifying that the main form and subform have been linked**

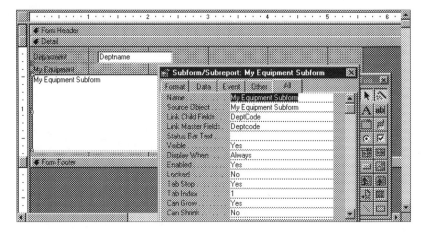

14. Close the property sheet and switch to Form view.

15. Click on the main form's **Next Record** navigation button several times. Like the Form window you saw earlier, as this window displays each department's name in the main form, it displays that department's equipment inventory in the subform.

16. Save the main form; then close the form. Notice that the Database window displays the names of the two forms you just created: *My Dept Equipment Purchased* and *My Equipment Subform.*

SUMMARY

In this chapter, you learned how to use control properties and various control styles to enhance the look and performance of your forms. You also learned how to use the Form Wizard to create two forms that work together in a single Form window.

Here's a quick reference guide to the Access features introduced in this chapter:

Desired Result	How to Do It
Display control's properties	In Design view, select desired control, and click on **Properties** button
Modify control's properties	Change desired property in control's property sheet
Display field list	In Design view, click on **Field List** button
Add text-box bound control to form	In Design view, click on Text Box tool, and drag desired field name from field list to form
Create calculated textbox control	In Design view, click on **Text Box** tool, click on form to add unbound control, click in unbound control, and type calculation expression
Modify label's text	In Design view, select label, and replace label's text as desired
Add rectangle control to form	In Design view, click on **Rectangle** tool, click mouse button at desired location on form, and size rectangle object using handles
Add list-box bound control to form	In Design view, make sure Control Wizard's tool is selected, click on **List Box** tool, and drag desired field name from field list to form; answer List Box Wizard prompts as desired; when completed, click on **Finish**
Set up one to-many relationship between two tables	Make sure all tables are closed, click on **Relationships** button, double-click on tables you want to establish link between, close Show Table dialog box, drag field from one table to field in other table, click on **Create**, close Relationships window
Create main form and subform	Display list of form object names, click on **New**, click on **Form Wizard**, and click on **OK**; select tables and fields that you want to appear, answer Form Wizard prompts as desired; when completed, click on **Finish**

In the next chapter, you'll learn how to use macros and command buttons to open and synchronize forms automatically.

CHAPTER 11: USING MACROS WITH FORMS

Creating a
Macro to Open a
Form Window

Creating a
Command Button
to Run a Macro

Synchronizing
Forms

Controlling Form
Window Placement

Macros are database objects that you can use to automate Access. For example, if you need to run a query and then print a report every time you open a certain database, you can create a macro to perform those tasks for you automatically.

Macros list a series of steps called *actions.* A single macro action, for example, can print a report. When you run a macro, Access uses it as a to-do list to perform that macro's actions in the order in which they are listed. The advantages of using macros over running the actions manually are twofold: Macros automate repetitive tasks, and they help ensure that those tasks are performed consistently and completely each time.

You can use macros in an almost unlimited number of ways to automate and customize Access. In this chapter, you'll discover the very basics of macros by learning how to create and use a simple macro that opens one Form window from within another Form window.

When you're done working through this chapter, you will know

- How to use a command button to run a macro from a Form window

- How to create a macro to open a Form window

- How to add a command button control to a form

- How to use a macro to synchronize two forms

- How to use a macro to control the placement of a Form window

CREATING A MACRO TO OPEN A FORM WINDOW

Macros can perform many of the steps you would perform manually while working with a database. Among other things, macro actions can

- Open a window

- Close a window

- Find a record

- Apply a filter

- Print an object

- Run a query

Access supplies over 40 macro actions; the two macro actions you'll learn about in this chapter are the *OpenForm* action, which opens a Form window, and the *MoveSize* action, which controls the placement and position of a window. (You'll learn how to get information about other macro actions later in this chapter.)

In Chapter 10, you learned how to use a main form and subform to view data from two forms in a single Form window. If you'd prefer, however, you can use a macro to view data from two forms in *separate* Form windows. For example, if you regularly use a form to enter and review employee records, you might want to open a second Form window in order to see the name of the current employee's manager.

Using a macro to view data in two separate Form windows provides two advantages over using a main form and subform:

- Because the Form windows are separate, you can move through records in either form independently.

- Using the above example, because Access does not need to determine and display the correct manager record for each and every employee record, you can scroll through employee records more quickly, viewing manager names only as needed.

Throughout this book, we have instructed you to maximize all Database windows and, when necessary, object windows. By maximizing windows, you reduce screen clutter and increase the available amount of window space for each object. At times, however, it's beneficial not to maximize windows; for example, when you want to view data in two Form windows at once. As you continue through this chapter, you'll learn some other advantages of working with nonmaximized windows.

To restore a maximized Database or object window to its former (nonmaximized) size, click on the window's Restore button. As you've no doubt already noticed, when you restore one Database or object window in Access, all Database and object windows are restored. When you maximize a Database or object window, all Database and object windows are maximized.

RUNNING A MACRO WITH A FORM'S COMMAND BUTTON

Access provides many ways to run macros, both from Database and object windows. One way of running a macro from a Form window is by using a command button that is bound to the macro. (You'll learn how to create your own command button control later in this chapter.)

If you do not have both the Access application and the Company Database windows opened and maximized, please open and maximize them now.

Let's work with a form that contains a command button that opens a second Form window:

1. Open the Payroll Managers form. Notice that the form contains a command button titled *Manager*. Notice also that the current record is of Gary Abel (Record 1), who works in the Electrical Engineering department.

2. Click on the Form window's **Restore** button to restore the window to its nonmaximized size, if necessary. It no longer completely fills the application window.

3. Click on the **Manager** command button. The Dept Managers form opens to display the manager of the Electrical Engineering department (see Figure 11.1). You may need to move the Dept Manager's dialog box up a bit in order to see the data. (You will learn how to fix this problem later in this chapter.)

Figure 11.1   **The Payroll Managers and Dept Managers forms**

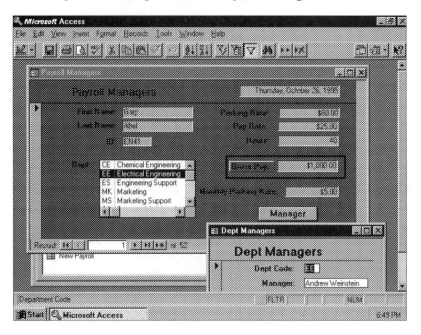

4. In the Payroll Managers form, view the next record, that of Murray Abel (Record 2), who works in the Chemical Engineering department.

5. Click on the **Manager** command button. The Dept Managers form now displays the manager of the Chemical Engineering department.

6. Close the Dept Managers form.

 EXAMINING A MACRO'S DESIGN

To determine the name of the macro that a command button runs when clicked, you can examine the command button control's *On Click* property, which determines what happens when you click on that button. You can view the properties of a command button control as you would any other control on a form:

• Switch to the form's Design view.

• Select the control.

• Open the control's property sheet.

Once you have determined the name of the macro, you can examine its design by opening the macro in Design view.

To open a macro in Design view:

• Click on the *Macro's* tab in the Database window to display the list of macro objects.

• Select the desired macro object.

• Click on *Design*.

Earlier, you learned that a macro lists macro actions, a series of steps to be performed. A macro in Design view lists these actions in the order in which they should be performed. As in the Design views of tables and queries, a macro in Design view is divided into an upper and a lower pane. The upper pane contains *Action cells* for specifying macro actions and *Comment cells* for your (optional) comments about those actions. The lower pane contains *argument boxes*, which enable you to specify arguments for each macro action. Arguments are similar to field and control properties: They determine the behavior of each action.

Let's examine the Manager command button control's On Click property to determine the macro that the command button runs, and then examine the design of that macro:

1. Maximize the Payroll Managers form, and switch to Design view.

2. Select the **Manager** command button control, and open the control's property sheet. Scroll to view the control's On Click property; notice that it is set to *Managers*, which is a macro (see Figure 11.2).

Figure 11.2   **The Manager control's properties**

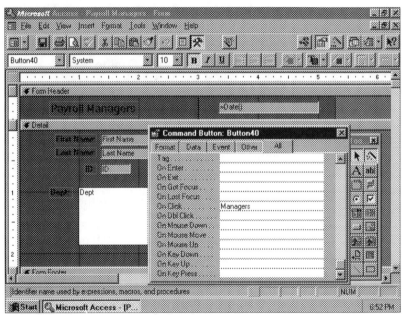

3. Close the property sheet, and then close the form.

4. In the Database window, click the **Macros** tab to display the list of macro objects. The Company database contains only one macro: *Managers.*

5. Click on **Design** to open the Managers macro in Design view. Notice that the Macro window is divided into an upper and lower pane. The upper pane lists the two actions that make

up the Managers macro: The *OpenForm* action opens the Dept Managers form, and the *MoveSize* action controls the placement of the form's window. Because the OpenForm Action cell is selected, the lower pane displays arguments for that action (see Figure 11.3).

6. Close the macro.

Figure 11.3 **The Managers macro OpenForm action arguments**

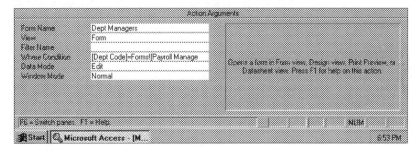

CREATING AND RUNNING A MACRO

Now that you've seen a macro in action and in design, you are ready to create and run your own macro. By the end of this chapter, your macro will perform the same tasks that the existing Managers macro performs: It will open the Dept Managers form, display the current employee's manager in that window, and move the window to the lower-right corner of your screen.

The first step in creating a new macro is to open a new Macro window. To open a new macro:

•Display the list of macro objects.

•Click on *New*.

Once you've opened a new macro, you can begin building the macro by specifying actions in the macro's Action cells. Like many cells you've seen throughout Access, each of a macro's Action cells displays a drop-down list, which enables you to select a macro action. (For information on macro actions not covered in this book, press F1 when an Action cell is selected.) Once you've selected an action, Access will display that action's relevant argument boxes in the Macro window's lower pane (as you saw in the previous exercise).

When your Database and object windows are not maximized, Access provides other alternatives for adding actions to macros. For example, if you want your macro to open a particular form, you can drag that form's object name from the Database window directly to an Action cell in your Macro window. When you do so, Access selects the OpenForm action and specifies that form's name automatically in the action's Form Name argument box.

To use this shortcut, you need to be able to view both the form object name in the Database window and the appropriate Action cell in the macro. One way to neatly arrange and view multiple windows—maximized or not—is to choose Window, Tile Horizontally or Tile Vertically. These commands tile all of the open windows so that they do not overlap one another. If necessary, you can use the scroll bars to scroll the desired area into view.

The Windows, Cascade command offers another way to arrange open windows neatly. This command arranges all open windows in an overlapping fashion, keeping each window's title bar visible. To activate any one of a set of cascaded windows, you need only click on its title bar.

Once you've added an action to a macro, you can test the macro from its window by clicking on the Run button in the toolbar.

Let's create a new macro and use the dragging method just described to instruct that macro to open the Dept Managers Form window:

1. In the Database window, display the list of macro objects. Click on **New** to open a new macro.

2. In the first Action cell, open the drop-down list and choose **OpenForm** (you'll need to scroll). In the lower pane, you can see that Access has automatically supplied default values for the View, Data Mode, and Window Mode arguments. However, it has not supplied a value for the Form Name argument.

3. Delete the OpenForm action (press **Delete**).

4. Choose **Window, Tile Vertically**. The Database and Macro windows are displayed side by side.

5. In the Database window, display the list of form objects. Then drag the **Dept Managers** form object name from the Database window to the first Action cell in the Macro window. The OpenForm action is added to the Action cell, and the action's Form Name argument is automatically set to *Dept Managers* (see Figure 11.4).

Figure 11.4 **The results of dragging the Dept Managers form object to the macro**

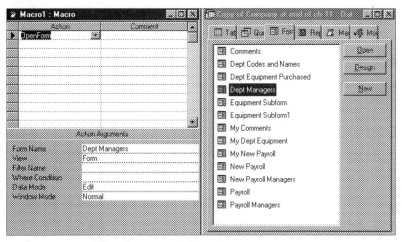

6. Save the macro as **My Managers**.

7. Run the macro (click on the **Run** button). The Dept Managers form is opened.

8. Close the form and the macro.

CREATING A COMMAND BUTTON TO RUN A MACRO

As you learned earlier in this chapter, once you have created and saved a macro, you can use a command button on a form to run that macro.

Using the techniques you learned in Chapter 10, you could manually add a command button control to a form by opening the Form window in Design view, opening the form's toolbox, clicking on the toolbox's Command button tool, clicking on the form to add an unbound command button control, and then setting the appropriate control properties to bind that control to the macro and provide the appropriate text for the face of the button. (For example, the Manager command button you used earlier was so titled because it ran a macro to display the name of the current employee's manager.)

Another alternative is to drag the macro's object name from the Database window to the location on the form design where you want to place the command button control. When you do, Access automatically creates a command button control, binds that control to the macro for you, and displays the name of the macro on the control's face. For macros with long names, Access sometimes displays only part of the macro's name; if this creates a problem, you can enlarge the control or select and edit the control's text.

ADDING A COMMAND BUTTON CONTROL TO A FORM

Let's use the dragging method described earlier to add to a form a command button that will run the My Managers macro:

1. Open the **New Payroll Managers** form in Design view. This form is similar to the My New Payroll form you created in Chapter 10.

2. Tile the open windows vertically (choose **Window, Tile Vertically**).

3. In the form, scroll to the right until the space below the Monthly Parking Rate controls is visible.

4. In the Database window, display the list of macro objects, and then drag the **My Managers** macro object from the Database window to the space on the form below the Monthly Parking Rate controls.

5. Access creates a command button control titled *My* (see Figure 11.5).

Figure 11.5   **The added My command button control**

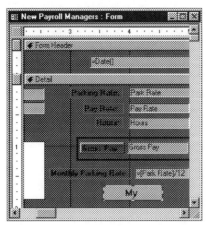

6. Click on the new **My** control to display the entire macro name, *My Managers*; then delete the word *My* to change the control's caption to *Managers*.

7. Press **Enter** to select the command button control; then open the control's property sheet. Notice that the On Click property is automatically set to *My Managers*. (You may need to scroll down to see it.)

8. Close the property sheet and save the form as **My Payroll Managers**.

TESTING THE COMMAND BUTTON

Now let's test our new command button to see how it works:

1. Choose **Window, Cascade** to layer the Form window over the Database window.

2. Display the form in Form view. The form displays the record for Gary Abel (Record 1), who works in the Electrical Engineering department.

3. Click on the **Managers** command button. The My Managers macro opens the Dept Managers form. Notice that the Dept Code control (CE) on the Dept Managers form does not match the Dept control (EE) on the My Payroll Managers form.

4. In the Dept Managers form, display the next record. The Dept Managers form now displays the correct manager.

5. In the My Payroll Managers form, display the next record, that of Murray Abel (Record 2), who works in the Chemical Engineering department.

6. Click on the **Managers** command button, and observe the Dept Managers form. The form does not automatically move to the record for the Chemical Engineering department manager. (We'll fix this problem in the next exercise.)

7. Close the Dept Managers form.

SYNCHRONIZING FORMS

As you can see from the last exercise, using a macro in one form to open a second form does not guarantee that the second form will display the record(s) relevant to the record in the first form.

When you used the Form Wizard to create a main form and sub-form in Chapter 10, the Form Wizard automatically synchronized the two forms so that the records in the subform were always relevant to the record in the main form. To accomplish the same thing using a macro and two forms, you need to use the OpenForm action's Where Condition argument in the macro's design.

SETTING THE WHERE CONDITION ARGUMENT

To synchronize two forms using the OpenForm action's Where Condition argument, you write an expression in the Where Condition argument box that equates a control on one form with a control on the other form (much as you would use two fields to create a relationship between two tables). This argument then behaves like a filter on the form that the action opens; the second form will display only those records that are relevant to the current record in the first form.

For example, suppose that you want the My Managers macro, run from the My Payroll Managers form, to open the Dept Managers form and display the correct department-manager name. To do so, you would set a Where Condition expression in the macro's design to equate the My Payroll Managers form's Dept control with the Dept Managers form's Dept Code control.

A Where Condition expression has two parts separated by an equal sign (=). On the right side of the equal sign, you specify the linking control on the form that controls the synchronization—that is, the form from which you run the macro. Using the previous example, that would be the Dept control on the My Payroll Managers form, because this form contains the macro's command button. On the left side of the equal sign, you specify the linking control on the form that the macro's OpenForm action opens. In this example, that would be the Dept Code control on the Dept Managers form. In the simplest of terms, then, your Where Condition expression would be

```
[Dept Code]=[Dept]
```

Because the macro's OpenForm action opens the Dept Managers form, Access assumes that the left side of this expression refers to the Dept Code control on that form. From this expression, however, Access cannot determine which form contains the Dept control. Therefore, you need to be more specific about the Dept control by using the following syntax:

```
Forms![formname]![controlname]
```

In the example we've been using, the Where Condition argument would therefore be

```
[Dept Code]=Forms![My Payroll Managers]![Dept]
```

Let's use this expression in the My Managers macro to synchronize the two forms:

1. Activate the Database window, and open the My Managers macro in Design view.

2. In the OpenForm action's Where Condition argument box, type **[Dept Code]=Forms![My Payroll Managers]![Dept]** to link the Dept Code control on the Dept Managers form to the Dept control on the My Payroll Managers form.

3. Save the revised macro; then close it.

4. Activate the My Payroll Managers form and move to Gary Abel's record (Record 1). Notice that Gary works in the Electrical Engineering department.

5. Click on the **Managers** command button. The Dept Managers form opens and automatically displays the record for the Electrical Engineering department manager (see Figure 11.6).

6. In the My Payroll Managers form, move to Murray Abel's record (Record 2). Notice that Murray works in the Chemical Engineering department.

7. Click on the **Managers** command button. The Dept Managers form now displays the record of the Chemical Engineering department manager.

PRACTICE YOUR SKILLS

1. Navigate through several records in the My Payroll Managers form, using the Managers command button on each record to test your macro.

2. In the My Payroll Managers form, return to Gary Abel's record (Record 1), and display the name of his manager. Your screen should once again resemble Figure 11.6.

Figure 11.6 **The synchronized forms**

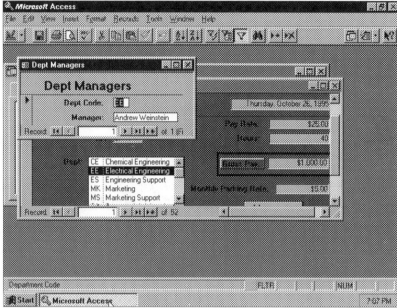

CONTROLLING FORM WINDOW PLACEMENT

When you use a macro's OpenForm action to open one form from another, Access by default places the new form over the upper-left corner of the existing one. This can be inconvenient if the new window blocks important controls on the existing window; each time you run the macro, you may need to move the new window manually to uncover those controls in the existing window.

When you ran the Managers macro earlier in this chapter, the macro automatically placed the Dept Managers form in the lower-right corner of the screen so that the window did not block controls in the Payroll Managers form. It accomplished this through the MoveSize action, which enables a macro to control both the placement and size of any window it opens.

The MoveSize action has four arguments:

- The *Right* argument controls the horizontal position of the new window, measured from the existing window's left edge.

- The *Down* argument controls the window's vertical position, measured from the existing window's top edge.

- The *Width* argument controls the window's width.

- The *Height* argument controls the window's height.

If you leave any of these arguments blank, Access uses defaults to determine the new window's position and size.

Because the Dept Managers form is already a good size, we'll leave the Width and Height arguments blank. However, we'll set the Right and Down arguments so that the form no longer blocks the My Payroll Managers form:

1. Observe the Dept Managers form. It may block Gary Abel's name and ID code controls (see Figure 11.6).

2. Switch to the Database window, and open the My Managers macro in Design view.

3. In the second Action cell, select **MoveSize** from the drop-down list. Observe the action's argument boxes. The MoveSize action enables you to specify the position and size of the Form window that the OpenForm action opens.

4. In the Right argument box, type **3.25** to instruct the macro to position the Dept Managers form $3^1/4$ inches to the right of the My Payroll Managers form's left border.

5. In the Down argument box, type **2.5** to instruct the macro to position the Dept Managers form $2^1/2$ inches down from the My Payroll Managers form's top border.

6. Save the revised macro; then close it.

7. Activate the My Payroll Managers form and click on the form's **Managers** command button. The macro opens the Dept Managers form in the lower-right corner of the screen. It no longer completely blocks any control on the My Payroll Manager's form (see Figure 11.7).

8. Close both forms; then close the Database window.

PRACTICE YOUR SKILLS

In Chapter 10, you learned how to use control properties and various control styles to enhance the look and performance of your forms, and how to use the Form Wizard to create two forms that work together in a single Form window. In this chapter, you learned how to create and use a macro to open, synchronize, and

Figure 11.7   **The Dept Managers form in its new position**

control the position of one Form window from within another Form window. The following two activities give you an opportunity to apply some of these techniques.

In this activity, you will add to a form a list box that displays health-company options:

1. Open the Practice database file and maximize the Database window (Chapter 2).

2. Open and examine the **Health Plan** form, and then display the form in Design view (Chapter 6).

3. Use the List Box Wizard to place below the form's First Name controls a list-box control that is bound to the Health field (Chapter 10). Create the list-box control according to the following criteria:

   • Use the **Health Codes** and **Names** table.

   • Select both the **Health Code** and **Health Carrier** fields.

   • Uncheck the Hide key column choice.

   • Size the columns for the best fit.

- Instruct the List Box Wizard to remember the **Health Code** column for later use.

- Name the label **Health Company**.

4. Size the label to make all of its text visible (Chapter 10).

5. Save the form as **My Health Plan** (Chapter 10).

6. Switch to Form view and compare your form to Figure 11.8 (Chapter 6).

Figure 11.8   The completed My Health Plan form

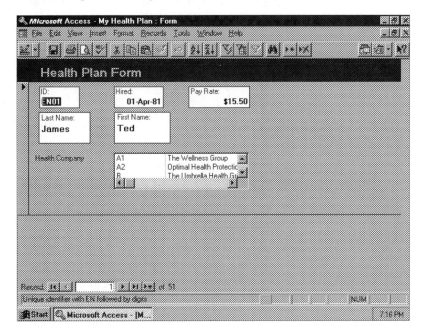

7. Close the form (Chapter 2).

In the next activity, you will create a macro and command button control to open one Form window from within another, synchronize the forms, and position the new Form window:

1. Open and examine both the **Vendor Contacts** and **Equipment** forms (Chapter 2).

2. Save the Equipment form as **My Equipment**, and then close both forms (Chapter 3).

3. Open a new Macro window, and tile the Database and Macro windows vertically.

4. Drag the **Vendor Contacts** form object from the Database window to the macro's first Action cell.

5. In the OpenForm action's Where Condition argument box, type an expression that equates the Code control on the Vendor Contacts form with the Vendor Code control on the My Equipment form.

6. Save the macro as **My Vendor**, and then close the macro.

7. Open the **My Equipment** form in Design view, and tile the Form and Database windows.

8. By dragging the **My Vendor** macro object from the Database window, add a My Vendor command button control directly under the My Equipment form's Vendor Code controls.

9. Change the My Vendor command button's caption to **Vendor**.

10. Save your form design changes, and cascade the Form and Database windows.

11. Display the form in Form view, and test the command button.

12. Close the Vendor Contacts form, and open the **My Vendor** macro in Design view.

13. Add the **MoveSize** action to the macro's second Action cell, set the action's Right argument to **3** and its Down argument to **1.5**, save the macro, and then close the macro.

14. Activate the My Equipment form, click on the **Vendor** command button, and compare your screen to Figure 11.9.

15. Close both forms and the Database window (Chapter 2).

SUMMARY

In this chapter, you learned how to use a command button from within one form to run a macro that opens a second form. You also learned how to create your own macro by setting macro actions and arguments for those actions, and how to add a command button to a form that enables you to run the macro.

Figure 11.9 **The Form windows after clicking on the Vendor command button**

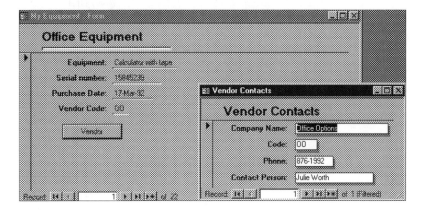

Here's a quick reference guide to the Access features introduced in this chapter:

Desired Result	How to Do It
View macro design	Select macro object, and click on **Design**
Open new Macro window	Display list of macro objects, and click on **New**
Design macro	Set macro actions in Macro window's Action cells, and set arguments for each action as necessary
Add OpenForm action to macro	Use Action cell's drop-down list to select **OpenForm** action, and set action's Form Name argument to form name; or, drag form object name from Database window to Action cell in Macro window
Tile open windows	Choose **Window, Tile Horizontally**, or **Window, Tile Vertically**
Run macro	In Macro window, click on **Run** button; from Form window, click on appropriate command button; from Database window, select macro object, and click on **Run** button

Desired Result	How to Do It
Add command button control to form	In Design view, drag macro object name from Database window to Form window
Change command button control's caption	In Design view, select command button control, select existing text, and type new text
Cascade open windows	Choose **Window, Cascade**
Synchronize two forms	In design of macro that opens one of the forms, set OpenForm action's Where Condition argument to expression that equates the two forms' common controls
Use macro to control window placement	In design of the macro that opens window, add **MoveSize** action, and set action's Right and Down arguments as desired

In Chapter 12, you'll learn how to enhance a report by creating calculated controls, by changing the report's page layout, and by adding a line control to separate visually the groups within that report. You'll also learn how to use the Mailing Label Report Wizard to create a mailing-label report based on a table, and then change that report's design in order to base that report on a query.

CHAPTER 12: ENHANCED REPORT DESIGN

Adding Controls
to a Report

Changing a
Report's Page
Layout

Creating Mailing-
Label Reports

In Chapter 7, you learned how to use the Report Wizard to create reports, and how to modify a report's design by using the toolbar to change some control properties. In Chapter 10, you learned how to use the property sheet to modify control properties in a form, and how to use the toolbox to add controls to a form. In this chapter, you are going to combine these skills with new skills to modify and enhance an existing report's design, and to create two mailing-label reports.

When you're done working through this chapter, you will know

- How to add a line control to a report

- How to add calculated controls to a report

- How to change a report's page layout

- How to use the Mailing Labels Report Wizard to create a mailing-label report

- How to change a report's record source

ADDING CONTROLS TO A REPORT

Most of the techniques you learned in Chapter 10 for adding controls to forms also apply to adding controls to reports. However, a report's different sections are more varied and more critical to a report design than a form's sections are to its design. Therefore, it's important to understand how a report design's different sections affect controls contained in those sections before you start adding controls to a report.

As you learned in Chapter 7, each report usually has at least five sections:

- A Report Header section, which contains controls that print at the beginning of the report

- A Page Header section, which contains controls that print at the beginning of each page

- A Detail section, which contains controls that print once for each record in the report's underlying table or query

- A Page Footer section, which contains controls that print at the bottom of each page

- A Report Footer section, which contains controls that print at the end of the report

A grouped report's design will also include a group header and group footer section for each of the report's grouping levels.

As you can see, some sections, such as the Report Header and Report Footer sections, use controls only once, while other sections, such as the Detail section, use controls over and over. Therefore, *where* you place a new control on a report will determine how often that report will use the control. For a calculated control that uses field values in its calculations, the placement of a control is particularly critical, not only for how often the control prints, but for what field values the control uses. For example, a calculated control in a Detail section uses field values from one record at a time, a calculated control in a group header or footer section uses field values from every record in that group, and a calculated control in a Report Footer section uses field values from every record in that report.

In this chapter, we'll add both unbound and calculated controls to different report sections to see how placement affects a control's use and behavior.

 ## ADDING A LINE CONTROL TO A REPORT

In Chapter 10, you learned how to add a rectangle control to a form. You also learned that a rectangle control is always an unbound control because it cannot display data but is instead used for its visual effect.

Access also offers a *line control*, which operates like the rectangle control but displays straight lines instead of rectangles. Your line control can be vertical, horizontal, or slanted at any angle. Because it can be difficult to drag a perfectly horizontal or vertical line control, you can use the Shift key while adding a line control to force the control to be perfectly horizontal or vertical.

To add a horizontal line control to a form:

- Display the report in Design view.

- Press and hold the *Shift* key.

- Click on the *Line* tool in the toolbox.

- Position the mouse pointer on the report where you want the line control to begin.

- Press and hold the mouse button and drag horizontally to where you want the line to end. Release the mouse button, and then release the Shift key.

As you have learned, where you place the line control determines where and how often that control will print. In the following exercise, you will add a line control at the bottom of a group footer section so that the line prints once at the end of each group.

If you do not have both the Access application and the Company Database windows opened and maximized, please open and maximize them now.

Let's preview a report with two line controls that each print once for each page; then we'll add a third line control that prints once for each group:

1. From the Database window, preview and observe the Pay Rates and Hours report. Horizontal lines are displayed above and below the column headings at the top of each page (see Figure 12.1).

Figure 12.1   **The previewed Pay Rates and Hours report**

Pay Rates and Hours				*Monday, October 30, 1995*	
Dept	First Name	Last Name	Pay Rate	Hours	Gross Pay
CE					
	Murray	Abel	$12.50	35.5	
	Ken	Beasley	$22.50	40	
	Bruce	Cassada	$21.50	40	
	Bill	Conner	$19.50	40	
	Hugh	Jones	$17.25	40	

2. Close the report; then reopen the Pay Rates and Hours report in Design view. Notice that the Page Header section contains two line controls above and below the column-heading controls.

3. Press and hold the **Shift** key, and then click on the **Line** tool in the toolbox. Your mouse pointer should change to crosshairs with the Line control icon attached.

4. While still holding Shift, place the mouse pointer near the lower-left corner of the Dept Footer section, press and hold the mouse button, drag horizontally to the 5-inch mark on the horizontal ruler, release the mouse button, and then release Shift. A perfectly horizontal line control appears in the Dept Footer section of the report (see Figure 12.2).

Figure 12.2   **The added line control**

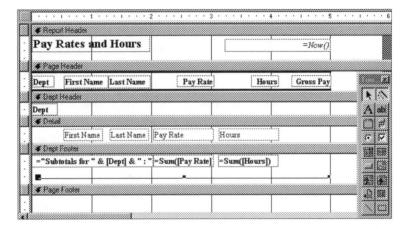

5. Preview and observe the report. It now includes horizontal lines that separate the department groups. (You'll need to scroll to see the lines.)

6. Save the report as **My Pay Rates and Hours**.

ADDING A CONTROL TO PERFORM A HORIZONTAL CALCULATION

In Chapter 5, you learned that you can use queries to perform both horizontal calculations (those that use field values within a single record) and vertical calculations (those that use field values from a group of records). In Chapter 10, we created calculated controls that performed horizontal calculations on forms. In reports, however, you can use calculated controls to perform both horizontal and vertical calculations. The placement of calculated controls determines whether the control can perform a horizontal or vertical calculation. To have a calculated control perform a horizontal calculation, place it in the Detail section.

For the most part, you can use calculated controls that perform horizontal calculations in place of a control bound to a query's calculated field. As you learned in Chapter 10, calculated controls save you the trouble of opening the design of an underlying query, creating a calculated field there, and then creating a control bound to that calculated field.

To add a calculated text-box control that performs a horizontal calculation:

- In a report's Design view, add an unbound text-box control and label to the Detail section and then, if desired, delete the unbound control's label.

- Select the unbound control; then click to place the insertion point in the control.

- Type a calculation expression that includes field names. Because this is a calculated control, remember to begin the expression with an equal sign. For example, an expression that multiplies the Pay Rate field by the Hours field would be =[Pay Rate]*[Hours].

- If you like, change the control's properties and position so that it displays its values appropriately and understandably. For example, if the control is to display dollar amounts, set the control's Format property to Currency.

Because our current report's underlying Report Data query does not have a gross-pay field, let's create a calculated field that calculates each employee's gross pay:

1. Observe the previewed report's Gross Pay column. It does not contain any values.

2. Close the preview window, then reopen the Pay Rates and Hours report in Design view. Observe that the Detail section of the report does not include a gross-pay control.

3. Open and observe the field list. The report's underlying Report Data query does not contain a gross-pay field. Close the field list.

4. To the right of the Detail section's Hours bound control, add an unbound text-box control and label. (Click on the **Text Box** tool, and then click in the Detail section.)

5. Select and delete your unbound control's label, and then select your unbound control.

6. Type =[pay rate]*[hours] to convert your unbound control to a calculated control that will display each employee's gross pay.

7. Press Enter to select the control, and then open and observe the control's property sheet. Notice that the control's Control Source property is set to the same expression you typed directly into the control.

8. Set the Format property to Currency, and then close the property sheet.

9. Align your control's right edge with the horizontal ruler's 5-inch mark. Then use the control's lower-left sizing handle to size the control to about 3/4-inch wide, so that it no longer overlaps the Hours bound control.

10. Preview and observe your report. Your new calculated control displays the gross pay for each employee (see Figure 12.3). Close the preview window (click on the Close button in the middle of the toolbar).

Figure 12.3   **The report with displayed gross-pay values**

Pay Rates and Hours   *Monday, October 30, 1995*

Dept	First Name	Last Name	Pay Rate	Hours	Gross Pay
CE					
	Murray	Abel	$12.50	35.5	$443.75
	Ken	Beasley	$22.50	40	$900.00
	Bruce	Cassada	$21.50	40	$860.00
	Bill	Conner	$19.50	40	$780.00
	Hugh	Jones	$17.25	40	$690.00
	Suzanne	Better	$21.50	40	$860.00

ADDING A CONTROL TO PERFORM A VERTICAL CALCULATION

To create a calculated control that performs a vertical calculation, place that control in the Report Header or Footer section, or in a group header or footer section. A calculated control in a Report Header or Footer section will use fields from every record in the report. A calculated control in a group header or footer section will use only the fields from records in that group. For example, the calculated control *=Avg([Pay Rate])* averages Pay Rate fields. In a Report Header or Footer section, it would average the Pay Rate fields of every record in the report; the same control in a group header or footer section would average the Pay Rate fields for each group separately.

Because calculated controls that perform vertical calculations provide summary, or *aggregate*, information, they use aggregate functions such as the Sum function, which totals values, and the Avg function, which averages values. (For a review of aggregate functions, see Chapter 5.)

In Chapter 7, Report Wizards automatically created calculated controls with aggregate functions. In this chapter, you'll create these controls manually. To use an aggregate function in a calculated control, use the syntax *=function(argument)*. For example, to use the Sum function to total the Hours field, use the expression =Sum([Hours]).

Besides using single fields, you can use expressions as a function's argument; for example,

```
=Sum([Hours]*1.07) or =Avg([Hours]* [Pay Rate])
```

Let's use the Sum function in a calculated control to total our entire report's gross-pay costs:

1. Observe the *=Sum([Pay Rate])* and *=Sum([Hours])* calculated controls in the Dept Footer section. They perform vertical calculations to total each department's Pay Rate and Hours fields. The =Sum([Pay Rate]) and =Sum([Hours]) calculated controls in the Report Footer section perform vertical calculations to total every Pay Rate and Hours field in the report.

2. Add an unbound text box and label directly to the right of the Report Footer section's =Sum([Hours]) calculated control.

3. Delete the new unbound control's label, and then select the unbound control. Type **=sum([pay rate]* [hours])** to convert

your unbound control into a calculated control that totals the overall gross-pay costs for every employee in the report.

4. Press **Enter** to select your calculated control. Then open the control's property sheet, set the control's Format property to **Currency**, and close the property sheet.

5. Make your calculated control's text bold (click on the **Bold** toolbar button).

6. Align your control's right edge with the horizontal ruler's 5-inch mark. Then use the control's lower-left sizing handle to size the control to about $^3/_4$ -inch wide, so that it no longer overlaps the =Sum([Hours]) calculated control.

7. Preview your report. Click the last page navigation button, then scroll to and observe the end of the report. Your newest calculated control has calculated the report's gross-pay total (see Figure 12.4). Close the preview window.

Figure 12.4   **The displayed gross-pay total**

SS				
Robert	Beaton	$12.50	35	$437.50
Sam	Binga	$13.30	35.5	$472.15
Wilma	Chase	$15.50	40	$620.00
Darren	Cline	$7.50	20	$150.00
Naja	Ellis	$13.50	40	$540.00
Susan	Hartle	$17.50	25	$437.50
Jason	Horn	$13.50	40	$540.00
Edward	Pierce	$12.50	40	$500.00
Randall	Vetch	$14.00	25	$350.00
	Subtotals for SS :	$119.80	300.5	
	Grand Total :	$891.42	1927	$33,985.35

PRACTICE YOUR SKILLS

1. Directly to the right of the Dept Footer section's =Sum([Hours]) calculated control, add an unbound text-box control and label.

2. Delete the unbound control's label.

3. Convert the new unbound control into a control that calculates each department's gross-pay total.

4. Select the control, use the property sheet to set the control's Format property to **Currency**, and then close the property sheet.

5. Make the control's text bold.

6. Align the control's right edge with the horizontal ruler's 5-inch mark. Then size the control so that it no longer overlaps the =Sum([Hours]) calculated control.

7. Preview and scroll through the report to observe each department's gross-pay subtotals.

8. Scroll to view the top of the report and the first department subtotal. Compare your screen to Figure 12.5.

Figure 12.5   **The previewed Chemical Engineering department subtotal**

Dept	First Name	Last Name	Pay Rate	Hours	Gross Pay
CE					
	Murray	Abel	$12.50	35.5	$443.75
	Ken	Beasley	$22.50	40	$900.00
	Bruce	Cassada	$21.50	40	$860.00
	Bill	Conner	$19.50	40	$780.00
	Hugh	Jones	$17.25	40	$690.00
	Suzanna	Petty	$21.50	40	$860.00
	David	Stevens	$15.00	40	$600.00
	Cristin	Warfield	$17.50	40	$700.00
	Joseph	Zambito	$15.50	40	$620.00
	Subtotals for CE :		$162.75	355.5	$6,453.75

9. Save the report.

CHANGING A REPORT'S PAGE LAYOUT

You can control the page layout of a report (or any object that you can preview, for that matter) through the Page Setup dialog box. A report's *page layout* affects the position of the report's data on paper. Page layout settings include margins, page orientation, and paper size.

To open the Page Setup dialog box from a previewed report's window or from a report in Design view, choose File, Page Setup. Once you have opened the Page Setup dialog box, you can view additional page-layout settings by clicking on the appropriate tab.

If you use the Page Setup dialog box from a previewed report's window, you will see the effect of those changes when you click on OK to close the dialog box.

Let's use the Page Setup dialog box to improve our report's page layout:

1. In the previewed report, click on the **Zoom** button, and observe the report's page layout. Most of the report is toward the left edge of the page.

2. Choose **File, Page Setup** to open the Page Setup dialog box, and observe the Left margin box. By default, Access sets all report margins to 1 inch.

3. Change the value in the Left margin text box to **1.75** to increase the report's left margin (see Figure 12.6), and click on **OK**. A dialog box opens, informing you that the section width is greater than the page width, and that some of the pages might be left blank.

4. Click on **OK**, and observe the previewed report. The report is now better centered on the page (see Figure 12.7).

5. Save and then close the report.

CREATING MAILING-LABEL REPORTS

You can use the Label Wizard to create reports that are designed for printing mailing labels. Like other Report Wizards, the Label Wizard asks you a series of questions, and then creates a report for you.

In Chapter 8, you learned how to use the toolbar's New Query button to create a new query based on the active or currently selected table or query. To create new reports, use the New Report button. (The New Form button, which is not used in this book, helps create new forms much as the New Query and New Report buttons help create new queries and reports.)

Figure 12.6   **Changing the report's left margin**

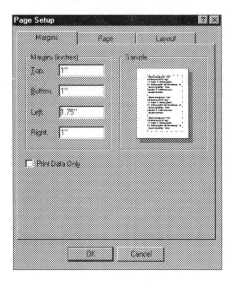

Figure 12.7   **The previewed report after changing its page layout**

To start the Label Wizard:

- Open the window for the table or query upon which you wish to base your report; or, in the Database window, select the desired table or query object.

- Click on the drop-down arrow next to the New Object button. Click on the *New Report* button. Access opens the New Report dialog box and automatically selects the active or currently selected table or query as the report's data source.

- Click on *Label Wizard*, then click on OK

DESIGNING MAILING LABELS

Once started, the Label Wizard asks you these three questions:

- What size mailing labels are you using?

- How do you want each mailing label to appear?

- How do you want your mailing labels sorted?

In the next pane, you will determine how each mailing label will appear. The Label Wizard provides a pane that asks you to build a sample label. To build the label, you use available field names and type text that you would like to appear on every label. To add a field name to the sample label, select the field name in the Available Fields list box and then click on the > button, or double-click on the field name. The next pane asks for information regarding the font of the label.

Once you complete the label's design and move to the next pane, select a sort order by moving the appropriate field or fields from the Available Fields list box to the Sort Order list box.

So that you can specify the size of the mailing labels you will use to print your report, the Label Wizard provides an extensive list of label sizes according to their Avery product numbers. If you are not using Avery brand labels, check your labels for an Avery equivalency number or use the measurements that the Report Wizard lists alongside each Avery product number.

Let's use the New Report button and Label Wizard to create a mailing-label report based on the Suppliers table:

1. Open and observe the Suppliers table. It contains seven records with all of the fields necessary for mailing labels (and then some): Company Name, Address, City, St, and Zip.

2. Click on the **New Report** button to open the New Report dialog box. (Click on the drop-down arrow next to the New Object button, then select New Report.) Because you used the New Report button from the Suppliers Table window, Access automatically selected *Suppliers* as the report's data source.

3. Select **Label Wizard**, and click on **OK** to start the Label Wizard. The Label Wizard dialog box is displayed (see Figure 12.8).

Figure 12.8   **The Label Wizard dialog box**

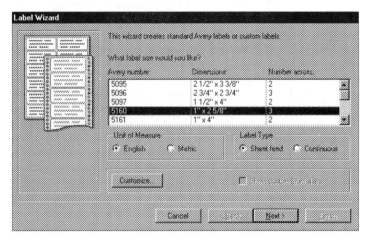

4. Select Avery number **5160**, and click on **Next** to advance to the next pane. You're prompted to select a font. The default font is Arial 8 point. (Your default font may differ.) Change the font size to **12**.

5. Click on **Next** to advance to the next pane. To the left is the Available Fields list box. To the right is the Prototype label box for building your sample label.

6. In the Available Fields box, double-click on **Company Name** to add the field to the Prototype label box.

7. Press **Enter** to add a new line to the Prototype label box.

8. Add **Address** to the Prototype label box, press **Enter** to add a third line, and add **City**.

9. Type **,** and press the **Spacebar** to add a comma and space after *City*.

10. Add **St** to the Prototype label box, press the **Spacebar** twice, and add **Zip** to complete the sample label appearance (see Figure 12.9).

Figure 12.9   **The Prototype label appearance**

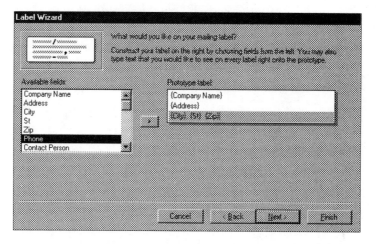

11. Click on **Next** to advance to the next Label Wizard pane. You are prompted to set the sort order.

12. Move **Zip** from the Available Fields list box to the Sort by list box to specify that your labels be sorted by zip code. Click on **Next** to advance to the final pane.

13. Type **My Supplier Labels** to change the name of the report. Click on **Finish** to display a preview of the printed report.

EXAMINING A MAILING-LABEL REPORT AND ITS DESIGN

No matter how many columns of labels there are in your mailing-label report, the Label Wizard uses a single set of controls. To specify that the report should use the single set of controls for more than one column of labels, the Label Wizard sets the value in the Page Setup dialog box's Items Across box to a number greater than 1. For example, to specify three columns of labels, the Label Wizard sets the Items Across text box to 3. To view the Items Across text box, open the Page Setup dialog box, and click on the Layout tab.

Take a look at the mailing-label report you just created, and then observe its design and settings in the Page Setup dialog box:

1. Maximize the report, and click on the previewed report to display the report in full-page view. Notice that the report contains three columns of labels. Because the Suppliers table contains only seven records, the report contains only seven labels (see Figure 12.10).

Figure 12.10   **The previewed mailing-label report**

2. Return to a close-up view. Notice that the labels are sorted by zip code.

3. Switch to Design view and notice that the report's Detail section contains controls for a single label.

4. Open the Page Setup dialog box (choose **File, Page Setup**), click on the Layout tab, and observe the Items Across setting: 3. This setting tells Access to construct three columns of labels from a single set of controls.

5. Close the Page Setup dialog box, and save the report.

CHANGING A REPORT'S RECORD SOURCE

If you need to generate mailing labels from more than one table or query, you could use the Label Wizard to create from scratch a new mailing-label report for each table or query. However, if your mailing-label designs are similar, you may find it easier to create and save a single mailing-label report, change that existing report's design so that it uses data from a different table or query, and then save the new report design with a different name.

To change a report's design so that it uses data from a different table or query, use the property sheet to change the report's Record Source property.

Because field names often vary among tables and queries, you may also need to change some of the control names in the report design and/or some of the field names in the design of the new table or query to ensure that the Record Source property change will succeed. For example, if you create a mailing-label report based on a query with a field named *Add* for address information, and then switch the report's Record Source property to a query that uses a field named *Address* instead, you will need to change either the name of the Add control in the report or the name of the Address field in the query.

Because query designs are more flexible than table designs, it's better to change a report's record source to a query rather than to a table. In a query, it's easier to rename and create fields as necessary for your mailing-label report.

Let's change our new mailing-label report's Record Source property from the Suppliers table to a query; then, we'll change the design of the query and of the report to make the property change a success:

1. Switch to the Database window. Then run the **Home Addresses** query and observe the query's resulting datasheet. Most of its fields have the same names as the fields you used from the Suppliers table for your mailing-labels report. However, this datasheet has separate First Name and Last Name fields; your mailing-labels report uses a single Company Name field.

2. Switch to Design view; then select and delete the design grid's First Name column.

3. In the Last Name field cell, replace *Last Name* with **Employee Name:[first name]&" "&[last name]** to create an Employee

Name field that concatenates the First Name and Last Name fields.

4. Run the query and observe the resulting datasheet. It now contains a single Employee Name field (see Figure 12.11).

Figure 12.11 **The modified query's datasheet**

Employee Name	Address	City	St	Zip
Ted James	34 Fields Street	Walworth	NY	14568
Hanna Harper	82 East Avenue	Adams Basin	NY	14410
Penny Packer	450 N. Madison St.	Holley	NY	14470
Julia Binder	10 Cory Drive	Hulberton	NY	14473
Maria Sanders	12 East Avenue	Leicester	NY	14481
Connie Easter	21 Stonecreek Rd.	Shortsville	NY	14548
Jane Martin	50 Smart Drive	Knowlesville	NY	14479
Allison Binga	50 Dallas Street	South Byron	NY	14557
Bill Conner	32 Ash Lane	Perkinsville	NY	14529
Dominick Osow	23 Lakeside Ave.	Pultneyville	NY	14538
Sam Binga	50 Dallas Street	South Byron	NY	14557
Murray Abel	127 Ford Avenue	Lakeville	NY	14480
Robert Abot	99 Stonecreek Rd.	Gorham	NY	14461
Joseph Zambito	81 Pleasing Lane	Rose	NY	14542
Peter McDonald	8165 Main Street	Oaks Corners	NY	14518
Wilma Chase	52 Pempleton Dr.	Wyoming	NY	14591
Arlene DeMarco	34 Sable Ave.	Gorham	NY	14461
Frank Desoto	P.O. Box 7234	Wayland	NY	14572

5. Save the query as **My Home Addresses**, close the query, and return to the report.

6. Open and observe the report's property sheet. The Record Source property is set to the Suppliers table.

7. Change the Record Source property to **My Home Addresses**; then close the property sheet. Notice that the =Trim[Company Name] control does not match the Home Addresses query's Employee Name field.

8. In the =Trim[Company Name] control, replace *Company* with **Employee**. Then compare your screen to Figure 12.12.

Figure 12.12 **The modified control name**

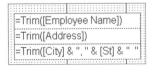

```
=Trim([Employee Name])
=Trim([Address])
=Trim([City] & ", " & [St] & " "
```

9. Preview your mailing-label report. The labels now contain data from the My Home Addresses query.

10. Click on the **Two Pages** button to display both pages on one screen.

11. Save your report as **My Home Address Labels**, close the report, and exit Access.

SUMMARY

In this chapter, you learned how to enhance reports by adding line controls and calculated controls, and by changing the report's page layout. You also learned how to use the Label Wizard to create a mailing-label report, and how to change that report's record source.

Congratulations! Having finished this chapter, you have completed your foundation of Access skills. You are now prepared to take all that you've learned and apply it to your own databases. Remember, in order to keep and master the skills that you've acquired, you must now supply the most important ingredient: *practice*. Good luck!

Here's a quick reference guide to the Access features introduced in this chapter:

Desired Result	How to Do It
Add horizontal line control to report	In Design view, press and hold **Shift**, click on **Line** tool, position mouse pointer where you want one end of control, press and hold mouse button, drag horizontally to opposite end of line control, release mouse button, and release Shift
Cause calculated control to perform horizontal calculation	Place control in Detail section
Cause calculated control to perform vertical calculation	Place control in Report Header, Report Footer, group header, or group footer section
Create calculated control that uses aggregate function	In unbound text-box control, type expression using =*function(argument)* syntax

Desired Result	How to Do It
Open report's Page Setup dialog box	Choose **File, Page Setup**
Change report's page layout	Change appropriate settings in report's Page Setup dialog box
Use New Report button to start Label Wizard	Open table or query upon which you wish to base report, or in Database window select table or query object; click on **New Object** button, click on **New Report**, click on **Label Wizard**, and click on **OK**
Design mailing label	In appropriate Label Wizard's pane, double-click on field names and type in punctuation
Change report's record source	Change Record Source property; then, if necessary, change control names in report and/or field names in the report's new table or query

Following this chapter are three appendices: Appendix A, "Installing Access 7.0," walks you through Access 7.0 installation. Appendix B, "Shortcut-Key Reference," labels the various toolbar buttons and drop-down list boxes, and lists many keyboard shortcuts available in Access and Windows. Appendix C, "Creating a Database," discusses creating your own database from scratch and importing existing data into that database.

APPENDIX A: INSTALLING ACCESS 7.0

Before You Begin Installing

Installing Access on Your Computer

Selecting a Printer for Use with Access

This appendix contains instructions for installing Access for Windows 95 on your computer.

BEFORE YOU BEGIN INSTALLING

Because Access is such a customizable program, you can change its screen setup and overall appearance by simply running and using Access. For this reason, we at PC Learning Labs have written this book on the assumption that you have just installed Access and have not yet run the program. If you have already installed and used Access, you may want to delete all of the Access files from your computer and then reinstall Access to guarantee that your version of Access will run as described in this book. If you use Access on a network or other shared computer system, check first with your network system administrator. In any case, be sure to back up important files before deleting them!

REQUIRED HARD-DISK SPACE

You need to have at least 4231MB (42,000,000 bytes) of free hard-disk space to install Access for Windows 95. (While this is the amount required for complete installation, not the installation we will perform, we recommend this upper limit to be safe.) If you do not have this much free space, you will have to delete enough files from your hard disk to bring the total free space up to 42MB. For help in doing this please refer to your Windows 95 manual.

Note: Remember to back up (copy to a floppy disk) any files you want to preserve before deleting them from your hard disk.

INSTALLING ACCESS ON YOUR COMPUTER

Follow these steps to install Access 7.0 for Windows 95:

1. Start Windows 95. (If you have not already installed Windows 95 on your system, please do so now; for help, see your Windows 95 reference manual.)

2. Insert the installation disk labeled Setup in the appropriate drive. If you are installing Access from a network, you will be prompted for the drive and folder later in the installation process.

3. In the taskbar, click on **Start**, point to **Settings**, and choose **Control Panel**.

4. Click on **Add/Remove Programs** icon, and verify that the Install/Uninstall tab is active.

5. Click on the **Install** button to begin the installation.

6. Follow the on-screen instructions to complete the installation. Here are some guidelines:

- For help understanding the contents of an installation dialog box, click on its **Help** button.

- In general, accept all installation defaults (by clicking on **Continue** or **OK**).

- When prompted to select an installation option, choose either **Typical** or **Custom** to install Access. The *Typical* option installs the basic Access setup, which will still give you access to many features. The *Custom* option allows you to install the Access components of your choice. The hard-disk space required for each component is listed next to it. (**Note**: Do not choose the Compact option, as doing so will prevent you from completing the exercises in this book!)

- If you discover that you don't have enough free hard-disk space to install the option of your dreams, either exit the installation procedure, free up some space on your hard disk and repeat the installation, or try life without it.

7. When the installation is complete, you are returned to Windows. To start Access, click on **Start**, point to **Programs**, and click on **Microsoft Access**.

SELECTING A PRINTER FOR USE WITH ACCESS

Before you can print from Access, you may need to select a printer. To do so, follow these steps:

1. Start Access for Windows 95. Open up any database.

2. Choose **File, Print** from the menu to display the Print dialog box.

3. In the Print dialog box, click on the **drop-down list arrow** in the Name field to display a list of the printers that are currently installed on your system.

4. If your printer appears in the list, select it.

5. If your printer does not appear in the list, install the printer on your system. (For instructions, refer to your Windows 95 documentation.) Then repeat this printer-selection procedure from step 1.

6. Click on the **Close** button (do not click on OK) to close the Print dialog box.

APPENDIX B: SHORTCUT-KEY REFERENCE

This appendix lists a number of shortcut keys available in Access for Windows 95.

In Access, virtually any action that can be performed with the mouse can also be performed with the keyboard using shortcut keys. Choose the method—mouse or keyboard—that works best for you.

Tables B.1, B.2, B.3, and B.4 describe the corresponding shortcut keys for Access actions covered in this book. For information on shortcut keys not covered in this appendix, search Help Topics, Index for "keyboard shortcuts."

Table B.1

Navigation and Selection Shortcut Keys

Shortcut Key	Action
F2	Switch between the insertion point and a selection
F5	Move to and select the Record Number box
F6	Move between the upper and lower panes of multiple-pane windows
Home	Move the insertion point to the beginning of a field or line; if an entire field is selected, move to the first field in the current record
Ctrl+Home	Move the insertion point in a multiple-line field to the beginning of the field; if a record is selected, move to the first field in the first record
End	Move the insertion point to the end of the field or line; if an entire field is selected, move to the last field in the current record
Ctrl+End	Move the insertion point in a multiple-line field to the end of the current field; if a record is selected, move to the last field in the last record
Up Arrow	Move the insertion point in a multiple-line field to the previous line; if the field contains only one line, move to the current field in the previous record

Table B.1 **Navigation and Selection Shortcut Keys (Continued)**

Shortcut Key	Action
Down Arrow	Move the insertion point in a multiple-line field to the next line; if the field contains only one line, move to the current field in the next record
Left Arrow	Move the insertion point one character to the left; if an entire field is selected, move to the previous field
Right Arrow	Move the insertion point one character to the right; if an entire field is selected, move one field to the right
Tab	Move to the next field in a record
Shift+Tab	Move to the previous field in a record
Shift+Spacebar	Select or deselect the current record
Ctrl+Spacebar	Select or deselect the current column

Table B.2 **Editing and Data Entry Shortcut Keys**

Shortcut Key	Action
Backspace	Delete the selection or the character to the left of the insertion point
Delete	Delete the selection or the character to the right of the insertion point
Ctrl+X	Cut the selection (same as Edit, Cut)
Ctrl+C	Copy the selection (same as Edit, Copy)
Ctrl+V	Paste the copied or cut selection (same as Edit, Paste)
Ctrl+Z or Alt+Backspace	Undo typing

Table B.2   **Editing and Data Entry Shortcut Keys (Continued)**

Shortcut Key	Action
Esc	Undo changes to the current field or record
Shift+F2	Open the Zoom dialog box
Ctrl+" or Ctrl+'	Copy the value from the same field in the previous record
Ctrl+–	Delete the current record
Shift+Enter	Save the current record
Ctrl+;	Insert the current date
Ctrl+:	Insert the current time
Ctrl+Alt+Spacebar	Insert the default value for the current field
Ctrl+Enter	Insert a new line in the current field, label, or Zoom button

Table B.3   **Print Preview Shortcut Keys**

Shortcut Key	Action
P	Print the active object
S	Open the Page Setup dialog box
Z	Zoom view
C or Esc	Close the Preview window
Page Down or Down Arrow	Move to the next page
Page Up or Up Arrow	Move to the previous page
Home	Move to the first page when in Zoom View
End	Move to the last page when in Zoom View

Table B.4   **Miscellaneous Shortcut Keys**

Shortcut Key	Action
F1	Open context-sensitive Help
Ctrl+F4	Close the active window
Alt+F4	Exit Access or close a dialog box
Ctrl+F6	Move between open windows
F11 or Alt+F1	Activate the Database window
F12 or Alt+F2	Open the Save As dialog box
Shift+F12 or Alt+Shift+F2	Save the current object
F7	Open the Spelling dialog box
F9	Recalculate the fields

APPENDIX C: CREATING A DATABASE

Creating a New
Database Table

Importing Data

This appendix explains how to create a database file from scratch and describes ways to bring existing data into a database.

CREATING A NEW DATABASE TABLE

Throughout this book, you have used Access database files that we supplied on the Data Disk. Now that you've nearly finished the book, you are ready to create your own database file.

To create a new Access database file:

- Choose *File, New Database* from the Access startup window or any Database window. Access opens the New dialog box.

- Select *Blank Database*, and click on *OK*.

- In the File Name text box, type a name for your new database file. Database file names can contain up to 255 characters, including spaces. They cannot contain many special characters, including periods, asterisks, and question marks.

- Specify the appropriate location to store your new database file.

- Click on *Create*. After a moment, Access will display a new, empty Database window bearing the name you provided in the File New Database dialog box.

Once you have created a new database file, you are ready to use any of the techniques you learned in this book to create new objects. Normally, you will create a number of tables, add data to those tables, and then build forms, queries, and reports based on that data.

IMPORTING DATA

If you have data stored in another Access database file or in a database file created by an application other than Access, you may be able to import that data into your new database file.

Access enables you to import data that is stored in the following formats:

- Microsoft Access (versions 1.X, 2.0, and 7.0)

- Paradox

- dBASE III, IV, and 5

- Microsoft SQL Server

- Text

- Microsoft Excel

- Lotus 1-2-3
- Microsoft Foxpro
- ODBC Databases

You usually can import any type of object from other Access databases. However, when you import from files created by applications other than Access, you usually can import only tables or table data.

Bear in mind that when you import Access objects such as queries, forms, and reports, you may also need to import the tables and/or queries upon which those objects are based. Otherwise, when you try to use your imported object, Access will report an error when the imported object cannot find the table or query upon which it is based.

Two ways to import data from one Access database to another are through the File, Get External Data, Import command and through the Copy, Cut, and Paste commands in the Edit menu. (See your Access documentation for other ways to move data into and out of Access databases.)

IMPORTING THROUGH FILE, GET EXTERNAL DATA, IMPORT

To import an object from one Access database to another using the File, Get External Data, Import command:

- Open the database into which you want to import an object.
- Choose *File, Get External Data, Import* to open the Import dialog box.
- Select the drive and directory where the database containing the object is stored, select the appropriate database file name, and then click on *Import* to open the Import Objects dialog box.
- Select the appropriate object type and object name.
- Click on *Options* to view your choices for importing. If you choose to import a table, you can also choose whether to import both the table design and the data stored in it, or just the table design itself.
- Click on *OK.* Your imported object's name will then be displayed in the Database window when you select the appropriate object button.

If the name of the object you import matches the name of an existing object, Access may rename the imported object. For example, if you import a table named *Employees* into a database that already includes an Employees table, Access might name the imported table *Employees1*.

Using the File, Get External Data, Import command, you can also import tables from Paradox, dBASE III and IV, Microsoft SQL Server, Microsoft FoxPro, and ODBC databases, and you can create tables by importing data stored in text, Microsoft Excel, and Lotus 1-2-3 files.

Once you've used the File, Get External Data, Import command to import an object from one Access database to another, you may want to delete the table from its original database.

To delete an Access database object:

- Open the database that contains the object you wish to delete.

- Select the name of the object.

- Press the *Delete* key or choose *Edit, Delete*. Access asks you to confirm the deletion.

- Click on *Yes*.

To remove an object from an Access database, you can also use the Edit, Cut command, which is described below.

IMPORTING THROUGH EDIT COMMANDS

To import an object from one Access database to another using the Edit menu's Copy, Cut, and Paste commands:

- Open the database that contains the object you wish to import.

- Select the appropriate object name.

- Choose *Edit, Copy* or *Edit, Cut*. The Edit, Copy command leaves the original object intact; the Edit, Cut command removes the object from the current database. (**Note:** Unlike using the Edit, Delete command described earlier, when you use the Edit, Cut command, Access does not ask you for confirmation. Therefore, you should be very careful when using this command.)

- Close the current database, and open the database into which you wish to import the object.

- Choose *Edit, Paste*. Access asks you for an object name. If you are pasting a table, the dialog box also enables you to choose to import just the table's design, to import the entire table, or to append the table's data to an existing table.

- Type an object name, choose a paste option if applicable, and then click on *OK*. Unless you choose to append data, your imported object's name will then be displayed in the Database window when you select the appropriate tab in the Database window.

INDEX

FOR THOSE HARD CHOICES.

PC MAGAZINE 1996 Computer Buyer's Guide

EDITED BY **JOHN C. DVORAK**

Completely updated for 1996!

- Comprehensive, state-of-the-art product comparisons from *PC Magazine* testing experts

- Dvorak's buying tips for multimedia computers, notebooks and laptops, CD-ROM drives, high-speed modems, software, and more

ISBN: 1-56276-343-1
Price: $19.95

Negotiating today's crowded hardware scene isn't easy. That's why *PC Magazine* and John C. Dvorak have teamed up to produce *PC Magazine 1996 Computer Buyer's Guide*. It's your one-stop source for unbiased analyses and easy-to-read comparison charts for hundreds of PCs, monitors, printers, input devices, and modems, all benchmark-tested in the world's most modern computer research facility.

Combining the latest laboratory results from *PC Magazine* with Dvorak's no-holds-barred commentary, *PC Magazine 1996 Computer Buyer's Guide* is an indispensable shopper's companion that will save you money and help you find the hardware that meets your computing needs.

ZIFF-DAVIS **ZD** PRESS

Available at all fine bookstores or by calling 1-800-688-0448.

■ TO RECEIVE 5¼-INCH DISK(S)

The Ziff-Davis Press software contained on the $3^1/_2$-inch disk included with this book is also available in $5^1/_4$-inch format. If you would like to receive the software in the $5^1/_4$-inch format, please return the $3^1/_2$-inch disk with your name and address to:

Disk Exchange
Ziff-Davis Press
5903 Christie Avenue
Emeryville, CA 94608